# Franz Boas
## *Social Activist*

Franz Boas, 1858–1942
Courtesy of Jack J. Augustin.

# Franz Boas
# *Social Activist*

## THE DYNAMICS OF ETHNICITY

# Marshall Hyatt

Contributions to the Study of Anthropology, Number 6

GP

GREENWOOD PRESS

*New York • Westport, Connecticut • London*

**Library of Congress Cataloging-in-Publication Data**

Hyatt, Marshall.
   Franz Boas, social activist : the dynamics of ethnicity / Marshall
Hyatt.
      p. cm. — (Contributions to the study of anthropology, ISSN
0890–9377 ; no. 6)
   Includes bibliographical references.
   ISBN 0–313–27320–0 (lib. bdg. : alk. paper)
   1. Boas, Franz, 1858–1942.   2. Anthropologists—United States—
Biography.   3. Anthropology—History.   4. Anthropologists—Germany—
Biography.   5. United States—Ethnic relations.   I. Title.
II. Series.
GN21.B56H93      1990
306'.092—dc20      89–25910

British Library Cataloguing in Publication Data is available.

Library of Congress Catalog Card Number: 89–25910
ISBN: 0–313–27320–0
ISSN: 0890–9377

First published in 1990

Greenwood Press, Inc.
88 Post Road West, Westport, Connecticut 06881

Printed in the United States of America

The paper used in this book complies with the
Permanent Paper Standard issued by the National
Information Standards Organization (Z39.48–1984).

10   9   8   7   6   5   4   3   2   1

# Contents

# Acknowledgments

Throughout the process of writing this biography of Franz Boas I have benefited immensely from numerous conversations, critiques and suggestions by a variety of individuals. In each case, these people have helped me form my assessment and have kept me going on the journey of finishing the project. I would like to thank them for their collective contributions.

Without question my greatest intellectual encouragement came from Professor Edward Lurie, whose vast knowledge of manuscript material in American intellectual history and constant admonition to be aware of historical processes significantly shaped my thinking. For me he represented all the positive aspects of being a historian, and he kindled my interest in both teaching and research. I hope in my own career I have been and will continue to be as dedicated to my students as he was to me.

I would also like to express gratitude to George Frick and Raymond Wolters, both of whom offered helpful suggestions along the way, and to acknowledge the help and encouragement provided by the late Joe Huthmacher. I will never forget his humanity, amity and wonderful sense of humor. He, much like Franz Boas, symbolized that rare breed of individual who fused his academic discipline with social action in a sincere effort to address inequality. I also profited from my contact with James Newton and Ron Lewis who made the resources of the Black American Studies Department at the University of Delaware available to me and welcomed frequent interruptions. During the process of expansion and revision I received additional advice from my colleagues at Harvard University's Afro-American studies and history departments. Specifically I would like to thank Eileen Southern, Nathan Huggins, James Jennings, Werner Sollors, Bernard Bailyn and Donald Fleming. Each of them offered meaningful suggestions along the way, as well as support and intellectual nourishment.

In conducting my research at the American Philosophical Society I benefited from early contact with Murphy Smith, the Manuscript Librarian at the time. His insights into the Boas Correspondence were most revealing. Also, in this connection, I would like to thank Whitfield Bell of the society, for allowing me access to the collection and to the American Philosophical Society Library itself for granting me permission to quote from the Boas Correspondence. The staffs of the Manuscript Division of the Library of Congress, the Morris Library at the University of Delaware, the Butler Library at Columbia University, the National Academy of Sciences Library, the American Museum of Natural History, the Smithsonian Institution, Harvard University's Widener and Pusey libraries, and the library at the University of Massachusetts-Amherst also provided important assistance.

Without much timely and efficient clerical assistance from key office professionals, I would still be laboring over a typewriter making revisions. I wish to thank Caren Betts, Marcelyn Dallis, Gail Brittingham, Chris Fenno and Maureen Spofford, for both their assistance and friendship. Ginny Gumz's involvement in preparing the final version has also been monumental. Lastly in this regard, I would like to thank my administrative assistant, Georgie Leone. Her dedication to her work, ability to keep me from being buried under an avalanche of paper, and wonderful comradeship have been deeply appreciated.

My involvement with Greenwood Press also deserves mention. Lynn Sedlak Flint and James T. Sabin have been helpful, encouraging and resourceful in helping me prepare the manuscript for publication.

Additionally, I would like to thank two colleagues who have played special roles in my development as a scholar. Charles A. Watkins, director of the Appalachian State University Historical Museum, has been both friend and colleague since graduate school. Our shared passion for historiography has enriched my understanding of American history, and I have valued the frequent crossing of our paths. Erness Bright Brody, Professor of Afro-American Studies at Wesleyan University's Center for Afro-American Studies, has been instrumental in keeping me from isolation in the final stages of revision. I thank her for her friendship and colleagueship and appreciate her real concern for teaching, research and the life of the mind.

Finally, I would like to thank my family for helping me make my dream a reality: first to my parents for stressing the critical importance of an education when I seemed least inclined to accept advice; second to my children, Adam and Rachel, for renewing my capacity to wonder and laugh and for not destroying the final copy of the manuscript; lastly to Cindy Hyatt, whose companionship has made the most difficult times much easier to bear and whose comments about this volume were the ones I respected most.

# Introduction

The life and thought of Franz Boas has had a profound impact on many diverse elements of American society. In a sense this German-born anthropologist can be viewed as a symbol of the age in which the United States responded to its rapid modernization at the onset of the twentieth century. Finding himself caught up in the whirlwind that resulted from such wholesale disequilibrium, Boas did his part to ease the national process of readaptation. During his long career in the United States, he responded not only to the shifting nature of American values but also to two world wars fought against his land of birth and a massive economic depression. Far from confining himself solely to science, he tackled problems fundamental to his new society. He fused science with political and social activism to ensure that his ideological contributions to anthropological thought also had practical relevance to issues facing the world.

In the second half of the nineteenth century, the nation experienced a major transformation of values, aims and perceptions. After emerging from a bloody civil war, which altered America's agrarian face irrevocably, the country encountered traumatic dislocations. In what has been variously termed "a response to industrialism" or "a search for order," Americans grappled with the assorted dilemmas caused by frenzied industrialization, mass immigration from Europe and chaotic urbanization. In reacting to these new forces, the Progressive movement collectively hoped to bring order out of the chaos on all fronts by addressing the ramifications of such intense change.

Although Boas himself did not arrive in the United States until the late 1880s, he soon became enmeshed in many of the problems that faced the general society. His reaction to the vast transformation of the country's political, social and intellectual landscape had significant influence on that very metamorphosis. Addressing a variety of concerns during the course of his career, Boas attempted to help solve some of the weighty dilemmas facing the nation as it sought to adjust to the forces that had caused that full-scale deracination.

As an intellectual, Boas attacked the misusers of science who promulgated theories of racial inferiority based on alleged mental differences between ethnic groups. As a scientist, he directed the professionalization of the field of anthropology, overseeing its evolution from an amateur hobby to its maturity as a rigorous academic discipline. As a social activist, he strove to eradicate prejudice and bigotry from American society, in an effort to ensure that the promise of American democracy was articulated in reality and practice.

The motivation behind Boas's actions and ideology was not monocausal. Certainly his devotion to a liberal creed significantly influenced his weltanschauung. Raised in a progressive German household that supported the revolution of 1848, Boas adopted political views similar to those of his parents. His education reinforced those sentiments. Accordingly, this liberalism lay at the root of his activity.

Combined with this, and every bit as influential, was his commitment to scientific accuracy and purity. This persistent dedication figured importantly in Boas's research and publication, and also accounted for his desire to rid anthropology of amateur control. It was this attribute that led inevitably to the personal battles Boas frequently fought with other individuals who did not share his passion.

The third major factor that determined his course was more defensive and personal in nature. It placed Boas in the position of reacting to insult and forced him into frequent confrontation. From early on in his university days in Germany, and throughout his life, Boas experienced anti-Semitism firsthand. These incidents left a lasting impression and molded his behavior and consciousness. The way in which these feelings were intertwined with both his liberal bent and scientific orthodoxy is a revealing aspect of the story of his life, because it accounts for many of his actions and beliefs.

It is imperative to understand Boas's life experiences in order to analyze his intellectual contributions. He merged science with politics because his upbringing was consistent with such a path. Moreover, his early years were most relevant in forming his philosophy; they help explain both the direction in which he embarked and his orientation as a thinker.

Boas left an indelible mark on anthropology. His work was not confined to one branch of the discipline; his research, thought, and teaching penetrated all facets of the field, including linguistics, archaeology and physical and cultural anthropology. In each component he infused scientific rigor, intent on questioning existing hypotheses. Among his numerous major contributions were challenges to evolutionary theory and arguments about race, mental ability and hierarchical ranking; major linguistic studies concerning the nexus between race, language and culture; insight into mental-cognitive paradigms; and explication of the plasticity of the human form and the primacy of environment in shaping both physique and mental behavior.

In constructing this thought, Boas overturned many of the existing theories under which amateur anthropologists had labored. As a result, he successfully reoriented the field itself along more precise methodological lines. He was, perhaps, the last major figure who cast so large a shadow on the discipline as a whole. Boas's impact so enhanced and expanded the field that specialization became the norm rather than the exception. Following him, anthropologists, including many of his own students, found sufficient scope to work within the subdivisions of the discipline.

The symbolic quality of Boas's life is an equally important facet of his legacy. Beyond his personal response to America's industrialization, he met head-on the various dilemmas of twentieth-century United States history. His pacifist sentiments during World War I embroiled him in controversy. His experiences during the war years brought into sharp relief the issue of personal liberty versus patriotism and underscored the hysteria extant in America during those turbulent times.

In a marked transition, the second world war offered Boas the opportunity to show his allegiance to the United States. Although arguing for American neutrality once again, his forceful, outspoken condemnation of Hitler led inevitably to support for the Allied effort against the forces of Fascism. Boas had understood sooner and more precisely than most American intellectuals how World War II would illuminate the paradoxical aspects of American racial attitudes. Although the United States commenced its assault against Nazi race theory by late 1941, the contradictory condoning of racism at home continued to detract from America's professed democratic ideals. Squaring the nation's attack on racism abroad with its maintenance at home remained a task for postwar activists.

That Boas recognized this discrepancy so early points to another crucial aspect of his legacy. His role in forging a new consensus on race theory and his efforts to eradicate bigotry characterized his entire adult life. His thought in this area had substantial impact on the Afro-American civil rights movement, particularly during the depression decade, when a heightened concern for racial equality compelled various groups and individuals to challenge segregation and racism. The forceful restatement of his many pronouncements on the equipotential of the races and his condemnation of pseudoscientists who honed their craft in the service of continuing the myth of racial inferiority paved the way for change.

In combination with the interracialism espoused by the National Association for the Advancement of Colored People (NAACP), the Communist Party of the United States (CPUSA), and organized labor, and with W. E. B. Du Bois's articulation of the need for black economic self-determination and his concern for the masses, Boas's argument helped bring a multidirectional civil rights movement to national attention. His forceful and repetitive attacks on racial injustice led inevitably to more research, and to the gradual invalidation over time of the racists' claim to scientific legitimacy. Once science had abandoned bigotry, the struggle for equality began to chip away at the legal and political hegemony of Jim Crow society. Boas's legacy in this regard was significant and enduring.

Racism, of course, outlived Boas. What he left to America were the intellectual weapons to combat it and recognition of the urgency of the task. What he left to anthropology was a cadre of well-trained scientists who collectively continued his approach. Not only did they argue against prejudice and any misuse of science as its justification, they also conducted individual research into various cultures, languages, customs and beliefs. Taken as a whole, their studies informed Americans about the way in which different societies contributed to civilization's advance, thus reinforcing Boas's belief in cultural relativism.

Certainly not all of Boas's students appreciated his domineering, professional style or his paternalistic concern for them. Many chafed under his tutelage, frustrated by his demands that they master all facets of their discipline. Nevertheless, out of Boas's classroom marched many of the new generation of professional American anthropologists. As they themselves rose to prominence in the academy, they carried forward Boas's desire to make anthropology useful in the service of society. Ruth Benedict, Ruth Bunzel, Melville Herskovits, Zora Neale Hurston, Alfred Kroeber, Robert Lowie, Margaret Mead, Edward Sapir, Leslie Spier and John Swanton were among those fortunate to work under Boas. Their combined efforts are yet another part of Boas's legacy.

Boas the scientist and Boas the social activist were dynamically intertwined. The story of his life explains why he fashioned his ideology, while conversely his thought and activity illustrate much about his own background. It is this book's intention to illuminate what Boas believed and why, and to analyze how he affected the intellectual and social milieu of his times. An assessment of his thoughts, actions and their motivations; his scientific acumen and academic discipline; and his concern for human freedom, provides a microcosmic view of twentieth-century American society and its history through the medium of one intellectual's voice in that process.

# Franz Boas
## *Social Activist*

# 1
# The Early Years

In the 1850s, American anthropology was largely an amateur science. There were no professional organizations or university-sanctioned graduate programs dedicated to the study of man. Anthropologists were "serious-minded amateurs or professionals in other disciplines who delighted in communicating across the boundaries of the several natural sciences and the humanities."[1] Not until 1892 did an American university award a doctorate in anthropology.

This landmark event not only foreshadowed a future of graduate education in anthropology in the United States, it also marked the beginning of the rise of anthropology's most prominent individual. Franz Uri Boas, the professor responsible for Alexander Chamberlain's doctorate from Clark University in 1892, would successfully raise anthropology from its infancy as a profession to a respectable, exacting and complex science by the early twentieth century.

Boas was born in Minden, Westphalia, Germany on July 9, 1858. As one of six children, and the only male to survive childhood, Boas was often overprotected. His correspondence with his parents during his university days reveals close maternal ties. His father, Meier, was a successful merchant who, according to Boas, was "liberal, but not active in public affairs."[2] Because his father travelled frequently in connection with his business, Boas had a closer relationship with his mother, Sophie. The founder of the first Froebel Kindergarten in Minden and an active supporter of the revolution of 1848, Sophie Boas was "idealistic, with a lively interest in public matters."[3] As a member of a revolutionary group she came in contact with other "forty-eighters" such as Carl Schurz and Abraham Jacobi, who married her younger sister.

Jacobi's own identification with revolutionary activity in Germany had led to his detention in Berlin and Cologne for high treason from 1851 to 1853.

He then resettled in New York City, where he established his practice as a physician. He assisted Boas in his eventual move to America and also offered him frequent career advice. Boas clearly respected Jacobi's opinion and often consulted with him instead of his parents, whose tendency toward overprotection limited their objectivity.

For Boas, his parents' support of the revolution became "a living force" during his early years and helped explain the formation of his own liberal ideas.[4] Boas was raised as an orthodox Jew, although he perceived that his religious education "was purely a sop for his grandparents, who were orthodox."[5] As Boas relates, "my parents had broken through the shackles of dogma. My father had retained an emotional affection for the ceremonial of his parental home, without allowing it to influence his intellectual freedom. Thus I was spread the struggle against religious dogma that besets the lives of so many young people."[6]

Yet, it is clear that Boas's ties to his religion, or more specifically, to his ethnicity, would profoundly affect him throughout his life. His Jewish upbringing and subsequent experiences with anti-Semitism left their mark on young Boas. Their influence helped account for much of Boas's later anthropological and political activity.

Early in life Boas developed an "intense interest in nature" and lived his early days "without speculation, naively enjoying every new impression."[7] During these formative years he began studying the piano, a hobby that gave him immense satisfaction throughout his life. He adored Beethoven's music, and was fascinated with musical composition. He once remarked, late in his life, that he would "rather have written a good poem than all the books he'd ever written—to say nothing of a movement in a symphony."[8] His daughter, Franziska, recalled that when asked what he would do if he had his life to live over, Boas was torn between a career as a mathematician or a pianist.[9]

Boas remained at home for nineteen years, receiving his primary education at the school and *Gymnasium* in Minden. His major focus in these years was on mathematics and physics, yet he also read poetry and literature. He was well-versed in the works of Schiller and Goethe, and enjoyed reading the poems of Homer and the histories of Herodotus and Thucydides in the original Greek.[10] He also studied Latin and English, as well as biology and other natural sciences. His favorite area of study in his *Gymnasium* education was geography, and he demonstrated an early desire to study cultural history, although the subject was not taught in his school.[11] His interest in culture and the possibilities of doing field research were manifest by age 13. In a letter to his sister in March 1870, he expressed a desire to travel to Australia or Africa. A year later he also spoke of doing research in "unknown lands."[12]

In addition to this early interest in the study of culture, the roots of Boas's later critique of the comparative method of studying cultures lay in his *Gymnasium* days. His own observations regarding his study of botany reflect this development. Expressing dismay at his concern for detail to the neglect of general observation, Boas wrote: "I learnt that true science does not consist in describing individual plants but in understanding their structure and life in comparing all the different groups of plants with one another.... I had already discovered that I preferred comparative science to the descriptive."[13]

At age 19 Boas began his university studies at Heidelberg. German universities at this time were immensely popular, attracting scholars throughout the world. The high degree of intellectual activity affected Boas profoundly, especially since he attended three academic institutions.

He spent one semester at Heidelberg before transferring to Bonn. This move brought him into contact with Theobald Fischer, a professor of geography. When Fischer moved from Bonn to the University at Kiel, Boas transferred there also, although there is no clear indication that Fischer inspired the move.[14] It was at Kiel that Boas settled down to become a serious student. His early university education, although rigorous in terms of coursework in physics and mathematics, was highlighted by frequent drinking and spending money.[15] At Bonn, for example, he was jailed for playing pranks.[16] In both Bonn and Heidelberg, he was involved in duels.[17]

These duels left Boas with several facial scars. In later life he humorously suggested that "an ice bear had scratched him" while he was engaged in field research in Baffinland.[18] The nature of these dueling incidents remains in doubt. It is possible that the duels occurred as a result of anti-Semitic remarks. Anti-Semitism was ascendant in Germany during Boas's college days. Given his inability to tolerate insults anti-Semitic in nature, such a challenge would appear inevitable. This characteristic, the constant drive to challenge beliefs with which he disagreed, remained with him throughout his life and could explain these early duels. Yet it was also the case that the duels were a common phenomenon of nineteenth-century German university life, and as such, were not necessarily motivated by prejudicial slurs but were instead part of each student's rite of passage.[19]

In the summer of 1880 Boas began to study the natural sciences at Kiel. By the fall he had renewed his childhood interest in geography under the tutelage of Fischer. The following year he received his doctorate in physics. His examiners awarded him magna cum laude status when he passed his examinations and a summa cum laude degree for his thesis.[20] His doctoral dissertation, "Contributions to the Understanding of the Color of Water," comprised two investigations: the polarization of light reflected from water and the absorption of light in water.[21]

The thesis incorporated the field of physics, yet it also illustrated Boas's ability to apply "analysis and a set of proofs" to a given project. This analytical method, deemed essential to physics, would later be of significance in Boas's studies of culture.[22] However, there was a crucial difference. In physics there was a body of laws that resulted from careful study and experimentation. Such was not the case in anthropology. Boas was always uneasy about generalizations regarding the study of culture. Insisting on rigorous, exacting methodology at all times, he was always hesitant to proclaim the discovery of a law. His critics often suggested that this trait impeded the growth of anthropological thought. Although the problem of generalization did not affect Boas in his university studies, he developed this concern for precise scientific study early in life.

In addition to Boas's main thesis on the color of water, he was also required to defend several minor theses. The last of these, "That Contemporary Operetta Was Equally to be Condemned on Grounds of Art and Morality," indicated Boas's aesthetic tastes and illustrated the range of his interest. In his own mind his university studies were a compromise between his intellectual and emotional desires. His emotional concern for the "phenomena of the world" led him to study geography, while his intellectual bent directed him toward mathematics and physics.[23] Both tendencies began to dissipate, however, in his last years as a student. As he suggested, his exposure to "the writings of philosophers stimulated news lines of thought," which led to "a desire to understand the relation between the objective and the subjective worlds."[24]

Boas's transition from physics and geography to anthropology was not final at the completion of his university training. However, several of his professors were extremely influential in the early stages of the transition. Theobald Fischer was most significant in this regard. From him, as well as through the readings of other great thinkers such as Karl Ritter and Alexander V. Humboldt, Boas became "preoccupied with actual phenomena in all their detail." In addition, he attained "a concept of diverse and multiple causes; an interest in the environment; a preoccupation with the interrelations of history, peoples, and their environments; and a strong sense of complexity of the historical process."[25] At the end of his university education Boas was still dedicated to the study of geography, physics and philosophy. Before he was to make a major shift in his thinking, however, military duty rudely interrupted his intellectual life.

In 1881 Boas began serving as a one-year "volunteer" in the German army. This military service was distasteful. He found it difficult to concentrate on his studies and actually began to fear a loss of his intellectual capabilities. He expressed his concern to his uncle, Abraham Jacobi: "I have really become so dull from my military duties that I can no longer think myself into my usual train of thought. . . . I am so overjoyed that the greatest part of my slavery is over—171 days more and I shall be free."[26]

During his military service Boas began to formulate plans for his future. His parents favored a teaching career at a Prussian *Gymnasium*, but Boas rejected the idea on two grounds. First, he complained that the profession was overcrowded and second, he cited the difficulty that a Jewish teacher would confront securing such a position.[27] Clearly, anti-Semitism was never far from his thoughts. Boas decided to continue his studies with the intention of dedicating himself to the study of "the mechanism of the life of organisms and especially of peoples."[28] Yet, he understood that he could not achieve such a goal in the immediate future, due both to his lack of knowledge in the field of ethnography and to the financial necessity of his finding immediate employment. Thus he contented himself with geography for the present. The decision was significant, however, in that it marked the first clear expression of Boas's intention to study people and their world.

In assessing his immediate options within geography, Boas chose to "study what influence the configuration of land has on the acquaintances of peoples with their near and far neighbors."[29] This topic led him inevitably to analyze aspects of the transmission of culture, a topic he would later incorporate into his anthropological studies.

Recognizing the need for field research to probe this question, and aware of his ignorance in physiology and sociology, Boas planned to "do nothing but study" until he achieved competency in these areas.[30] Studying, however, paid him no salary. Due to pressing financial need, he contacted Jacobi in New York inquiring about the prospect of attaining a fellowship at Johns Hopkins University in Baltimore.[31]

After communicating with Daniel Coit Gilman, president of Johns Hopkins, Jacobi informed Boas that Gilman would definitely entertain his fellowship application. Boas responded to Gilman with a detailed explanation of his intended geographical study. What emerged from his discussion was the clear indication that culture was beginning to dominate his thought.

Boas flatly rejected the materialistic point of view that had dominated his thinking during his training in physics. Recognizing the "importance of study-ing the interaction between the organic and inorganic, above all the relation between the life of a people and their physical environment," he proposed a new focus for his life's work. Specifically he hoped to investigate "how far may we consider the phenomena of organic life from a mechanistic point of view."

To initiate this project, Boas informed Gilman of his immediate research plans: "At present I am studying the relationship of the migration of the present day Eskimo to the configuration and physical conditions of land. This is, of course, a very extensive piece of work and cannot be finished so soon. I am taking it up chiefly from a methodological standpoint, in order to discover how far one can get studying a very special, and not simple, case, in determining the relationship between the life of a people and environ-ment."[32]

In mid-summer, 1882, Johns Hopkins rejected Boas's application; at the advice of his professors, he remained in Berlin and continued studying.[33] His family supported him financially during this time. The economic drain on his parents dismayed him, and he expressed profound unhappiness over his failure to secure the fellowship, which would have lightened the burden on his father. The fellowship would also have afforded Boas the possibility of joining an expedition to the American Polar Region, or helped him secure a position with the United States Geological Survey.[34] Since the plan did not materialize, he chose to delay this first field trip until the following year.

Having heard of an expedition ship that would sail to Lady Franklin Bay in the summer of 1883, Boas asked Jacobi if he could use his influence to secure Boas's passage on the ship. There is no indication that Jacobi was able to help Boas in this matter; however, Boas finally found transportation with the German Polar Commission vessel *Germania*. The ship would sail to Baffinland in June 1883. The Polar Commission not only promised Boas transportation, it also offered him the use of a house and instruments located in Cumberland Sound.[35] Confident that he would embark on his initial field expedition in the summer, Boas spent the winter and spring of that year with Rudolf Virchow at the Pathological Institute in Berlin practicing anthropological measurements and readying himself for his maiden ethnographic voyage.

Virchow, a left-wing political leader in Germany, had perhaps the greatest influence on Boas. Although trained as a physician and pathologist, Virchow published a number of articles related to anthropological inquiry. He translated his radical political beliefs into his science, as he attempted to professionalize German scientific endeavor. In this respect, his influence on Boas is significant. Boas's concern with the professionalization of anthropology in America, although clearly the result of many diverse forces, was at least partially initiated by Virchow's own activity. Additionally, Virchow's political beliefs and his constant protest against injustice mirrored Boas's philosophy. Both attacked the problem of race prejudice without concern for reprisal. As Clyde Kluckhohn and Olaf Prufer have written, "the motto attributed to Pericles, 'Prosperity lies in freedom alone, and freedom lies only in courage,' was equally that of Virchow and Boas."[36]

From a scientific standpoint, Virchow's attitudes were also critical to Boas's development. His "relative lack of interest in Darwinian evolution and his skepticism about Mendelian heredity" created the reserve Boas always displayed when treating these subjects.[37] Virchow also influenced Boas regarding the development of races. His belief in the plasticity of races foreshadowed Boas's own findings, as delineated in his report for the Dillingham Immigration Commission in 1911.[38]

Perhaps the most significant contribution that Virchow made to Boas's development was the gift of skepticism. Throughout his life Boas hesitated to generalize from specific cases for fear of finding the one exception to the rule. As such he maintained a skeptical stance toward the formulation of any general unifying law concerning man and culture. No doubt recognizing his debt to Virchow in this regard, Boas praised his mentor's wariness:

His position rests on the general scientific principle that it is dangerous to classify data that are imperfectly known under the point of view of general theories, and that the sound progress of science requires of us to be clear at every moment, what elements in the system of science are hypothetical and what are the limits of that knowledge which is obtained by exact observation. To this principle Virchow has adhered steadfastly and rigidly, so much so that many an impetuous student has felt his quiet and cautious criticism as an obstacle to progress. On this account he has suffered many hostile attacks—until generally the progress of research showed that the cautious master was right in rejecting the far-reaching conclusion based on imperfect evidence.[39]

Boas's initial opportunity to collect data from his own "exact observation" approached rapidly. In May 1883 he prepared for his first field trip. After some difficulty procuring financial support, he finally gained the backing of a German newspaper, the *Berliner Tageblatt*, which paid him 3,000 marks for a series of reports he would write and send to the paper during his trip.[40] As Boas explained to Jacobi, his primary reason for making the expedition was to compile data for more general study. He hoped to ascertain the extent of indigenous peoples' knowledge of local geography and how that knowledge influenced migratory patterns.[41]

Aside from his pending trip, Boas contemplated his future. Although his fondest aim prior to his Baffinland expedition was to secure a German professorship, he continued to weigh the possibility of settling in America.[42] He was torn between his determination to further his scientific career, his dream of teaching in Germany and his desire to marry Marie Krackowizer, who resided in New York City.[43] Marie, born in America of German parents, had settled in New York after spending some time in Germany. Boas met her during her visit to Germany in 1881. Her return to the United States affected Boas greatly, for he had fallen in love with her. When she again visited Germany in 1883, they became engaged. Accordingly, these conflicting desires raged within young Boas, as he prepared to embark on a voyage that would change the course of his study as well as the course of his life.

His one-year study of Eskimo culture began in July 1883. He concentrated on both ethnological and geographical problems, although it is clear that ethnography was becoming his dominant interest. The contributions he made to the field of geography, however, were significant. Although forced to use imprecise instruments, Boas greatly improved upon the existing map of the Baffinland region. Additionally, he did much to support the proposition that geography was a "separate scientific discipline."[44]

Personally, Boas was disappointed with his ethnographic research during the trip. He had sought to "add to the knowledge of unknown regions" and to "understand the reaction of the human mind to natural environment." He considered his results "shallow" and felt that he had not discovered anything of value concerning the "forces that mold behavior."[45] Perhaps his most important accomplishment during the expedition was the solidification of his commitment to ethnography as his future course of study. While career opportunities would force him to delay an actual shift into anthropology, he recognized that his trip to Baffinland profoundly affected his intellectual outlook. He believed this experience moved him away from his former scientific interests, "toward the desire to understand what determines the behavior of human beings."[46]

Apart from the trip's significance for Boas's transition from physics and geography to anthropology lay revealing insights into the nature of Boas's personality. As Melville Herskovits explained, in discussing the Baffinland adventure:

We see here his scientific integrity and intransigence, which made compromise on any level unthinkable. We see his fertility of mind and his ability to grasp and phrase a problem, which caused him to develop the many innovations in theoretical analysis and methodological techniques for which he became famous. We see the mathematical ability that gave the analytical bent to his approach to all questions, and the point of view which insisted that theory not outrun inductively derived proof.[47]

A more emotional side of Boas's character also surfaced during the expedition. He enjoyed his life among the Eskimos and wrote of them with much sentiment. He valued their love of nature and the importance they placed on friendship. Although he felt the quality of their life was rude in comparison with his own, he stressed that "the Eskimo is a man as we are; his feelings, his virtues and his shortcomings are based on human nature, like ours."[48]

In September 1884, after completing his research in Baffinland, Boas made his initial journey to America. Residing with Jacobi throughout the winter, he desperately hunted for employment in the United States. Jacobi, presumably at Boas's urging, inquired about the possibility of Boas lecturing at Columbia College. The trustees, however, refused to open the lecture rooms of the college to strangers, and consequently, Boas's affiliation with Columbia remained in the future.[49] Since he found no job prospects in America, Boas returned to Germany in the spring. He had not, however, abandoned his desire to live in America.

This yearning to settle in the United States caused Boas's parents much consternation. The closeness of the family and the strength of parental ties were most apparent during this period of Boas's life. His mother, writing to Jacobi, expressed her concern about losing her only son to America, although clearly she recognized that such a move might be beneficial to his future. Exclaiming that she could not stand it if Boas settled in America, she also admitted that "parents and sisters now take second place, when it is a matter of establishing a home."[50] Boas felt the conflict as well. His love for Germany and parents clashed with his yearning for his fiancée Marie and his realization that his future as an anthropologist would be brighter in the United States.

Boas returned from America "down-hearted and discouraged."[51] His failure to find work combined with the separation from Marie made him uncertain about his future and unhappy about his current predicament. He busied himself recording the results of his Baffinland research, and delivered an occasional lecture on anthropology. Soon after his return to Germany, he became an assistant to ethnologist Adolph Bastian at the Royal Ethnographic Museum in Berlin. Boas's principle duty there was to design and build displays illustrating Alaskan and northwestern Canadian culture. Additionally, he became a docent in geography at the University of Berlin in 1886.

During this uncertain time, Boas studied the Indian tribes of the North Pacific Coast. His previous contact with the Bella Coola Indians in 1883 and his work on a Bella Coola display at the museum triggered a desire to continue his research in British Columbia. Consequently, he began to formulate plans for another expedition. Recognizing the limitations of a single year's research in an unknown region, Boas planned a four-year trip to study Indian and Eskimo tribes of the British Northwest. Utilizing a comparative methodology, he hoped to observe the Naskopi and Eskimos of Labrador, the Indian tribes of Chesterfield Inlet and Alaska, and the Indians of Vancouver. He understood that the various tribes of the British Northwest "must be studied in relation to one another and that only someone who understands The East will be able to thoroughly understand The West."[52]

Finding no opportunity to "make his knowledge of value for science," Boas turned to Bastian to support his research proposal. He requested 9,000 marks a year for a four-year period. Bastian, however, was unable to grant him the necessary amount, which increased Boas's discouragement and frustration about continuing to live and work in Germany.

Further disappointment followed shortly thereafter. Johns Hopkins University again rejected his application for a fellowship;[53] the Geological and Natural History Survey of Canada declined to fund his four-year research proposal.[54] Financial worries and uncertainty about his career continually distressed Boas. Since he had received his doctorate, his life had been unsettled. Pushed by a desire to begin meaningful scientific work in America and plagued by the insecurity of financial insolvency, Boas was extremely depressed.

In May 1886, his prospects grew brighter. Robert Bell, assistant director of the Geological Survey of Canada, secured Boas's passage on the S. S. Alert, which would sail from Halifax to explore Hudson Bay.[55] Although the survey could not grant Boas money for the trip, Bell was confident that funds would be forthcoming, once Boas proved his competency and the importance of his research.[56] Determined not to be deterred by economic problems, Boas financed the trip through his own resources and a modest gift from Jacobi.

Boas spent autumn 1886 in the Hudson Bay region working under the auspices of the Canadian government. His enthusiasm for research remained unabated during his trip, but he became lonely for Marie and his parents. He travelled by rail to Victoria where he reported that his life in British Columbia was "monotonous," since he spent most of his time listening to stories that dealt with the mythology of the region.[57] During his three-month expedition he not only collected museum specimens, skulls and Indian tales, but also compiled some linguistic material and made an ethnographic map of Vancouver Island.[58]

Clearly, Boas viewed this trip as "his entree to a museum position in America."[59] During the trip he contacted Carl Schurz in New York. Schurz, a close friend of Jacobi's and himself a forty-eighter, was influential in the scientific community in New York. Boas sought his aid in obtaining a position at the American Museum of Natural History.[60] Schurz's inability to secure such employment further frustrated Boas. Settlement in America preoccupied him toward the close of his three-month research trip. Although scheduled to lecture at the University of Berlin on the geography and ethnography of North America upon his return to Germany, Boas hoped instead to remain in New York.[61]

On the basis of Boas's work on the Northwest Coast, Daniel G. Brinton, a prominent Philadelphia ethnologist, supported his effort to stay in the United States. Believing it to be a "decided advantage to American ethnology if you can secure a position in the United States which will induce you to remain," Brinton offered his unqualified help and endorsement.[62] Boas, on the basis of such support and his own belief in future opportunities in America, resigned from his position at the University of Berlin and, in February 1887, accepted employment as an assistant editor of *Science*, a New York-based journal.

Many factors influenced Boas's decision to settle in America. His expectation of better opportunities for career advancement was a primary motivating force. He saw science developing rapidly in America and felt confident that he could secure either a teaching position or a museum job. Additionally, Boas had found "the intellectual atmosphere" of Manhattan attractive.[63] Through Jacobi, Boas had made contact with prominent members of the German-Jewish community, who were active in various academic, scientific and cultural circles. This led him to believe that he could more easily establish contacts necessary for a promising career in America than elsewhere. The other major factor contributing to his resettlement was his desire to marry Marie Krackowizer. Separated from her while in Germany and during his Baffinland trip, Boas refused to leave her again.

Although these reasons are sufficient to explain his move, there was another factor of considerable importance. The anti-Semitism and political repression that characterized late nineteenth-century Germany constantly weighed on Boas. His early experience with anti-Jewish feeling, which may have precipitated the dueling incidents, left psychic as well as physical scars. Also, the recognition of the difficulty he would encounter as a Jew teaching in Germany influenced his decision. He viewed America as "politically an ideal country," where he could be free to do as he pleased.[64] Enthralled with the ideal of democracy, which complemented his republican and individualistic tendencies, Boas was enthusiastic about the promise of American life.[65] Finally, his fear of the draft in Germany and the necessity of declaring a religious affiliation also played minor roles in his decision.[66]

Boas's immigration to the United States in 1887 marked the beginning of a new stage in his life. Not only did he marry Marie and begin his job as assistant editor of *Science*, he also made the final leap from physics to anthropology as his major field of study.

The transition had been a slow one. His desire to shift to ethnology preceded his opportunities. Although it has been argued that "the shift in his orientation was gradual and continuous" from 1880 to 1887, this ignores the divergence of his thought and action.[67] Clearly Boas did not actively change the focus of his study prior to his arrival in America. The financial constraints that burdened him throughout his early life forced him into compromises that made ethnographic activity difficult. Fearing that he was a drain on his parents, he lectured in geography at the University of Berlin. Requiring money to further his researches, he concentrated on geography in his Northwest Coast explorations, primarily to please his employers.[68] And yet, Boas had committed himself to anthropology prior to 1887. As early as 1883, during his trip to Baffinland, he recognized the change in his own thinking. He wanted to understand "what determines the behavior of human beings."[69] The beginnings of this shift were discernable even prior to this initial expedition. The proposal Boas made to Jacobi when applying for the Johns Hopkins fellowship indicated his desire to study man. Concerned with his lack of the necessary ethnographic knowledge to conduct research properly, Boas delayed making an actual shift in his work, although he had clearly made the transition in his thought.[70]

Boas's avid interest in human beings accounted for the shift in his field of study. "He passed rapidly through geography to anthropology...due to his being humanly interested in human contacts."[71] The sentiment he expressed toward the Eskimos with whom he lived in Baffinland illustrated this point. The frequent protests against racism that would characterize his entire life also point to his concern for humanity. The origins of this concern are complex. However, the influence of his parents, to a certain degree, explained his desire to study man:

His methods were from the laboratories of the physical sciences and his inspiration, according to his own account, came from the "spirit of liberalism," as interpreted by his mother. That calculated and militant spirit of liberalism just about closed out the old-fashioned father who maintained an "emotional affection" for the traditions of a great people. It is just possible, however, that it was his father that turned Boas's retreat from the active world of people into an assault on the problems and mysteries of that world. Lacking a natural *feeling* for people, he sought to make up for that loss by *knowing* more about them than anyone else. Without the small but critical inheritance from his father he would not have felt his loss, and the determination—stronger for being blind—to make up for it would never have been born.[72]

Whatever the roots of his shift to anthropology, Boas embarked on a new career when he came to America in 1887. The beliefs he held and the areas he wished to explore would both be affected by his new surroundings. He came to America as "a nineteenth-century scientist" who believed that "scientific laws are found in nature rather than formulated by the scientist."[73] The great enthusiasm he held for "the discovery of laws of cultural development" would diminish before the advent of modern science.[74] And yet, although Boas would be changed by modern science, he would significantly transform it as well.

## NOTES

1. Frederica Delaguna, ed., *Selected Papers from the American Anthropologist, 1888–1920* (Evanston, Ill.: Row, Peterson, 1960), p. 91.

2. Franz Boas, "An Anthropologist's Credo," *The Nation* 147 (August 1938): 201.

3. Ibid.

4. Ibid.

5. "The Reminiscences of Franziska Boas," Oral History Research Office, Columbia University, 1972, p. 10.

6. Boas, "Credo," p. 201.

7. Ibid.

8. Margaret Mead, *An Anthropologist at Work: Writings of Ruth Benedict* (Boston: Houghton Mifflin, 1959), p. 74.

9. "Reminiscences of Franziska Boas," p. 69.

10. Clyde Kluckhohn and Olaf Prufer, "Influences during the Formative Years," in *The Anthropology of Franz Boas: Essays on the Centennial of His Birth*, ed. Walter Goldschmidt, American Anthropological Association, 62, no. 5, part 2, Memoir no. 89 (October 1959): 6.

11. Ibid.

12. Ibid.

13. Ibid., p. 7.

14. There is some disagreement on this point. Alfred Kroeber contends in "Franz Boas: The Man," *American Anthropologist* 45, no. 3, Part 2, Memoir no. 61 (July-September 1943): 5–26, that Boas did, indeed, follow Fischer to Kiel for the purpose of studying geography with him. Kluckhohn and Prufer disagree. Based on a letter from Boas to his mother on September 28, 1879, they assert that Boas's family wanted him to go to Kiel and that Boas considered staying there for only one term. In light of the evidence, most notably the fact that Boas did not make mention of his relationship with Fischer until after his transfer, it seems apparent that he went to Kiel at the urging of his parents, and not because of Fischer.

15. Kluckhohn and Prufer, "Influences," p. 8.

16. "Reminiscences of Franziska Boas," p. 25.

17. Kluckhohn and Prufer, "Influences," p. 8.

18. "Reminiscences of Franziska Boas," p. 11.

19. Abram Kardiner and Edward Preble, *They Studied Man* (New York: World Publishing, 1961), p. 137.

20. Kluckhohn and Prufer, "Influences," p. 8.

21. Kroeber, "The Man," p. 5.

22. Ibid.

23. Boas, "Credo," p. 202.

24. Ibid., p. 203.

25. Kluckhohn and Prufer, "Influences," p. 20.

26. Franz Boas to Abraham Jacobi, April 12, 1882, American Philosophical Society, Library, Boas Correspondence. (Hereafter cited as APS/BC.) Written in English.

27. Boas to Jacobi, January 2, 1882, APS/BC.

28. Ibid.

29. Ibid.

30. Ibid.

31. Ibid.

32. Boas to Jacobi, April 10, 1882, APS/BC.

33. Sophie Boas to Jacobi, July 22, 1882, APS/BC.

34. Boas to Jacobi, November 26, 1882, APS/BC.

35. Boas to Jacobi, February 8, 1883, APS/BC.

36. Kluckhohn and Prufer, "Influences," pp. 21–22.

37. Ibid.

38. Erwin H. Ackerknecht, *Rudolf Virchow, doctor, statesman, and anthropologist* (Madison: Wisconsin University Press, 1953), p. 235.

39. Franz Boas, "Rudolf Virchow's Anthropological Work," *Science*, n.s. 16, No. 403 (September 1902): 442; Kluckhohn and Prufer, "Influences," p. 23.

40. Boas to Jacobi, May 2, 1883, APS/BC.

41. Ibid.

42. Boas to Jacobi, November 26, 1882, APS/BC.

43. Boas to Jacobi, May 9, 1883, APS/BC.

44. Saul Benison, "Geography and the Early Career of Franz Boas," *American Anthropologist* 51 (1949): 523–24.

45. Boas, "Credo," p. 204.

46. Ibid.

47. Melville J. Herskovits, *Franz Boas: The Science of Man in the Making* (New York: Charles Scribner's Sons, 1953), pp. 10–11.

48. Kardiner and Preble, *They Studied Man*, p. 137.

49. O. N. Rood to Abraham Jacobi, January 30, 1885, APS/BC.

50. Sophie Boas to Jacobi, February 4, 1885, APS/BC.

51. Sophie Boas to Jacobi, April 20, 1885, APS/BC.

52. Boas to Adolph Bastian, January 5, 1886, APS/BC.

53. T. R. Ball to Boas, January 8, 1886, APS/BC.

54. George M. Dawson to Boas, February 23, 1886, APS/BC.

55. Robert Bell to Boas, May 23, 1886, APS/BC.

56. Bell to Boas, May 15, 1886, APS/BC.

57. Boas to Sophie and Meier Boas, October 23, 1886, in *The Ethnography of Franz Boas: Letters and Diaries of Franz Boas Written on the Northwest Coast from 1886 to 1931*, ed. Ronald Rohner (Chicago: University of Chicago Press, 1969), p. 45. (Hereafter letters from this work will be cited as RR/FB.)

58. Rohner, *Ethnography of Franz Boas*, p. 17.

59. Ibid.

60. Boas to Carl Schurz, October 27, 1886, APS/BC.

61. Boas to Sophie and Meier Boas, November 19, 1886, RR/FB, p. 62.

62. Daniel G. Brinton to Boas, January 2, 1887, APS/BC.

63. Herskovits, *Franz Boas*, p. 12.

64. Boas to Toni Boas, December 8, 1930, RR/FB, p. 295.

65. Kroeber, "The Man," p. 11.

66. Boas to Toni Boas, December 8, 1930, RR/FB, p. 296.

67. George W. Stocking, Jr., *Race, Culture, and Evolution: Essays in the History of Anthropology* (New York: Free Press, 1968), pp. 156–57.

68. Robert Bell to Boas, May 25, 1886, APS/BC. This letter suggests that Bell and the Geological Survey of Canada expected Boas to focus on the geology of the area. Although the trip was not funded by the Canadian government, Bell assured Boas that impressive results, with a geological bent, would influence the survey to support him financially in the future.

69. Boas, "Credo," p. 204.

70. Franz Boas to Abraham Jacobi, January 2, 1882, APS/BC.

71. Kroeber, "The Man," p. 11.

72. Kardiner and Preble, *They Studied Man*, p. 145.

73. Kluckhohn and Prufer, "Influences," p. 24.

74. Ibid.

# 2
# The Quest for Stability

Boas's employment as an assistant editor of *Science* commenced in February 1887. His principle duties included working with the journals published by Science, Inc., and the preparation and supervision of map printing.[1] Specifically, he took charge of the geographical department of the company, although he also edited anthropological material. Receiving a salary of $150 per month, Boas felt financially stable for the first time since he had left the University of Kiel. This new security prompted him to marry Marie Krackowizer on March 10, 1887. The couple moved into a small apartment on the east side of Manhattan.

Although primarily concerned with his editorial responsibilities, Boas engaged in other scholarly activities as well. He began his first formal association with the American Museum of Natural History in late February 1887. The museum commissioned him to catalogue H. R. Bishop's collection of British Columbian artifacts.[2] Additionally, he continued his association with prominent members of the Canadian scientific community. At the urging of Robert Bell, the man responsible for his 1886 expedition, Boas journeyed to Canada for the spring meeting of the Royal Scientific Society.[3] This Canadian connection remained useful throughout the late nineteenth century, as Boas expanded his own field research.

Boas's arrival in America, then, represented a fresh, distinct phase of his life. He began a family, settled into his own home, and established contacts in the professional world that would later be instrumental in his own rise as a scientist. These first years in America also revealed the beginning of a dichotomy that characterized his entire life. As Melville Herskovits has pointed out, there appeared to be two sides to Boas, "the personal and professional, which stand in such marked contrast—the first calm, conventional, warm in human relations, the second turbulent, courageous, wherein Boas was the supreme individualist, who dominated the scene in which he for so many years played his role."[4]

The first evidence of Boas's professional courage and individualism occurred soon after his arrival at *Science*. That spring he openly challenged several prominent members of the Smithsonian Institution by debating their theories of museum classification.

In 1886, Otis Tufton Mason of the United States National Museum had published a report on the organization of museum exhibits, examining the problem of the appearance of similar inventions in areas geographically distant from one another. He attributed this phenomenon to one of several factors. Either the race of people initially responsible for the invention had migrated, thus taking their creation with them, or the ideas and techniques of invention itself were taught to other tribes, by the originating people.

A third possibility, Mason suggested, was that the same conditions were present in two or more different and distinct tribes. This led Mason to the hypothesis that "like causes produce like effects."[5] In arguing for a system of classification based on this theory, Mason believed that organizing museum displays by individual objects would allow for comparison between them and would illustrate the evolution of the product to fit human needs.[6]

Mason's logic rested firmly on his strong adherence to evolutionary doctrine. Although similar inventions among different races could be the product of cultural diffusion, and have either physical or intellectual origins, if no such contact existed, then the similar invention must be the result of a similar level of civilization. For evolutionists, such as Mason, "the regular, independent occurrence of the same idea in similar circumstances seemed to offer direct evidence that the development of human reason was governed by natural laws."[7]

In his response to Mason, "The Occurrence of Similar Inventions in Areas Widely Apart," Boas challenged his classification of "human inventions and other ethnological phenomena in the light of biological specimens."[8] He also dissented vigorously from the hypothesis that "like causes produce like effects." Boas suggested that each ethnological specimen should be studied individually in terms of its own history. He rejected Mason's idea that classifying an object in relation to another subject of similar form and use would help explain its origin and purpose within a specific society.

Frustrated by the National Museum's method of display, which grouped together similar types of objects, Boas argued for the reorientation of the museum's entire system. Claiming that "the marked character of the North-West American tribes is almost lost" in the National Museum display, he advocated arranging the collection according to individual tribes, "in order to teach the peculiar style of each group."[9] Emphasizing the importance of each invention's history, Boas insisted on classification by tribe, rather than by object. This would illustrate the object's origin, history and development, and would also show its relationship to the culture as a whole.[10]

Admiring the "candid spirit" with which Boas expressed himself, Mason promised to reply through the pages of *Science*.[11] There he defended his classification method as one of many viable systems used by museums. He explained that different methods worked to different purposes, and that the aim of the National Museum was well-served by his system in this particular instance. Then, taking a staunchly evolutionist posture, he dealt with Boas's theoretical assault on the like causes–like effects principle. He dismissed as irrelevant, although ingenious, Boas's counter-theory that unlike causes could also produce similar effects. He again emphasized his own point of view in this regard, while at the same time defending his biological methodology. He expressed his conviction "that inventions of both customs and things spring from prior inventions, just as life springs from life, and that the sooner we recognize the fact that in the study of arts, institutions, language, knowledge, customs, religions, and races of men, we must always apply the methods and instrumentalities of the biologist, the sooner will our beloved science stand upon an immovable foundation."[12]

Boas warmed to the debate. He offered his own definition of the study of ethnology. He stressed that the purpose of "our science is to understand the phenomena, called ethnological and anthropological, in the widest sense of those words—in their historical development and geographical distribution, and in their physiological and psychological foundation."[13] He then sought to examine the method that must be used in ethnological research. Stating that "ethnological phenomena are the result of the physical and psychical character of men, and of its development under the influence of the surroundings," Boas posed two problems for study.[14] The initial inquiry, he said, must deal with an investigation into the people's surroundings. This study should yield an understanding of the "laws and history of the development of the physiological and psychological character of mankind."[15] Additionally, Boas urged consideration of other crucial variables, such as the history of the people, the influences that affected the people during migration, and the individuals with whom the migrating group came into contact.

Beyond this initial phase of research, Boas detailed a second, more challenging area of study. It was imperative, he said, to determine the interplay between an ever-changing environment and the physical and psychical character of the people under study. Since "each stage in the development of a people leaves its stamp," Boas thought it crucial to discern each step and its relation to the final cultural form.[16] By this process the anthropologist could fashion a realistic explanation for the appearance of similar inventions in distant cultures.

Boas described two ways of handling this problem. One method, advocated by Mason, was "to compare the phenomena, and to draw conclusions by analogy."[17] Boas labelled this the deductive method. The second research paradigm, the inductive approach, studied "phenomena arising from a common psychical cause among all tribes and as influenced by their surroundings; i.e., by tracing the full history of the single phenomenon."[18] Clearly, Boas advocated the latter approach. Arranging museum objects by tribes fit neatly with this inductive theory, since it permitted the study of phenomena within a particular culture. Although admitting that Mason's deductive technique was useful in pinpointing problems, Boas asserted that "induction must scrutinize the ideas found by deduction."[19]

Boas was also critical of Mason's reliance on a system based on analogy. He cautioned that phenomena appearing to be similar on the surface are actually vastly different in their "immanent qualities." Consequently, the "same phenomena may originate from unlike causes." Although accepting that similar causes can have like effects, Boas also contended that like effects often evolve from totally different causal factors.[20]

What emerged from this round of the debate was Boas's adherence to the inductive method as it applied to museum exhibits. He firmly maintained that "in ethnology all is individuality." Arranging an exhibit by tribe rather than by object highlighted the relative nature of civilizations and also demonstrated the degree to which each culture was influenced by its "geographical and historical surroundings." Furthermore, this system alone illustrated the state of a civilization at any given historical moment, which for Boas was of paramount importance in understanding cultural progress and development.[21]

This detailed rebuttal of Mason's position elicited yet another reply from the National Museum. John Wesley Powell, head of the United States Geological Survey and a prominent member of the Bureau of American Ethnology of the Smithsonian Institution, entered the debate. The central focus of his argument was an attack on Boas's system, which he claimed was contradictory in nature. Powell praised Mason's method as the most workable paradigm. Himself an ardent evolutionist, he naturally subscribed to classification by analogy.[22]

In a style typical of his entire career, Boas had the last word. He responded to Powell tersely by explaining that displaying objects by tribe highlighted individual phenomena, while Mason's system made "classifications that are not founded on the phenomenon, but in the mind of the student."[23] Although this note in *Science* concluded the public exchange, Boas and Mason continued the debate privately. Boas stressed the importance of taking history into account before drawing conclusions, an emphasis he found sadly lacking in Mason's desire to compare particular phenomena apart from their originating cultures.[24] Unlike later acrimonious scientific squabbles, however, this debate ended with the major combatants still on cordial terms.

The Mason-Boas controversy was significant for several reasons. First, it shed crucial light on the development of Boas's anthropological thought. Boas directly attacked the underpinning of the evolutionist argument, both by elevating the importance of historical particularism and by arguing for a holistic paradigm in displaying tribal artifacts. Mason and Powell's system of museum classification represented the evolutionist's dedication to comparativism, which Boas criticized as "premature and arbitrary."[25] Accordingly, this intellectual exchange graphically revealed a fundamental difference between evolutionist and antievolutionist thought. Boas's method, which highlighted the complexities of the entire culture and revealed subtleties extant below its surface, would later gain ascendancy in anthropological circles.[26]

Boas's hesitancy to generalize in formulating unifying laws was apparent throughout the course of the debate. This distrust of general laws and emphasis on individual phenomena and their history constituted "the best expression of Boas's fundamental attitude toward science."[27]

Additionally, in challenging Mason, Boas displayed a good bit of courage. His theories were not yet part of the scientific mainstream, although anthropology as a discipline eventually followed Boas's method, rather than Mason's.[28] This movement within the field away from wide-ranging generalizations highlighted a distinction between two different groups of scientific thinkers. In one category were "generalizers or theory-builders," including men such as Charles Darwin, Thomas Hunt Morgan, Edward B. Tylor, Emile Durkheim and Charles S. Peirce. A second group, which explicitly rejected generalizations, featured Boas and William James. These "particularists" contended that "generalizations are never valued in the field of man and culture because there is always some particular fact that doesn't fit the theory."[29]

Since late nineteenth-century society witnessed an implicit rejection of materialism and naturalism in interpreting the world, it is not surprising that social sciences such as anthropology followed the particularist approach advanced by Boas and James.[30] Anthropology, specifically, adhered to Boas's method not because of his dynamism as a leader of scientific thought, but because his theories meshed with the existing zeitgeist. Boas became a spokesman for society's current beliefs.

Boas's dispute with Mason and Powell represented in microcosm the clash that would take place, late in the century, between amateur and professional anthropologists. Both Mason and Powell, although certainly enlightened ethnologists, were not trained as such. Mason deplored the advent of professionalization, especially because of his connection with the Anthropological Society of Washington.[31] Boas, on the other hand, represented the thoroughgoing, university-trained professional. In his later efforts to found an anthropological association, he would condemn and belittle the activity of amateurs as detrimental to serious scientific research. Together, the disagreement with Mason and anthropology's eventual shift to Boasian particularism marked that science's nascent professionalization. Boas, advocating a more intensive, and hence more demanding, research methodology, was slowly formulating the course that twentieth-century anthropology would follow.

Apart from this distinction between amateurs and professionals, the debate underscored the inroads that Jewish scientists would make in American social science. Anthropology in the United States began as a science under the control of white, Anglo-Saxon males. Boas significantly expanded the ethnic and gender makeup of this membership to include not only Jews but blacks and women as well. This transition, of course, was no smoother or less acrimonious than the one from amateur to professional.

Beyond the concern with historical particularism and the development of anthropology, the controversy depicted other elements of what would become Boasian thought. The debate set the stage for Boas's initial rejection of "premature" or "arbitrary" classification.[32] He would intensify his critique of the method and the dangers of the comparative theory before the close of the century. At this early stage in his career, he had already developed a concern for meticulous, detailed research. Furthermore, the debate reflected Boas's commitment to individuality in ethnological study. His concern for the history and development of a single phenomenon and the role of environment in that development would remain a central thrust of his thought.[33]

In the fall of 1887, Boas embarked upon a plan to establish an ethnological society in New York City. After gaining support from Judge Charles Daley, president of the Geographical Society of New York; Professor Newburry, president of the New York Academy of Sciences; Abraham Jacobi, president of the Academy of Medicine (Boas's uncle); and Carl Schurz, Boas contacted Powell seeking endorsement of his project.[34] He hoped that the new society would promote interest in ethnology, provide a forum for the publication of ethnological treatises, and help fund field research.[35]

Many prominent scientists supported this goal. Frederick Ward Putnam of Harvard University's Peabody Museum thought the plan desirable, but urged caution. Recalling abortive efforts to establish the American Ethnological Society of New York several years before, Putnam suggested that Boas use great care in organizing his society. Specifically, Putnam was concerned that the membership could lack the dedication vital to success. Consequently, he advised Boas to consider limiting entrance into the society to workers in anthropology.[36] This suggestion mirrored Boas's later sentiments concerning the requirements for membership in the American Anthropological Association, and foreshadowed the conflict between amateur and professional anthropologists that occurred around the turn of the century.

Daniel G. Brinton, an early admirer and supporter of Boas, also supported the plan, and accepted Boas's invitation to write an article for the first volume of the society's journal.[37] Brinton approved Boas's idea to merge his society with the extant, but inactive American Ethnological Society.[38] Boas had previously contacted Alexander J. Cotheal, president of the dormant society, in an attempt to procure his membership roster.[39]

Suggestions and enthusiastic support for the society came from Washington as well. Mason, recalling his own experience as one of the founders of the Anthropological Society of Washington, suggested changing the name from "ethnological" to "anthropological."[40] Unlike Putnam, Mason favored an open membership policy rather than restricting membership solely to individuals actively engaged in anthropological research. Explaining that a new society needs "patrons as well as talkers, men who like to see their names among intellectual people," Mason advocated the active recruitment of "doctors, lawyers, architects, engineers, clergy, rabbis," and anyone else expressing avid interest.[41]

Mason, representing Washington-based anthropology, adhered to the idea of a conglomeration of professionals and amateurs. Juxtaposed to him stood Putnam, who preferred a more professional, intellectual group. Although part of Mason's motive for the inclusion of amateurs was financial, the divergence of opinion was nonetheless significant. Anthropologists from the Washington area generally were not committed to the professionalization of their science. This was not the case with Boas and Putnam. The disagreement, however, did not become a major issue at this time. In the final analysis, Boas did not listen to either man. The struggle between Washington's open membership policy and Putnam's concern for professionalization smoldered under the surface of anthropological organizations. It would not come to the fore until the creation of an association of national scope. Boas proceeded with the establishment of his ethnological society, grateful for the interest and advice of others, but seemingly unmoved by their suggestions.

Boas's former connection with the Geological Survey of Canada reaped additional benefits in the winter of 1888. Impressed with his earlier work during the Northwest Coast expedition, the British Association for the Advancement of Science asked if he was interested in collecting information on aboriginal tales of Canada.[42] The committee under whose auspices Boas would work was chaired by the noted British ethnologist, Edward B. Tylor, although the local director, Horatio Hale, a former member of the Wilkes expedition, would actually supervise Boas's research. After two months of deliberation, Boas accepted the invitation and made plans to begin research at the end of May 1888.

Despite his editing responsibilities at *Science*, his efforts on behalf of the ethnological society, and preparation for his summer journey, Boas continued to extend himself in other directions. In the spring of 1888 he joined William Wells Newell of Cambridge, Massachusetts, in founding the *Folk-Lore Journal*. Although Newell handled most of the publishing and administrative duties, Boas was in close contact with him, and together the two men assembled the contents of each issue.

In late May Boas left for the field. Hale instructed him to "confine his linguistic research to the collection of limited vocabularies and brief grammatical sketches."[43] He was also asked to draw an ethnographic map of northwestern Canada and to make anthropometric measurements of the various Indian tribes he encountered. Finally, Hale expected him to give "a brief description of the country insofar as it helped to understand 'the condition and mode of life of the different tribes.' "[44] In addition to the work outlined by Hale, Boas collected anthropological material for his own use. Although considering the job unpleasant, Boas took bones from Indian graves. He wrote to the United States National Museum in Washington inquiring whether they would consider purchasing the skeletons for the sum of $600.[45]

Critics have contended that Boas's lack of respect for the Indian tribes precipitated these forays into "grave robbing." On occasion he did complain both about the conditions under which he had to live and the irresponsibility of the Indians with whom he worked. Yet, on the whole, Boas respected the Indians, feeling that he could learn a great deal from them. The success of his research and the vast quantity of data he amassed can be attributed to the rapport he established with them. Herskovits writes of the ease with which Boas was able to relate to the tribes he studied:

[It] stemmed from the recognition he accorded values in the life of the peoples with whom he dealt, the deep pity he felt for the difficult times on which they had come, and his honest humility in the face of those who commanded information whose importance he understood, and which he had come to them to learn. In his own culture, Boas, though a man of broad human sympathy, was proud, with a sense of position that derived from the early days of his childhood training. He would concede what he felt to be his due to no man; but where he was the student, he took the position that those who taught him merited the respect that he gave them.[46]

Boas was satisfied with the results of his trip, although he believed he achieved far less than in his 1886 expedition.[47] His major accomplishment concerned the structure of the Indian languages he studied. It was during this expedition that he discovered that the Haida and Tlingit languages were similar in structure to Asiatic languages, rather than to Indian ones.[48] Although not proven conclusively at this time, the theory excited Boas about the possibility of further research.

Returning to Manhattan in the summer, Boas again confronted a future of financial insecurity. His two-year contract with *Science* would expire the following February, and financial constraints prohibited the publisher from renewing his contract.[49] Despite this impending economic problem, Boas remained optimistic. He had received notification that the committee of the British Association for the Advancement of Science required his services again for the following summer. Additionally, John W. Powell promised Boas $450 to bring back information on the Salish people, for the Bureau of American

Ethnology in Washington.[50] Moreover, before his contract with *Science* expired, Boas entered into a new agreement with N. D. C. Hodges, the journal's publisher. Boas agreed to furnish three columns of geographical and ethnological material and notes, including maps, for each week's edition. Hodges would pay him $50 a month for the service.[51] This added income partially offset the loss of the editing job, although it did not ease Boas's financial worries.

When Boas wrote up the results of his most recent field trip for Tylor's committee, he recognized that more research was necessary, and took the liberty of outlining the areas that required more data. The report he submitted became a source of conflict with Hale. Hale criticized several aspects of the maps. He also accused Boas of failing to follow the detailed instructions given him prior to the expedition. Attributing this attack to Hale's own lack of experience with mapmaking, Boas urged Hale to trust Boas's judgment.[52]

Boas was extremely distressed by Hale's displeasure. Accordingly, prior to his planned trip to Europe in April, Boas restructured his summer research plans. He set aside a few weeks to work in British Columbia for Tylor's committee, but made his major commitment to Powell and the Bureau of American Ethnology. Boas accepted Powell's offer to continue working in the Washington and Oregon areas. In attempting to justify this move, Boas delineated the "many annoyances" he endured while working under Hale's direction.[53] He was upset by the "numerous restrictions imposed by Professor Hale regarding the arrangement of the reports."[54] He also believed that Hale's detailed instructions, given at the "very last moment," hindered the field work. Accordingly, Boas recommended that Alexander F. Chamberlain of Toronto take over the bulk of the committee's research, so that Boas would no longer have to deal with Hale directly.[55]

Boas did not, however, abandon the British Columbia research project. Returning from Europe in early July, he prepared to depart for Canada by the middle of the month. He planned to begin his expedition in Alert Bay north of Vancouver Island, hoping "to settle a number of doubtful points on the sociology of the tribes of that region, but principally to obtain translations of a number of songs of members of secret societies."[56] He also expected to travel to Bella Bella to study the Indian tribes of that region.

His proposal clearly indicated that despite his annoyance with Hale his research took precedence. It is difficult to determine whether this is attributable to Boas's sense of professional obligation, his need for financial security, or the coaxing of Tylor, with whom Boas conferred during his recent European trip. At any rate, Boas did not sever his ties with the committee.

He began his second summer of research for the British Association for the Advancement of Science in Victoria, British Columbia, in July. Again plagued by the detailed, often contradictory instructions of Hale, Boas found his research impeded. As he complained to his wife: "When I come back I shall make excerpts from Hale's most juicy letters and send them to Tylor, explaining that I cannot go on working with Hale. . . . The old man is simply so forgetful that he forgets from letter to letter what he has said before and then accuses me of having not followed his instructions. . . . Besides, his special instructions are very childish and show clearly that he knows nothing about general ethnology."[57] The results of the expedition were, in Boas's own words, "meager." Hampered by Hale's "useless instructions," Boas wasted valuable research time.[58] Nevertheless, he did collect important material on the Nootka, Salish and Kwakiutl tribes.

Moreover, during this second expedition Boas laid the foundation for his future career. He contacted G. Stanley Hall, president of the newly established Clark University, regarding a possible appointment as a professor of anthropology. Hall, explaining that a department of anthropology was "an experiment not yet tried in this country," offered Boas a docentship in the psychology department, beginning in the fall of 1889.[59] The position, "intended primarily as an honor but yielding an income larger than that of a Fellow," would allow Boas to lecture in anthropology and still continue his research.[60] Boas accepted the offer on the condition that Hall would permit him to continue his field research during the summer months.[61] Hall agreed to the terms and enthusiastically welcomed him to Clark.

At Clark, Boas taught anthropology in "the broadest possible way by a hasty preliminary survey," expanding into the special ethnological problems with which he was most familiar.[62] In addition to his teaching duties, Boas began publishing papers on his varied anthropological research. An article on anthropometry appeared in 1888, along with five papers covering folklore and traditions. He also published an essay on the aims of ethnology.

In 1889 Boas wrote a linguistic piece "On Alternating Sounds," which drew together his "experience in physics, psychology, and ethnology, his work in the laboratory at Kiel and in the field in Baffinland and British Columbia."[63] The article "foreshadowed a great deal of modern anthropological thought on 'culture.' "[64] Viewing cultural phenomena as the result of the interplay between traditional meaning and changing conditions, Boas discussed the influence of history on cultural change.[65] This was clearly one the foundations of Boas's anthropological thought, which he first hinted at in his debate with Mason.

Boas became increasingly interested in physical anthropology while at Clark. Although partially self-trained in anthropometric techniques, he fused his own mathematical ability acquired during his training in physics with knowledge gleaned from Rudolf Virchow. Sir Francis Galton, who helped create the science of biometrics in the 1890s, also influenced him to some degree.[66] By the 1890s Boas had invented his own techniques. Influenced by G. Stanley Hall's studies in child psychology, he measured school children in Worcester, Massachusetts. Boas's major purpose was to determine patterns of growth. Discovering that the differences were minimal among younger children, but more varied later in life, he began to develop a critical theory.

Instead of attributing divergent development to heredity, he looked to the influence of environmental factors. It appeared that healthier environments produced healthier children.

The study itself created something of a scandal. The local Worcester population, anxious to criticize the newly established college located in its midst, attacked Boas' research. The *Worcester Telegram* "directed its spleen against the 'professor' of German birth and education whose face was marred by a cruel mesur scar," inaccurately reporting that Boas could only measure the children in the nude.[67] Nevertheless, Boas finished these preliminary studies and also conducted growth studies in Toronto and Oakland.

This preliminary research foreshadowed his extensive work for the Dillingham Immigration Commission. Contending that racial types were not static, but were "the products of the processes of heredity and growth within specific environmental situations," Boas "was less interested in describing or classifying types than in understanding the processes that had produced them."[68] The early study in Worcester led Boas later to question theories of racial inferiority. He would champion the causes of so-called inferior races, arguing that environment rather than heredity accounted for racial differences.

These years at Clark also afforded Boas the opportunity to cultivate professional relationships. His association with biologist Henry H. Donaldson, who later directed Philadelphia's Wistar Institute, grew in the fertile intellectual soil of the Clark experience. Boas and Donaldson remained close personal friends for many years. Additionally, he developed a camaraderie with A. A. Michelson, whose contributions to physics Boas admired.

In the summer of 1890 Boas returned to British Columbia. This trip was financed solely by the Bureau of American Ethnology, who gave Boas $1,100.[69] Correspondingly, Horatio Hale's directions became less demanding. Hale simply requested that Boas fill in some research gaps left over from the previous years, and he promised "not to hamper [Boas] with any specific instruction."[70] During the summer excursion, Boas compiled anthropometric measurements and linguistic notes among the Chinook and Salish people. He provided the Bureau of American Ethnology with extensive Salish material as well as measurements of other northwestern tribes. Additionally, he drew a possible genetic link between the Nootka and Kwakiutl tribes, based on the "practical identity of the suffixes in the two languages" and the "peculiarities in the two vocabularies."[71] The following summer, again under the auspices of the bureau, he added further information to his linguistic texts.

Clark University renewed his docentship in 1890, and again in 1891. During this time Boas achieved a milestone in the history of American anthropology. In 1892 the university conferred on Alexander Chamberlain a doctorate in anthropology. It was the first such academic honor bestowed in America, and Boas took pride in having directed Chamberlain's study.

In the spring of 1891, Boas sought to broaden his professional contacts.

Living in close proximity to Cambridge, Boas had come into contact with Frederick W. Putnam. At the latter's invitation, Boas began a new research project, preparing physical charts of various Indian tribes for the upcoming World Columbian Exposition, to be held in Chicago in 1892. Additionally, Boas, with Hall's permission, agreed to give a series of eight ethnographic lectures at Harvard's Peabody Museum.[72]

Boas was particularly fortunate in securing this part-time employment, because the tranquil intellectual atmosphere at Clark was shattered in the fall of 1891. For his own part, Boas had begun to complain about the time required of him in developing a department of anthropology. Arguing that his duties were those of a docent, he decided to limit himself to lecturing and to conducting his research.[73]

Boas sensed his growing importance. Powell had promised him funds for another summer's research in Canada, and Nicholas Murray Butler, then editor of the *Educational Review of the Columbia College*, had asked Boas for an article on anthropometric measurement of school children.[74] With his reputation growing, Boas became more independent. Clark University willingly accepted his new provisions, and Hall urged him to stay on as a docent. And yet, Boas's career at Clark was short-lived. General faculty displeasure with Hall's administrative policies caused a major crisis at Clark, which had serious ramifications for Boas.

The initial turmoil at the university was financial in nature. Jonas Clark, the school's founder, withdrew a substantial amount of support two years after the school opened, fearing that the college was specializing too much in graduate training at the expense of undergraduate education. Hall, attempting to ensure the university's survival, covered up the financial problems. He tightened his control over appropriations, which substantially caused suspicion among members of the faculty. Not the economic situation itself, "but Hall's methods of effecting economies and general deviousness...antagonized" the faculty.[75] By the fall of 1891, the faculty was aware of the school's financial condition, and it attempted to negotiate with Hall.

The professors were cognizant of the fact that the college was "incompletely endowed," and they felt that Hall "had evidently much to learn, but may improve by experience."[76] Boas's conflict with Hall concerning his duties as docent was a case in point. Clearly, Hall attempted to use Boas to his maximum capacity, while paying him a minimal salary. Had it not been for Boas's unwillingness to continue under those conditions, Hall certainly would not have instituted any change in his responsibilities. Other faculty members received similar treatment. Additionally, Hall often "acted without consulting the professors concerned, constantly shifted positions, and frequently interfered with the faculty's work."[77] When confronted with these charges, Hall shifted the blame to Clark, explaining that the founder exercised a powerful veto. The ploy was unsuccessful. The faculty not only understood Hall's role in the conflict, but condemned him further for implicating Clark.[78]

These criticisms of Hall smoldered under the surface until the fall of 1891, when they became public. Two incidents, one external and one internal, called attention to Hall's troubles. The outside force was the creation of the new University of Chicago. Backed by Rockefeller money and directed by William Rainey Harper, the new institution actively recruited disgruntled members of the Clark faculty.[79] Meanwhile, within Clark itself, Hall continued his arbitrary policies. For example, he penalized C. O. Whitman's fellow in zoology for not reporting to campus on time. This economic sanction widened the chasm between the faculty and their president. Whitman immediately intensified negotiations with Harper. He proposed that Chicago hire himself, Frank Mall, Donaldson, Boas and several others. However, Harper's reticence to do this immediately afforded Hall a chance to work out his problems with the faculty.[80]

The winter of 1892 witnessed a series of clandestine faculty gatherings, as well as several general meetings that included Hall. Boas was directly involved in the proceedings. His notes for January 1892 illustrate the bargaining process and the compromise proposals developed by the faculty. Aware of the existing danger to the university's future, the faculty forced Hall to agree to five major points aimed at reducing his power:

1. The Faculty and other Academic appointees are governed by only such rules as have been publicly brought to their notice.

2. At the written request of two or more members of the Faculty, stating the object of the meeting, the President will call a faculty meeting.

3. Members of the Faculty may propose for discussion any subject concerning the University or its members.

4. In matters pertaining to their studies, Assistants, Fellows, scholars and students shall be responsible to the instructors by whom their work is directed.

5. The Faculty may elect their officers and committees, President excepted.[81]

Hall later exacerbated tensions considerably when he reversed himself and rejected the proposals. The faculty, led by Michelson, resigned on January 21, 1892.[82] The professors believed this would bring the matter to the attention of the Board of Trustees.[83] Compromise attempts were quickly renewed. Hall proposed "a mutual redetermination of powers, rules, and methods of the Faculty" and "open negotiations in the future."[84] The faculty agreed to resume the talks, but Hall's evasiveness continued.

Finally, C. O. Whitman, realizing the futility of further meetings, wrote privately to Hall. Although claiming to speak for himself alone, his sentiments mirrored those of most members of the faculty engaged in the controversy. Expressing regret that the problems, misapprehensions and distrust could not be eliminated, Whitman informed Hall of his intention to leave the university.[85] This was the beginning of the end. By the close of the spring term of 1892, "two-thirds of the faculty and 70 percent of the students left Clark."[86]

Boas was among them.[87] While many of the departing faculty and students transferred to the University of Chicago, Boas did not.[88] Finding himself without full-time employment or a stable income, his newfound independence quickly ebbed. Once again his future seemed uncertain and the support of his family became a major concern.

Ironically, Boas resettled in Chicago after the Clark controversy. He was not, however, associated with the university. Rather, he became the chief assistant to Frederick Putnam of the Department of Anthropology at the Chicago World Columbian Exposition. Boas's previous association with Putnam, preparing physical charts of Indians tribes for the exposition, played a significant role in this appointment. Abraham Jacobi, meanwhile, attempted unsuccessfully to use his influence to secure Boas a teaching position in anthropology at Columbia College.

Chicago was a perfect place for Boas in the 1890s. It had "become a laboratory for the study of social movements and the new ideas which the recent immigrant strains had served to introduce."[89] Prominent intellectuals resided there. Jane Addams of Hull House, Thorstein Veblen at the university, Theodore Dreiser and Boas himself, represented a new generation of thinkers with new ideas. Additionally, Veblen, Dreiser and Boas stood as reminders to America of the value of foreign thinkers.[90] Their contributions stood in marked contrast to the nativistic expectations and xenophobic reactions that came to the fore in the wake of the 1886 Haymarket Riot.

At the exposition, Boas worked primarily on displaying Indian materials. He continued to catalogue anthropometric measurements of Indians, while also assuming a large part of the exposition's administrative responsibilities. It was at this time that Boas made his first contact with the Canadian Indian George Hunt. He trained Hunt in the basics of phonological transcription and sent him into the field to collect information. This long-enduring relationship provided Boas with much significant ethnographic material.

Although the position at the exposition afforded Boas valuable experience, a decent salary, and excellent professional contacts, it was obvious that the fair would eventually end. Consequently, Boas continued to seek future employment. He sought, unsuccessfully, to continue his anthropometric work for the Bureau of American Ethnology.[91] He hoped for employment at the University of Pennsylvania, which did not materialize due to unforeseen administrative difficulties.[92]

A further option was to stay on in Chicago as curator of the new museum that was established at the exposition's close. The Field Columbian Museum, incorporated in 1894, would house many of the extensive ethnographic collections of the fair. Since Boas had assisted in the organization and arrangement of these displays, he logically assumed that he stood a good chance of remaining at the museum in an administrative capacity. This assumption, however, was not shared by the museum trustees.

The search for a new curator for the anthropological department touched off a controversy that involved not only Boas and the museum officials, but also the major centers of anthropological endeavor in the United States. Scientists from Boston, New York and Washington entered the conflict. The resulting argument had ramifications beyond Boas's personal career, creating animosity and distrust among distinguished anthropologists. In Boas's case, antagonisms developed that would never subside.

Ironically, during the course of the conflict a permanent friendship developed between Boas and W J McGee of the Bureau of American Ethnology. McGee had come to the bureau as the chief assistant to Powell and appeared to be his logical successor as bureau head. Boas, distressed at the Columbian Museum's hesitancy in making its appointments, became increasingly uneasy about the future.[93] He shared this concern with McGee and inquired again about employment in Washington, D.C. Explaining that the bureau's financial constraints precluded anthropometric work for the time being, McGee vowed to investigate the Columbian Museum matter, if he could do so inconspicuously.[94] Meanwhile, during January and February of 1894 Boas helped Putnam clean up the administrative details left over from the fair. Putnam, "anxious to get this whole Indian circus off [his] hands," relied heavily on Boas.[95] Consequently, Boas remained connected with the ethnological department of the museum, still waiting word on his hoped-for appointment to head the department.

The situation intensified in mid-February. Boas confronted the museum's director, F. V. Skiff, about the appointment. Skiff was far from definitive, leading Boas to seek out other sources of information. William Harper of the University of Chicago provided the missing details. The museum trustees had decided to offer the position to William Henry Holmes of the Smithsonian Institution and the Bureau of American Ethnology. The reasons were complex. Skiff thought that Holmes could be easily influenced to associate the museum with the University of Chicago, and thus he sought his appointment.[96] Another Washington scientist, Charles D. Walcott, had also persuaded Holmes to take the Chicago job.

Boas, understanding that this was far from the entire story, eagerly pressed his own investigation. McGee confirmed these suspicions when he informed Boas that Holmes had been offered the position and was "holding the matter under advisement."[97] He went on to explain that the offer was still confidential, and assured Boas that "none of the Washington ethnologists have taken or will take any stand inimical to you."[98]

Boas, however, did not share McGee's view. Prior to receiving McGee's letter, Boas again met with Skiff. Claiming that an "authoritative source" had now confirmed Holmes's pending appointment, Boas asked for an explanation. Skiff agreed to a private meeting with Boas, but remained reluctant to discuss the subtleties of the affair. At that session, Boas, explaining that he had not yet finished installing the anthropological collections in the museum, demanded more money to stay on until the display's completion. Clearly, he was reacting to being slighted by the museum. Skiff brought the matter to the attention of the executive committee, which approved a $1,100 salary for Boas to finish his work.[99] This decision did not end the incident. Boas also informed Holmes of the slight, and Holmes, apparently unaware of the matter, assured Boas that he had great respect for him and wanted to maintain cordial relations.[100]

The affair's impact carried over into the spring. Henry Donaldson, Boas's former colleague at Clark and now a professor of neurology at the University of Chicago, regretted the situation.[101] Putnam was far more upset. Not only did he deplore the treatment accorded Boas, he also felt personally slighted by the museum trustees. Believing himself responsible for establishing the museum for Chicago, Putnam felt his advice should have been followed regarding Boas's appointment to head the anthropology department. He complained that after "squeezing all the juice out of me they [the trustees] threw me aside as a used up orange."[102] He expressed his disgust to Boas: "I feel that I have been very shabbily treated by Mr. Skiff and the trustees, after the protestations which were made to me and all the work I did for the Museum, the conception of which was mine and which would never have been accomplished had I not worked for it as I did. Such ingratitude I have never heard before and I am very much disappointed."[103]

Boas later suspected that the museum incident was part of a general shake-up in the Washington scientific community. Powell had left the Geological Survey under mounting criticism. He took refuge at the Bureau of American Ethnology, and he appointed Walcott to succeed him at the survey. Walcott then returned the favor by influencing Holmes to leave the bureau for the Columbian Museum, thus making room for Powell as a salaried official.[104]

The ramifications of the incident were significant. Although McGee explained to Boas that Holmes was hired due to his "experience and ability in museum work" and not as a slight to Boas, tensions did not subside.[105] Boas harbored resentment toward both Holmes and Walcott. Putnam was equally upset with the trustees of the museum. The conflict further reflected the tensions within the anthropological community at large. The fight had produced two hostile camps that viewed each other's activities with suspicion. Putnam of Cambridge, Boas of New York and Daniel Brinton of Philadelphia represented one group that cautiously guarded against the ascendancy of Washington anthropologists into a position of national importance, at the expense of other regional groups. The other contingent, centered in the Anthropological Society of Washington and the Field Columbian Museum, jealously protected its self-perceived hegemony, prestige, and close relationship with the Bureau of American Ethnology.

The one Washingtonian who attempted to mediate between the two factions was W J McGee. He alone sought to appease both Boas and the museum throughout the conflict. He alone would initiate a movement to create a national organization for all individuals interested in anthropology. The fight between Boas and Putnam on one side and the Field Columbian Museum on the other illustrated the difficulties he would encounter.

Boas left Chicago in May and returned to New York. His future looked bleak. Although he had made many contacts, he had no prospects of employment. Putnam, however, aided in the search. Having recently been placed in charge of the anthropological department of the American Museum of Natural History in Manhattan, Putnam gave Boas hope that eventually he might secure a position there.[106] Yet for the time being, Boas was unemployed. To compound his worries, personal tragedy intervened. He and Marie lost a child in early June.

Despite Putnam's constant efforts, the Museum of Natural History would not commit itself to Boas. In July, acting on his own initiative, Boas secured part-time work in Washington. Otis Mason asked him to work with the Smithsonian's collections from British Columbia and to make a descriptive catalogue of the museum's holdings in this area.[107] The job brought Boas needed income, but did not alleviate his despair. Putnam continued to console him, assuring him that "after the cloudy days the sunshine is coming."[108] Nevertheless, when Boas began his research work in British Columbia in late August, he had only dim prospects for employment, and no assurances.

Prior to his departure for British Columbia, Boas, as outgoing vice president of Section H of the American Association for the Advancement of Science, delivered his first pronouncement on the subject of racial differences and their effects. Boas's speech, "Human Faculty as Determined by Race," illustrated many of the standard arguments he would continue to develop throughout his career in attacking racial prejudice and injustice.

His speech was significant in that it represented his first public attack on race prejudice. He employed arguments in this address that he would develop continually throughout the next thirty years. What also emerged from the speech was Boas's emphasis on culture as a determinant of behavior. Rather than attributing differing mental abilities to differences in race, Boas concluded that environment and the historical process were responsible for such characteristics. Thus he launched his scientific crusade against bigotry, well in advance of public opinions.

The timing of his polemic against prejudice is instructive. Having recently tangled with Washington, the center of white Anglo-Saxon Protestant–controlled anthropological study, over the museum appointment, Boas was still licking his wounds. Despite evidence suggesting that an internal shake-up at the bureau had forced the Holmes appointment, Boas conceivably read the incident in ethnic terms. Given his heightened sensitivity to persecution, which colored much of his life in Germany, and the dominant influence of white, Anglo-Saxon Protestants in anthropology, this was not surprising. Accordingly, he began his assault on prejudice soon after his own disappointment over the Columbian Museum job. However, rather than call attention to his own plight and risk accusations of subjectivity, Boas chose another aspect of bigotry, that directed against Afro-Americans, at which to vent his distress. This camouflage became part of Boas's raison d'etre for attacking all forms of human prejudice.

Boas left for British Columbia in late August. This 1894 field trip was the final one Boas made under the direction of the British Association for the Advancement of Science. He received additional support from both the American Museum of Natural History and the United States National Museum. Putnam played a prominent role in securing funds for him from the natural history museum, believing such support would open up the possibility of employing Boas at the museum. Consequently, Putnam persuaded Morris K. Jesup, president of the New York museum, to provide funds for the trip.

The expedition's purpose was to collect customs and folktales, although Hale allowed Boas great latitude in his research. Putnam and Powell were interested in both anthropometric data and the languages and customs of the Indian tribes. Based on this research, Boas postulated that language patterns and physical types did not go hand in hand, thus helping to shatter the view that racial classification could be based on such a union. During the trip Boas met another individual, James Teit, who with George Hunt provided him with valuable information about the tribes. James Teit of the Shetland Islands resided in Spences Bridge, British Columbia, and aided Boas in writing reports and gathering information on the languages of the various tribes.[109] Boas also worked with Hunt during this expedition but found him "hard to get along with" and "too lazy."[110]

The trip, however, was a success. Boas collected important information on the Kwakiutl Indians, as well as anthropometric data on other tribes. Combined with past work on the physical anthropology of Canadian tribes, this new information aided Boas in a groundbreaking theory concerning Indians. His anthropometry suggested that rather than originating from a single type, Canadian Indians represented several physical varieties, each displaying different forms.[111] Additionally, he took numerous photographs of both the region and the peoples he studied. By late November, however, he was anxious "to get back to civilization."[112] No doubt worried about a steady job, he returned to New York in December.

The new year brought a rise in Boas's fortunes. James McKean Cattell resumed the publication of *Science* and requested Boas's assistance in contributing to the journal.[113] Although offering no pay, Cattell's invitation confirmed Boas's growing reputation in American scientific circles. In the spring Boas left for Europe, still uncertain about his future. During his absence a skirmish ensued between anthropologists in Washington and New York concerning his future.

Powell offered Boas a job editing the reports of the Bureau of American Ethnology at the salary of $1,800 for the first year.[114] Boas, upon receiving Powell's offer cabled Putnam to pass along the news. Upset at the information, Putnam explained to Boas that Seth Low, president of Columbia College, was considering hiring Boas for the anthropology department in the fall. Furthermore, Jesup, as Putnam had predicted, wanted Boas to work for the American Museum of Natural History. Consequently, Putnam advised Boas to delay accepting Powell's offer. He candidly expressed himself concerning Boas's employment at the bureau: "I should hate to have you go to Washington, where I do not believe you would be either as happy or as free as you would be in New York."[115] Accordingly, Boas put Powell off, explaining that he could not accept the job until December. Powell, anxious to add Boas to his staff, agreed to wait.[116] McGee then attempted to force Boas's hand, urging him to terminate his work in Berlin and return home to take up his position at the Bureau of American Ethnology.[117] Boas delayed, prolonging the intrigue.

Boas clearly preferred to work in New York. However, Putnam's inability to secure promises from either Low or Jesup threatened to frustrate these wishes. Explaining to Putnam that he would have to accept Powell's offer if no other employment seemed likely, Boas sought to finalize the matter prior to his return to America.[118] He even contemplated a move to the West Coast, inquiring if Stanford University's president, David Starr Jordan, could use his services.

Returning home in mid-October, Boas agonizingly waited for Putnam's reply. Finally, in early December, Jesup offered Boas the position of Special Assistant for the Ethnological and Somatological Collections of the American Museum of Natural History. The salary would be $3,000 a year, with the proviso that if Columbia College appointed Boas to a professorship, his museum pay would be reduced by half.[119] Boas cheerfully accepted the offer and prepared to begin his new career.

The position at the museum ended the financial and emotional instability that had plagued Boas during his early years. Since his graduation from Kiel and throughout the first nine years in America, he had never known the security of a permanent position. The appointment at the museum was a dream come true. Never again would Boas have to scramble for work or peddle his services. Through his position in the museum and his subsequent appointment in 1896 to Columbia College's department of anthropology, Boas was able to establish himself, over the next thirty years, as the leading light in American anthropology. The end of 1895, then, marked a transition in Boas's life. No longer concerned with economic survival, he began to concentrate on the science of anthropology and its many applications.

## NOTES

1. N.D.C. Hodges to Franz Boas, January 27, 1887, American Philosophical Society, Boas Correspondence. (Hereafter cited as APS/BC.)

2. H. R. Bishop to Albert Bickmore, February 23, 1887, APS/BC.

3. Robert Bell to Boas, April 19, 1887, APS/BC.

4. Melville J. Herskovits, *Franz Boas: The Science of Man in the Making* (New York: Charles Scribner's Sons, 1953), pp. 12–13.

5. Otis T. Mason, "Resemblances in Arts Widely Separated," *American Naturalist* 20 (1887): 246–51.

6. Ibid.

7. George W. Stocking, Jr., *Race, Culture, and Evolution: Essays in the History of Anthropology* (New York: Free Press, 1968), p. 205.

8. Franz Boas, "The Occurrence of Similar Inventions in Areas Widely Apart," *Science*, O.S. (old series) 9 (1887), p. 485.

9. Ibid., p. 486.

10. Ibid.

11. Otis T. Mason to Boas, May 19, 1887, APS/BC.

12. Otis T. Mason, "The Occurrence of Similar Inventions in Areas Widely Apart," *Science*, O.S. 9 (1887): 534–35.

13. Franz Boas, "Museums of Ethnology and their Classification," *Science*, O.S. 9 (1887): 588.

14. Ibid.

15. Ibid.

16. Ibid.

17. Ibid.

18. Ibid.

19. Ibid.

20. Ibid., p. 589.

21. Ibid.

22. John W. Powell, letter to editor, *Science*, O.S. 9 (1887): 612–14.

23. Franz Boas, letter to the editor, *Science*, O.S. 9 (1887): 614.

24. Boas to Otis T. Mason, June 26, 1887, APS/BC.

25. Stocking, *Race, Culture, and Evolution*, p. 205.

26. Ibid., p. 156.

27. John Buettner-Janusch, "Boas and Mason: Particularism versus Generalization," *American Anthropologist* 59 (1957), p. 322.

28. Ibid.

29. Ibid., p. 323.

30. Ibid. Buettner-Janusch's explanation answers the criticisms advanced by Murray Wax in his 1956 article, "The Limitations of Boas' Anthropology," *American Anthropologist*, 58 (1956): 63–74. Wax believed that Boas restricted anthropological research through his conservative, particularist methodology. Buettner-Janusch's article defends Boas. The author claims that no personality alone could account for anthropology's shift to Boasian methodology. Rather, the scientists of the late nineteenth century were "spokesmen for the sociocultural forces" of their time. Hence the shift that occurred in anthropological thought mirrored Boas's particularist philosophy, but was not transformed by it alone.

31. J. Kirkpatrick Flack, *Desideratum in Washington: The Intellectual Community in the Capital City, 1870–1900* (Cambridge: Schenkman Publishing, 1975), p. 116.

32. George W. Stocking, Jr., ed., *The Shaping of American Anthropology, 1883–1911: A Franz Boas Reader* (New York: Basic Books, 1974), pp. 2–3.

33. Ibid., p. 4.

34. Boas to Charles Scribner's Sons, February 8, 1888, APS/BC.

35. Boas to John W. Powell, November 16, 1887, APS/BC.

36. Frederick Ward Putnam to Boas, November 17, 1887, APS/BC.

37. Daniel G. Brinton to Boas, November 20, 1887, APS/BC.

38. Daniel G. Brinton to Boas, November 26, 1887, APS/BC.

39. Boas to Alexander J. Cotheal, November 19, 1887, APS/BC.

40. John Wesley Powell also suggested a change of names. In a letter to Boas on December 15, 1887, he argued that the term ethnology was "gradually being restricted to the study of classification of peoples, especially by biological characteristics, such as are found in the skeleton, the hair, eyes, etc." Anthropology, on the other hand, was being employed "by scholars as the proper name for the general science of mankind." In order to keep "principal scientific terms" in alignment with current usage, Powell recommended that the organization be renamed the Anthropological Society. Boas, it appears, did not follow this suggestion.

41. Otis T. Mason to Boas, December 3, 1887, APS/BC.

42. Horatio Hale to Boas, end of 1887 (no date), APS/BC.

43. Ronald Rohner, ed., *The Ethnology of Franz Boas: Letters and Diaries of Franz Boas Written on the Northwest Coast from 1886 to 1931* (Chicago: The University of Chicago Press, 1969), p. 81. (Hereafter letters and diary entries from this work will be cited as RR/FB.)

44. Ibid.

45. Boas diary, June 6, 1888, RR/FB, p. 88.

46. Herskovits, *Franz Boas*, p. 64.

47. Boas diary, July 24, 1888, RR/FB, p. 103.

48. Boas diary, July 9, 1888, RR/FB, p. 98.

49. N.D.C. Hodges to Boas, August 1, 1888, APS/BC.

50. Boas to John W. Powell, November 23, 1888; Powell to Boas, December 21, 1888, APS/BC.

51. Boas to N.D.C. Hodges, January 30, 1889; Hodges to Boas, January 31, 1889, APS/BC.

52. Boas to Horatio Hale, March 13, 1889, APS/BC.

53. Boas to Edward B. Tylor, April 25, 1889, APS/BC.

54. Ibid.

55. Ibid.

56. Boas to Horatio Hale, July 6, 1889, APS/BC.

57. Boas to Marie Boas, July 23, 1889, RR/FB, p. 107.

58. Boas to Marie Boas, July 28, 1889, RR/FB, p. 109.

59. G. Stanley Hall to Boas, August 8, 1889, APS/BC.

60. Ibid.

61. Boas to G. Stanley Hall, August 20, 1889, APS/BC.

62. G. Stanley Hall to Boas, August 30, 1889, APS/BC.

63. Stocking, *Race, Culture, and Evolution*, p. 159.

64. Ibid.

65. Ibid.

66. Ibid., p. 167.

67. Dorothy Ross, *G. Stanley Hall: The Psychologist as Prophet* (Chicago: University of Chicago Press, 1972), p. 210.

68. Stocking, *Boas Reader*, p. 190.

69. John W. Powell to Boas, March 10, 1890, APS/BC.

70. Horatio Hale to Boas, Spring 1890, RR/FB, p. 82.

71. H. W. Henshaw to Boas, November 25, 1890, APS/BC.

72. G. Stanley Hall to Boas, April 6, 1891, APS/BC.

73. Boas to G. Stanley Hall, June 4, 1891, APS/BC.

74. Nicholas Murray Butler to Boas, December 18, 1891, APS/BC.

75. Ross, *G. Stanley Hall*, p. 216.

76. Memo from Clark University faculty, APS/BC.

77. Ross, *G. Stanley Hall*, pp. 217–18. Among those who seem to have had the most problem with Hall, regarding such interferences, were Boas, Frank Mall in anatomy and Donaldson in physiology. Ross explained that Mall and Donaldson were annoyed with Hall's "suggestions to their fellows," and they believed he disrupted their work.

78. Ibid., p. 219.

79. Ibid., p. 220. Ross suggested that C. O. Whitman and Mall were the two professors that Harper actively recruited. Whitman, in a letter to Hall in the spring of 1892, made it clear that two offers had been made by Harper. Contending that he hoped for an improvement in conditions at Clark, Whitman rejected both offers.

80. Ibid., p. 222.

81. "Propositions as Presented and Amended in the Faculty Meeting of January 1892," Memo, APS/BC.

82. Faculty members of Clark University to G. Stanley Hall, January 21, 1892, APS/BC. The professors listed in the letters were: A. A. Michelson, Whitman, Donaldson, P. Lombard, J. Nef, Mall, A. Bolza, S. Baur and Boas.

83. Ross, *G. Stanley Hall*, p. 224.

84. Ibid.

85. C. O. Whitman to G. Stanley Hall, April 12, 1892, APS/BC.

86. Ross, *G. Stanley Hall*, p. 227.

87. The crisis at Clark created long-standing animosities between the faculty members and Hall. Donaldson, Michelson and Whitman never forgave Hall for his actions. Boas, according to Melville Herskovits, also reacted intensely to Hall's irresponsibility and this feeling "never diminished" (Herskovits, *Franz Boas*, p. 15). Herskovits, however, has misstated the case. In the fall of 1920, upon Hall's decision to retire from academic life, Boas paid him a tribute that belies any negative feeling. Writing to Hall on September 10, 1920, Boas expressed his "thanks for your serious attempt to develop the highest ideals of scientific achievement in our university life. Even if circumstances did not permit the realization of your great plans to their fullest extent, I feel certain that your work has given a stimulus to research that is even now bearing fruit." Boas was not a man capable of rendering false praise. His entire life was highlighted by bold criticisms of people and theories to which he took exception. Had he felt animosity toward Hall, he would not have been capable of such a tribute. Hall apparently realized the sincerity of Boas's words. After his retirement he wrote to Boas, explaining the burden he still carried from the 1892 incident. Without dwelling on "the most painful memories of my life," Hall turned to his relationship with Boas. Thanking Boas for his courtesy in corresponding, Hall concluded by expressing "my profound appreciation of the fact that you are the only one of those who left us at the close of the third year who has a kind word for me. I can only hope that with the years all those who survive will have a little of the same feeling and insight that you do" (G. Stanley Hall to Boas, January 27, 1921, APS/BC).

88. Ross lists some of the professors who left for Chicago. Among them were Whitman, Mall and Michelson.

89. Van Wyck Brooks, *The Confident Years, 1885–1915* (New York: E. P. Dutton, 1952), p. 168.

90. Ibid.

91. Boas to William Henry Holmes, October 7, 1893, APS/BC.

92. Boas to W J McGee, December, 1893, APS/BC.

93. Ibid.

94. McGee to Boas, January 30, 1894, APS/BC.

95. Frederick Ward Putnam to Boas, February 2, 1894, APS/BC.

96. Boas to Putnam, February 18, 1894, APS/BC.

97. McGee to Boas, February 19, 1894, APS/BC.

98. Ibid.

99. F. V. Skiff to Boas, February 23, 1894, APS/BC.

100. William Henry Holmes to Boas, February 21, 1894, APS/BC.

101. Henry Donaldson to Boas, March 6, 1894, APS/BC.

102. Frederick Ward Putnam to Samuel A. Crawford, March 7, 1894, APS/BC.

103. Frederick Ward Putnam to Boas, March 7, 1894, APS/BC. Putnam did not let the matter rest. He continued to complain that the museum ignored his advice, and constantly criticized the "shabby way" things were being handled.

104. Stocking, *Race, Culture, and Evolution*, p. 281. Although Boas adhered to this explanation, which accounted for much of his animosity toward the Washington anthropological community, his information may have been wrong. Curtis M. Hinsley and Bill Holm surmise that Holmes's appointment was the handiwork of geologist Thomas C. Chamberlain, himself a former member of the Geological Survey. They postulate that Chamberlain wanted to create a vital scientific "complex in Chicago" that would be "dominated by his former colleagues in the Survey." Accordingly, they argue that Holmes went at Chamberlain's request and that Boas was ineffective in blocking the move because of Chamberlain's substantial political clout. See Curtis M. Hinsley and Bill Holm, "A Cannibal in the National Museum: The Early Career of Franz Boas in America," *American Anthropologist* 78 (1976), p. 311.

105. W J McGee to Boas, March 21, 1894, APS/BC.

106. Frederick Ward Putnam to Boas, April 30, 1894; Putnam to Boas, May 14, 1894, APS/BC.

107. Boas to Putnam, July 25, 1894, APS/BC.

108. Putnam to Boas, August 3, 1894, APS/BC.

109. Boas to Marie Boas, September 21, 1894, RR/FB, p. 139; Boas to Marie Boas, December 15, 1894, RR/FB, p. 196.

110. Boas to Marie Boas, November 22, 1894, RR/FB, p. 183. Boas's relationship with both Hunt and Teit has been the subject of some controversy. As his dealings with them span many years, it would perhaps be best to examine this problem in light of later evidence. Consequently, his feelings toward his informants will be discussed in a later chapter.

111. Franz Boas and Livingston Farrand, "Physical Characteristics of the Tribes of British Columbia." *Report of the British Association for the Advancement of Science*, 1898.

112. Boas to Marie Boas, November 28, 1894, RR/FB, p. 187. Some critics have pointed out these types of remarks as proof of Boas's prejudice. Contending that Boas

did consider white civilization to be the highest form of life, they attempt to show the racist undertones of this thought. Boas's statements, however, have been blown out of proportion. Rather than viewing the remark as proof of prejudice, critics should examine it within the totality of Boas's correspondence to Marie during his field expeditions. From these letters emerges the picture of a man who deeply missed his wife and family. His longing to return to them was obvious. The intention of his remark was not prejudice. He simply wanted to return to his own civilization. There is reason to criticize Boas for some biased feelings, but not in this instance.

113. James McKean Catteal to Boas, December 17, 1894, APS/BC.

114. John W. Powell to Boas, June 7, 1895, APS/BC.

115. Frederick Ward Putnam to Boas, June 19, 1895, APS/BC.

116. Powell to Boas, July 3, 1895, APS/BC.

117. W J McGee to Boas, July 6, 1895, APS/BC.

118. Boas to Putnam, September 6, 1895, APS/BC.

119. Putnam to Boas, December 10, 1895, APS/BC.

# 3

# The Rise of the Professional

Boas's arrival at the American Museum of Natural History greatly pleased Frederick Ward Putnam. He had begun his own work as the museum's curator in 1894, spending one week each month in Manhattan, while continuing to hold his professorship at Harvard. The New York museum's ethnological collections were in complete disarray at the time of Putnam's arrival. After attempting to bring a modicum of order to that chaos, he advised Morris K. Jesup, the museum's president, to hire two young men who could develop collections of North American, Mexican and Central American objects. Marshall Saville was hired to assist in the development of the Mexican and Central American displays, while Boas was charged with organizing the North American Indian exhibits. Jesup, fearful of Boas's youth, had been hesitant. Convinced by Putnam's persistence, however, he added Boas to the museum staff.[1]

The Bureau of American Ethnology had lost the battle to gain Boas's services but harbored no animosities. W J McGee regretted the loss but was satisfied that Boas would continue to work in America. He assured Boas that the bureau regarded him as one of their "strongest allies in scientific work," and made it clear that he anticipated future collaboration between Boas and the bureau.[2]

In addition to the museum appointment, Boas also obtained his long-sought-after teaching position. In May of 1896, Seth Low, president of Columbia College, offered Boas a post as a lecturer in physical anthropology. Although Columbia did not have an autonomous anthropology department at that time, Boas would join Livingston Farrand and William Z. Ripley, both of whom also lectured on anthropological topics. Low advised Boas that the formation of a separate department was under consideration and that he hoped Boas would play a role in its creation.[3] Boas accepted the offer, thus beginning a mutually beneficial association between himself and Columbia.

This newfound economic security eased Boas's mind. He threw himself wholeheartedly into this teaching at Columbia. He also began organizing the Indian objects at the museum. Employing his system of tribal classification, so carefully explained in his debate with Otis Mason, Boas developed a rational display of North American ethnographic material. He began to illustrate the life-styles of the Indian tribes that he had studied during his connection with the British Association for the Advancement of Science, and he attempted to reconstruct the history and migration patterns of the various tribes by careful arrangement of the artifacts in the museum's possession. Impressed by Boas's zeal and expertise, Jesup and the museum trustees made additional funds available to him for future field work. Boas quickly hired several research assistants and made significant contributions to the museum's collections. "Jesup and the Board of Trustees were 'amazed and delighted' by Boas's energy, and supported his researches generously."[4]

Despite his time-consuming duties at the museum and at Columbia, Boas continued to publish material covering a broad range of anthropological topics. In 1895 alone, for example, he wrote some thirteen articles, including Indian linguistic texts, anthropometric studies of Indian tribes, and head form studies of children in the United States. The following year he increased his publication output, extending his range to include decorative art and folklore.

Finally relieved of nagging unemployment woes, Boas, in these early years at Columbia and the museum, fashioned his own anthropological style. Grounded on a repudiation of nineteenth-century cultural evolutionism and a rejection of the uniform working of the human mind, his theory stressed the important influence of specific history on culture. His holistic treatment of each culture revealed clues concerning specific events and migratory experiences that escaped the attention of evolutionists bent on proving the uniformity of the human mind. If similar phenomena existed in apparently separate cultural settings, Boas demanded a more thorough investigation. In contrast, the prevailing evolutionist theory was content to attribute similarities to the idea that the human mind obeyed the same laws everywhere.

In essence, Boas was concerned with more than artifacts and their cross-cultural development. He envisioned his museum display as models for "detailed study of customs in their bearings to the total culture of the tribe practicing them."[5] Rather than relying on a comparative methodology that ignored both individual experience and the function of objects within a civilization, this holistic structure pinpointed "the historical causes that led to the formation of the customs in question and to the psychological processes" responsible for their creation.[6]

Boas desired to study each distinct culture in its entirety, rather than concentrate on single artifacts in isolation, in order to understand a people's psychology. Thus he sought to investigate customs, language and social systems, and even to collect physical measurements of an individual civilization. Merging these together, the anthropologist could then penetrate the "psychological factors" that shaped a culture and ascertain the extent to which "historical connections" contributed to the lifestyle of a given society.[7] Such a methodology would further highlight the impact of environment on cultural elements. Significantly, however, Boas downplayed environment as a primary formative agent in shaping culture. He contended that surroundings did have a "certain limited effect upon the culture of man," but warned against exaggerating its overall importance.[8]

This research paradigm provided a "means of reconstructing the history of the growth of ideas with much greater accuracy than the generalizations of a comparative method."[9] Boas fashioned this philosophy in opposition to both the comparative methods favored by evolutionists and the attempts to develop generalized theories on the basis of limited study. Guarding against the "indiscriminate use of similarities of culture for proving historical connection," he emphasized the particular rather than the general.

Obviously, much of his motivation for developing this critique derived from a desire to justify his own method of museum display. Recalling his earlier debate with Mason, Boas built up a method of study to support his system. His historical bent was the more cautious, and yet less prone to error. Comparative methodologies, "ingenious vagaries" to Boas, were "barren of definite results" and would remain so until anthropologists moved beyond "the vain endeavor to construct a uniform systematic history of the evolution of culture."[10]

The development of this theoretical critique was significant. It marked the culmination of ten years of thought, beginning with the Mason debate. Boas did not "consciously set himself the task of championing the proposition that there were no regularities in history, but rather . . . he felt that the amount of regularity had been grossly overestimated."[11]

Beyond reshaping the course of twentieth-century anthropology, Boas's critique of evolutionary theory provided insights into his own character. Nineteenth-century evolutionary theory utilized science to argue for the "presumed superiority of white-skinned civilized men to dark-skinned savages by placing them both on a single developmental ladder extending upward from the apes."[12] Evolutionists compared cultural phenomena, reconstructed "the process of development" and placed it "within a deterministic scientific framework, thereby legitimating the cultural superiority that had been assured at the outset."[13] Significantly, these evolutionists all fell into the white, Anglo-Saxon Protestant category themselves; they benefited most from their own theoretical paradigms. Boas rejected this philosophy because it did not conform to his own scientific investigations. However, his own background as a Jewish immigrant and his intellectual successes led him to defend non-Wasp individuals, who either fared poorly at the hands of evolutionary theory, or were excluded entirely. Thus a personal as well as a scientific motivation shaped Boas's thought, leading him to attack the notion that the progress of culture could be "correlated with any presumed hierarchy of racial types."[14]

During his attack on evolutionists' adherence to a comparative framework, Boas also announced his hesitancy to generalize when developing anthropological laws. This insistence on precise methodology became a central tenet of his thought. It evoked criticism from other anthropologists who believed that Boas's rigorous scientific method was detrimental to anthropological endeavor precisely because he made no attempt to draw even tentative generalizations.[15] Concerned with the reconstruction of history but not with the formation of laws derived from it, Boas appeared to be hindering the growth of anthropological thought. These critics held Boas's particularist philosophy responsible. Ever fearful of finding the exception to the rule, Boas avoided generalization.

His critics were correct. He consistently shied away from the establishment of cultural laws. He left no "Boasian school" of anthropological theory, save that committed to historical particularism. Yet, he "surpassed most anthropologists before or since in his concern to present to others the evidence from which enthnographic statements could be constructed."[16]

Boas's commitment to methodological puritanism represented the "one great reformatory movement necessary to further the progress of the science of culture."[17] In placing Boas within the context of late nineteenth-century anthropological thought, it is clear that he was responsible for raising the standards of professional anthropological research and thus for eliminating untrained amateurs.

However, as some of his critics averred, his emphasis on "patient accumulation of historical data" did not "lead automatically to the improvement of anthropological theory."

As Marvin Harris explains:

He never conceded that a choice must be made between history and science; rather he conceived of science as having historical and generalizing components, formally disallowing any invidious comparison between them. Regardless of his attempt to maintain an interest in the problem of formulating lawful principles, it is obvious from the research strategy he followed throughout his career that he was perfectly content to continue his particularist studies in complete independence of their nomothetic payoff.[18]

Boas's shortcoming here lay not in his exacting methodology, but in his refusal to formulate generalizations based on such extensive evidence. He worked in a world void of laws, content simply to gather data on the assumption that these facts would lead automatically to the discovery of general truths. His emphasis on the collection of historical facts should not be read as an outright rejection of the comparative approach. He merely sought to bring the two systems of research and display into equilibrium. "The historical method was thus to be harnessed to the service of the comparative method. By so doing, anthropological theory would be purged of its puerile amateurism, and a new and sounder basis for generalization would be established."[19]

This early stage of Boas's historical particularism was characterized by a denial of "universal unilinear sequences, but not to the extent of rejecting more limited forms of parallel sequences." Boas optimistically believed that laws governing these uniformities could be found, and consequently, he felt that they should be the most important goal of anthropological research.[20] Yet, the fact that he, himself, could not formulate these laws for fear of discovering contradictory evidence did impede anthropological development. However, his commitment to an exacting methodology aided rather than hindered the maturation of anthropological research.[21]

Boas's success at the Museum of Natural History validated his methodology. Jesup continued to express joy at his efforts and more importantly, continued to fund research projects. In 1897, at the suggestion of both Putnam and Boas, Jesup financed a major expedition to the North Pacific Coast. Designed to investigate the history of Indian tribes "of the coast of the North Pacific Ocean, beginning at the Amoor River in Asia, and extending northeastward to the Bering Sea, then southeastward along the American coast as far as the Columbia River," the Jesup North Pacific Expedition became an ongoing concern for Boas.[22] Although he did not make frequent field trips himself, Boas tended to the administrative aspects of the project and directed the research. He also took charge of publishing the expedition's results.

Boas's prior British Columbian research had hinted at a possible connection between American Indian tribes and those of northern Asia. The expedition, he felt, might verify this hypothesis and explain whether this affinity was "due to mixture, to migration, or to gradual differentiation."[23] Accordingly, Boas urged the formation of the expedition and agreed to supervise it. In 1897, he made one of only two personal field trips under the auspices of Jesup's project, joining Livingston Farrand of Columbia University and Harlan I. Smith of the American Museum of Natural History. Assisting the three researchers were Filip Jacobsen of Clayoquot, British Columbia, and Boas's former Indian informants, James Teit and George Hunt.[24]

The four-year expedition, which concluded in 1901, centered on fieldwork in British Columbia, Oregon, California and Washington. Concurrent with this research, Boas organized a Siberian expedition under Russian-born scientists Waldemar Bogoras and Waldemar Jochelson. The project became both a source of pride and irritation for Boas. On the positive side, the expedition was immensely successful in yielding new information and in establishing the nexus between Pacific Indian tribes and people of northern Asia. In the first year alone, the researchers under Boas's charge collected extensive specimens "illustrating the archaeology of the interior and of the Coast of British Columbia."[25] The objects added significantly to the depth of the displays of the museum, which naturally pleased Jesup. Boas received congratulations from many scientists both in America and abroad.

The published results of the expedition, however, were another matter. Due to poor communication and the researchers' lackadaisical attitude toward writing up their results, the completion of the published volumes was postponed continuously throughout the first quarter of the century. Jesup, displeased with the frequent delays, hounded Boas about the continual tardiness, which exacerbated tensions between them.

The expedition also reestablished Boas's faith in the abilities of George Hunt. Convinced of Hunt's incompetence during his 1894 field trip to British Columbia, Boas reassessed his position during the Jesup expedition. He found Hunt competent and thorough, believing him "quite dependable."[26] In fact, the correspondence between Hunt and Boas depicts a warm relationship between two friends. The Jesup expedition had marked a turning point in that relationship. Impressed with Hunt's ability and desire, Boas entrusted more and more responsibility to his Indian colleague.

The Jesup expedition, despite its enormous administrative duties, was not Boas's main concern during this period. Troubled by the lack of organization among anthropological societies in the country and by the inadequacy of the current journals in the field, Boas planned to reorganize anthropology's major publication, the *American Anthropologist*. Established in 1888, the journal was run by the Anthropological Society of Washington. Boas felt that the publication did not represent American anthropology generally, but was rather a local organ for the Washington area. Thus, he sought either to revise the journal giving it a more national flavor, or to create a new journal entirely. In December 1897 at the Ithaca meeting of Section H of the American Association for the Advancement of Science, Boas was appointed chairman of a committee to establish a new journal. WJ McGee assumed the role of secretary for the committee, which included William Henry Holmes, Daniel G. Brinton and Frederick Ward Putnam.

The committee's initial meeting took place in Philadelphia. All members agreed that the new journal would publish "high grade papers, pertaining to all parts of the domain of anthropology," "general scientific notes," and a bibliography.[27] Following the May meeting of the Anthropological Society of Washington, it became apparent that that organization wished to transform its own journal, instead of creating a separate, competing publication. Consequently, the board of managers of the Washington group voted in favor of revising the journal, and proposed to keep the current name. The board suggested a nine-member editorial committee, with at least four individuals, including the managing editor, drawn from the membership of the Washington society. However, the board assured Boas that the journal would not be "the exclusive organ of any one society."[28]

Nonetheless, dissenting opinions quickly arose following the plan's formulation. Brinton withdrew his support from the project, contending that the membership quota on the editorial committee would make the journal "the exclusive organ" of the Washington group. As a compromise, he proposed a reduction to three Washington members, with the managing editor to be selected annually by the committee as a whole. So strongly did Brinton fear Washington control that he preferred to establish a new journal without Washington support, and its $600 in subscriptions, rather than permit one area of anthropological activity to control all publications.[29] Putnam agreed with these objections. He advised limiting Washington representation to three committee members, suggesting that three others be selected from Section H, with the final three to be chosen jointly by the first six.[30]

Responding to these ideas, McGee sought a compromise. He proposed that no quotas be set for committee membership. Stressing that the journal should be "American and not sectional," he favored a general election of members rather than placing any restrictions on those eligible to serve.[31] McGee suggested a meeting of the journal committee at Washington's Cosmos Club to finalize plans. Agreement was reached by late summer on the general structure and control of the journal. All that remained was the difficult procedure of transferring control of the publication from the Washington group to the new editorial board.[32] By late November the new committee was officially organized, and the Anthropological Society of Washington turned over the *American Anthropologist* to the new editorial staff.[33]

The establishment of a national anthropological journal was highly significant. It signalled the growing realization among leading American anthropologists that consolidation was necessary for the future well-being of the profession. In this respect the reorganization paved the way for the creation of a national anthropological society. And yet, the dispute over the new journal emphasized the deep divisions and petty jealousies extant within the anthropological community. The fear of Washington control loomed larger than ever in the anthropological circles of Cambridge, New York and Philadelphia. Similarly, the Washington contingent was troubled by the prospect of being usurped on the national scene.

These status anxieties had come to the fore during the negotiations. They simmered down upon reorganization, but did not die. The mutual wariness that remained was well illustrated by a decision regarding the new journal's ownership. Since neither group was willing to surrender its responsibility, co-ownership was proposed. McGee and Boas assumed legal responsibility for the publication. One man from Washington, one from New York, they stood as testimony to the insecurities that plagued the anthropological community. Tensions would rise again, ironically heightened by Boas and McGee, the two men most responsible for creating the new series of the *American Anthropologist*.

At the outset, Boas and McGee sought to widen support for the journal by launching a massive subscription drive. Boas personally contacted many universities and private individuals, hoping to ensure the publication's financial stability. Despite these efforts, the first year produced a deficit. To rescue the fledgling journal, Boas and McGee began a campaign to raise a guarantee fund. Displaying the same zeal that he brought to his research, Boas secured over $450 in pledges to help defray the journal's debts. Due to Boas's initiative, Charles Bowditch of Boston became one of the journal's most prominent financial supporters.

The work of the journal was only one of a myriad of interests for Boas. He also continued his research and teaching, and he resumed his linguistic studies for the Bureau of American Ethnology. During 1899 he worked on Tsimshian and Chinook vocabularies, and also continued his anthropometric publications on North American Indians. He attempted to renew interest in the American Ethnological Society of New York, which had merged with his smaller society. He continued to publish anthropological articles as well, many of which restated his commitment to both history and an exacting methodology, while at the same time attacking evolutionary theory.

His enthusiastic commitment to professional anthropology was not confined to research. Boas's efforts to improve the discipline's stature covered a broad spectrum of activity. From the "philological evenings" held at his home to his work at Columbia University, Boas exemplified the professional anthropologist. His election to the National Academy of Sciences in 1900 was a fitting tribute. His 1899 appointment as Professor of Anthropology in the newly created Department of Psychology and Anthropology at Columbia gave him the opportunity to expand his sphere of influence.[34] The new department gave Boas enhanced status and provided his profession the impetus for growth. Boas, quite naturally, would continue to be instrumental in that process.

Prior to the turn of the century, however, anthropology was not considered a necessary graduate offering at American universities. Rather, it was confined to an "institutional framework" represented by the Smithsonian Institution's Bureau of Ethnology, the United States National Museum, the Anthropological Society of Washington and other museums and private societies.[35] "Only Museum archaeology and ethnology had any connection with universities, and neither Museum curators nor anthropologists looked to the Graduate School as the proper place for anthropological research, training, and publication."[36]

Washington was the early hub of anthropological investigation, beginning with John Wesley Powell's establishment of the Bureau of American Ethnology in 1879. From the outset the bureau was controlled and staffed by amateurs, who made their livelihoods elsewhere. For them the bureau "served as a last bastion of defense for the individual investigator against the sweeping cultural changes of the late nineteenth century."[37] Evolutionism was clearly the dominant theory of the Washington group, as evidenced by Mason and Powell in their philosophical exchange with Boas over museum classification.

This link between evolution and the amateur status of the men who preached it ironically aided Boas in his successful attack against the theory's underpinnings. The popularity of the bureau was not synonymous with anthropology's "acceptance as a profession." Rather the ethnology practiced at the bureau resembled "a democratic hobby."[38] Bureau anthropologists who gravitated to the study of man attempted to popularize evolutionary theory at a time when America's landscape was being transformed by the forces of industrialization and immigration. Whether or not these evolutionists pressed their case due to anxiety over their patrician status in a changing world, it is certain that bureau members defended the white, Anglo-Saxon Protestant against all challengers. By popularizing their theories, they surmised, perhaps they could convince the nation not only that they were correct but that they deserved an ascendant place in the new order. Ironically, popularizing anthropology to justify Wasp hegemony in America detracted from the seriousness and credibility afforded to ethnology in general. "Professional status and a degree of exclusiveness in science," which the bureau lacked, "required first to be taken seriously, which in turn required having serious public purpose."[39]

Prior to the last decade of the century, "anthropology in America was quite content" with this position. During the 1880s, not even Boas advocated the establishment of graduate departments in anthropology.[40] His arrival at Clark University changed his mind. He petitioned G. Stanley Hall, requesting the formation of an anthropology department. When Alexander Chamberlain received his doctorate under Boas at Clark it marked the dawn of graduate anthropology in the United States. However, much developmental work remained before the transformation from amateur to professional status would be complete. Boas had been present at the creation and was eager to play a prominent role.

His arrival at Columbia in 1896 did not automatically spark the growth of graduate work. Appointed as a lecturer in physical anthropology, attached to the faculty of pure science, Boas lacked an administrative base from which to work. The creation of an anthropology department, albeit connected to the psychology department, resolved this dilemma. Moreover, Boas's promotion to the rank of professor not only solidified his position within the university, it also represented a giant step forward in the growth of graduate anthropology.

Boas's plan for Columbia was complex and ambitious. It envisioned the establishment of "a well-organized school of anthropology, including all the different branches of the subject."[41] To this end it sought to utilize the collections of the American Museum of Natural History as a tool for the training of graduate students. In this way the museum and the university would be able to serve each other's needs. Boas suggested to Putnam that the museum appoint Livingston Farrand of Columbia to a position as an archaeological assistant, because Farrand's training would benefit the museum, and since he held a professorship at Columbia, the appointment would also strengthen the university's connection to the museum.[42] Boas also planned to expand the university's Department of Anthropology. He hoped to hire specialists in both physical and comparative anthropology, as well as in American ethnology and in the research fields of China, the Malay Archipelago, the East Indies and Africa.[43]

This desire to create such a broad program illustrated Boas's displeasure with America's present generation of anthropologists. Claiming that most current anthropologists were "deficient in certain lines" of inquiry with which they should be familiar, Boas sought to rectify the problem in the future by producing well-trained, complete students.[44] Although aware of the huge financial cost of such a program and of the government's inability to lend support, Boas was confident that he could secure funds from other institutions.

Boas's loyalty to Columbia and his desire to keep the organizing power centered in New York under his control were put to the test in the summer of 1901. Phoebe Apperson Hearst, a regent of the University of California, became interested in developing a museum for her university, similar to the American Museum of Natural History. Zelia Nuttall, one of Hearst's early advisors in this matter, contacted Boas clandestinely, since he himself had been appointed to an advisory position for the new project. Nuttall inquired whether Boas would consider leaving New York to head the anthropological center at the University of California.[45] Boas declined; however, he attempted to take advantage of the offer. Rather than establishing a research center in California with no one qualified to direct it, Boas suggested to Nuttall that Hearst fund four fellowships in ethnology at Columbia and two in archaeology at Harvard. After five years the fellowships could be transferred to California, at which time there would be individuals of sufficient training to ensure the West Coast center's success.[46] In this way Boas hoped to gain California's moral and financial support for his own project and maintain control of graduate education in anthropology at the same time.

Hearst and the advisory committee ignored Boas's scheme. Putnam, a member of the committee, assumed the direction of the California center. Boas was excluded at his own request, and was no longer consulted. In fact, the members eliminated his name from the committee of advisors.[47] Ironically, Boas played a major role in Hearst's future plans. The man who eventually took charge of the California center was Alfred L. Kroeber, one of many anthropologists to receive a doctorate from Boas at Columbia.

The turn of the century, then, marked the beginnings of anthropology's growth. This "classical period" in which Boas built "a science of man in America" signalled that professional anthropologists would enter and eventually dominate a field previously run by amateurs.[48] The university became the "vital center of professionalization with Washington's scientists slipping to a secondary importance."[49] Washington-based anthropology, with its concern for the amateur, would soon be outdated. Accordingly, the intellectual community of the nation's capital looked to the future with increasing anxiety, fearful of becoming "an anachronism, a throwback to the nineteenth-century ethos of genteel culture."[50] The professionalization of a discipline was underway, and Boas was directing its course.

In the summer of 1900, Boas journeyed to Northwest Vancouver on his second expedition for the Jesup project. Moreover, he continued working for the Bureau of Ethnology, proposing to prepare a handbook of North American languages, which would include all the linguistic material he already had in his possession, and which would also encompass additional research he did for the museum or any other institution.[51] The bureau not only paid him a salary for incurred research expenses, but through the efforts of McGee, also appointed Boas as Honorary Philologist.[52]

The winter of 1902 witnessed a development of profound proportions for the future professionalization of anthropology. In early January, McGee contacted Boas to discuss the foundation of a national anthropological organization. Prompted by a discussion held at Chicago's Field Museum in December and by a conversation with James McKean Cattell, McGee informed Boas that the time was right for such a move.[53] The Chicago meeting had dealt primarily with the financial status of the *American Anthropologist*, although McGee had apparently desired to discuss national organization at that time. The length of the meeting precluded such consideration and forced postponement of the issue.[54] Consequently, McGee now hoped that the matter could be taken up at the upcoming meeting of Section H of the American Association for the Advancement of Science, to be held in June in Pittsburgh.

Anticipating that summer gathering, McGee contacted all the participants of the Chicago meeting. Included in the group were Boas and Livingston Farrand, representing the American Ethnological Society of New York; George A. Dorsey, George C. MacCurdy, Frank Russell, Frederick Starr and Stewart Cullen, representing Section H; and J. Walter Fewkes and McGee from the Anthropological Society of Washington. McGee proposed that the group, which he considered a good nucleus for an American anthropological association, formulate plans for the development of an organization. Acting as a clearinghouse, McGee invited comments prior to the summer meeting. He also mailed a rough draft of a constitution for the new organization, hoping to evoke constructive criticism of it. The constitution stressed that the new association would not impinge upon the workings of any local society. It depended upon the establishment of a council, or administrative body, of sufficient size to include "all active professional workers in anthropology in the country." McGee also suggested that the new association take over the *American Anthropologist*, making the journal its official organ.[55]

Boas was most enthusiastic about the formation of such an association, although he thought the move a bit premature. Nevertheless, he agreed to proceed in such a direction if others were in accord. This hesitancy was surprising given Boas's previous feelings. As early as 1896, he himself proposed such a national organization to McGee. At that time it was McGee who balked, insisting that the time was not right.[56] Now their roles were reversed. Boas, however, was happy to support McGee.

Therefore, Boas immediately set down the criticisms that McGee had invited. Most significantly, he attacked the criteria for membership in the association. Claiming that he understood the financial need for including amateurs who would contribute money to the organization, Boas urged caution. He felt that amateurs would "endanger the permanent interests of science."[57] The entire question of the popularization of science profoundly disturbed him. He recognized the need to garner public support, without which science would stagnate. Aside from economic participation, however, Boas feared amateur activity. He stated the dilemma precisely, pointing out that when amateurs outnumbered professionals in a scientific society, there was a natural "tendency towards lowering the scientific value of discussion" by omitting technical data. Boas believed such information was vital to the best interests of "the advancement of science," and worried that popularization of the association would seriously undermine the quality of scientific study. Particularly in anthropology, he believed, was this danger "ever imminent," and thus he took great pains "to protect the purely scientific interests."[58]

Weighing most heavily on Boas, no doubt, were the implications of eliminating technical data from anthropological discussion. Such omissions could make his work vulnerable to pseudoscientific generalizations that attempted to prove a hierarchy of racial or ethnic types based on unproven differences in mental ability. Boas frequently attacked these arguments during his career, motivated by his liberal ideology, his concern for pure scientific inquiry, and most importantly, by his own reaction to personal encounters with prejudice. Accordingly, it is not surprising that he would both fear the elimination of data and disapprove of any scholarly treatise that was not properly substantiated.

Since both the American Ethnological Society and the Anthropological Society of Washington contained many amateurs, Boas felt that the national organization could exclude them for professional reasons and yet not suffer any economic loss. Accordingly, he proposed that all prospective members of the new association have prior experience either teaching or publishing scholarly articles in anthropology.[59] Lest he be viewed as totally uncompromising, Boas did concede that in the future, expansion of the membership to include amateurs could be considered, but he still argued that this should not be an initial step.

McGee gathered this and other suggestions from most of the men who had met in Chicago and sent out a letter recapitulating them for all the participants. Besides Boas's objections, McGee was able to report favorable comments from Cullen, Dorsey and Fewkes. He also noted that Russell, MacCurdy, Starr and Roland B. Dixon, who was eliminated from McGee's initial list but who did attend the Chicago meeting, all agreed with Boas's desire for an exclusive organization. Despite these opinions, however, McGee still desired a broader membership. Claiming to have sought the opinions of a "few anthropologists outside the Chicago nucleus," McGee reported that most favored a broader policy. In a postscript, McGee reported that MacCurdy had reconsidered his position and now called for an open membership policy.[60] With his addition to those already in favor of a more liberal policy, McGee felt certain that he had won the point.[61]

He wrote to Boas explaining that the amateur element of the organization would do more than simply provide economic assistance. He believed that they could be stimulated by the association to help promote scientific activity throughout the country. Furthermore, if the membership believed that amateurs were detracting from the scientific integrity of the association, they could always vote for exclusivity at a later time.[62]

McGee moved ahead with his plan, pressing for incorporation. Aware of the opposition to his open membership policy, he mailed the provisional constitution to his supporters first. He instructed them, upon ratifying it, to forward it until all members had a chance to accept or reject it. By this "rather transparent flanking maneuver" McGee hoped to have a majority in favor of his position before Boas, Dixon or Farrand received the document.[63] His plan appeared to be successful. The first four recipients ratified the constitution. Dixon, Boas and Farrand refused to do so. Boas wrote to McGee suggesting a private meeting in Washington in mid-April.[64] He explained that he now preferred to modify the organization of one of the existing anthropological associations rather than create a new one. Clearly, Boas was disturbed by the possible duplication of functions of two large associations.[65]

McGee did not wait for Boas's trip to Washington. On March 24, 1902, he and several others incorporated themselves as a national organization.[66] Essentially, the American Anthropological Association was formed behind Boas's back. George Dorsey, one of McGee's cosigners, travelled to New York to deliver the news to Boas in person. Angered and surprised by McGee's "mode of procedure," Boas attacked McGee's lack of openness and his failure to allow for a fair expression of opinion. He equated McGee's action to "the warfare of political parties." Further, Boas raised the issue of the political methods of Washington science. He informed McGee that the secret incorporation could easily be seen as a power play to ensure Washington hegemony in the new national organization.

After venting his rage, Boas stated the terms under which he would still cooperate with McGee. First, he insisted that the incorporation should be "the basis of formally bringing this matter before the attention of anthropologists." He also demanded that McGee send out the provisional constitution to other anthropologists, whose names Boas would furnish, and that their suggestions be embodied in the final constitution.[67]

Negotiations continued. Boas still advocated a merger with Section H rather than the creation of a new organization, and adhered to an exclusive membership policy. McGee, hoping for a compromise, agreed to the provisions Boas had suggested. He mailed the provisional constitution to a number of other American anthropologists, making it clear that he would take no further action until the Pittsburgh meeting.

The conference of Section H of the American Association for the Advancement of Science was held in late June. On July 1, the constitution was adopted, and the American Anthropological Association was formed. The constitution differed little from McGee's original draft, except that "McGee's view of the organization as a confederation encouraging the development of local societies was modified."[68] Also, the council's powers were enlarged.[69] All the founders of the organization were entitled to the "privileges of the American Association for the Advancement of Science" and would receive the *American Anthropologist.*[70]

The ratification of the constitution and the formation of the association were historic events. The discipline now had a strong national base. However, the future trend of professionalization emanated from university anthropology departments rather than from the newly-created association. Clearly the future belonged to Boas. The present, however, was McGee's, since he received most of the credit for the association's birth. Although Boas had suggested such a national enterprise in 1896, McGee carried the plan to fruition.

McGee was less than candid during the negotiations, engaging in some "double dealing."[71] Since he controlled the mailing of documents and the tabulation of the votes, he held a powerful veto. His manipulative course may be attributed to his "aggressive and ambitious" personality. Being an amateur anthropologist himself, he stressed an open organization simply to guarantee his own future and leadership.[72] Coupled with this, moreover, was McGee's realization that anthropology was becoming a profession. With the establishment of university departments of anthropology, it was obvious that trained students would soon emerge. Since McGee was only second in command at the bureau, and the future looked bleak, he needed a power base from which to operate. He could not rely on possible promotion following John W. Powell's retirement or death. His actions, then, stemmed from a desire both to ensure the future role of amateurs in anthropology and to secure for himself a position of power. As the founder of the association, McGee seemed guaranteed a role in its development.

The dire forecasts made by Boas regarding inclusive membership policies and duplication of efforts did not transpire. The association did not retard the development of anthropology. This was so principally because professionalization was channelled through academic circles, not through scientific organizations. The amateur members of the association could not harm real scientific progress, since it was carried on elsewhere.

The chaos surrounding the creation of the association reflected divergent values within anthropology. Boas represented professional anthropology,

McGee the amateur concern. The conflict over the membership policy illustrated the state of the science. Most anthropologists were amateurs, thus most voted for an inclusive policy. The rising class of trained scientists was still small at the turn of the century. The attempt to professionalize the association was premature. Those in favor of amateur participation carried the day. These men, led by McGee, were in no sense unexperienced or amateurish in their research. They were professionals in their treatment and understanding of anthropological problems, although not in their education. As anthropology became more complex, their lack of formal training became both more apparent and more of a liability. Anxious over their status due to the emergence of trained anthropologists, they felt sufficiently threatened to insist on amateur inclusion. Contrary to Boas's prediction, this did not harm the association in the long run. It did, however, signal the demise of Washington anthropology's control over the science. The future belonged to the professionals.

Yet, because of its membership policy, Boas remained dismayed and worried over the future of the association. Thus he plotted the course of anthropology's maturation through Columbia rather than through the association. In an ironic twist, the men who came to control the association in the twentieth century were not of McGee's ilk. With the rise of graduate training in all areas of anthropology, the untrained anthropologist became an anachronism. The individuals who soon assumed control of McGee's creation were trained professionals. All possessed doctoral degrees, many having studied under Boas at Columbia.

Several factors explain why professionalization and the desire for a national organization came to the fore at the turn of the century. American society had come to revere science. In an age of increasing technological expertise, this was not surprising. America's industrial and urban growth had triggered an increase in the applications of science. Scientists, consequently, were more in demand. Not only technological adjustments, but a general replanning of society became necessary. Against this background the rise of the social sciences, such as anthropology, should be viewed as a "response to industrialism." Coupled with this trend was the rise of the university, which functioned as "a potent catalyst in fields where academic credentials could serve as universally recognized symbols of professional competence."[73]

Moreover, the national organization was created out of necessity. The science of man had grown too complex for local organizational control. Academic anthropology and amateur anthropology took off in opposite directions. McGee and others believed that a national association could bring some measure of order to the chaos of the growing science.

Professionalization was a reaction to the same confusion. In the nineteenth century, anthropology had been run strictly by amateurs. Largely self-trained, these individuals founded and controlled the major institutions and societies devoted to anthropology. Professionals were in the minority. By the advent of the twentieth century, circumstances had changed dramatically. "The relationship between amateur and professional social science was exactly the reverse of what it had been at the close of the Civil War."[74] Again the university was responsible, since the establishment of graduate education had profoundly transformed the social sciences. Trained individuals sought to replace amateurs. The struggle occurred earlier in some fields than in others.[75] It began in anthropology by 1900.

These professionals were not motivated solely by the need for employment. The same desire to bring order out of chaos that prompted McGee to push for the establishment of the American Anthropological Association also affected them. American society was changing immeasurably under the weight of the forces of urbanization, immigration and industrialization. The peaceful agricultural nation of the Jefferson era was transformed into a complex, often enigmatic society. Many individuals reacted by engaging in a "search for order."[76] Viewing the efficiency with which the business sector conducted its affairs, reformers attempted to apply the same techniques to other areas. Accordingly, efficiency experts soon tackled the problems of corrupt government and municipal mismanagement. The late nineteenth century witnessed the development of professional urban planners.

Anthropology underwent a similar conversion. Boas, a man dedicated to efficient and meticulous research, was the natural individual to lead the way. Constantly critical of wasteful generalizations and imprecise methodologies, he urged more patient investigation. His fear of amateur involvement in the American Anthropological Association stemmed from the belief that chaos would result. For Boas, the future of his discipline rested with professionally trained researchers. Only through their expertise, he felt, would efficient, precise investigation produce accurate and worthwhile results.

In this respect, Boas was a reformer responding to change. Intolerant of inaccuracies and aware of a need for order, he led the drive for a reorientation of American anthropology. His commitment to professionalization was an outgrowth of his desire to rationalize and improve the study of man in America. From his office at Columbia he succeeded in transforming anthropology from an amateur to a professional science. The achievements of the men and women he trained became the benchmarks of his vision.

By the turn of the century, the demise of Washington-controlled anthropology was inevitable. Nothing expressed this passing so vividly or abruptly as the death of John Wesley Powell on September 28, 1902. Powell had been a mainstay of the Washington scientific community. His work as director of the Bureau of American Ethnology and his contributions to the United States Geological Survey stood as major achievements in nineteenth-century science. He had been a prominent member of Washington's Cosmos Club, the center of intellectual activity in the nation's capital. His death, then, created a vacuum within Washington scientific circles. Most importantly, the Smithsonian Institution needed a new director for the Bureau of American Ethnology.

Upon learning of Powell's death, Boas immediately contacted S. P. Langley, the secretary of the Smithsonian Institution. He recommended that Langley appoint McGee, Powell's close friend and second in command at the bureau, to the position of director. Boas's action suggested that there was no animosity between the two friends as a result of the debate over the founding of the American Anthropological Association, and also illustrated that Boas was still content to let an amateur run the Washington-based anthropological establishment.

Langley, however, did not heed Boas's advice. He felt it was necessary to "alter the method of administration" of the bureau.[77] Concerned that in Powell's last years his health had affected the bureau's operation, Langley sought to eliminate the position of director, with its pervasive power. In an attempt to ensure more consistent administration, he decided to run the bureau from the Smithsonian Institution itself, "through some immediate personal representative acquainted with the Institution and the Bureau."[78] Langley designated William H. Holmes to fill the position of chief of the bureau. Holmes, who had replaced Boas at the Field Columbian Museum after the Chicago exposition, had returned to Washington and was currently the head curator of the department of anthropology in the United States National Museum. Langley expressed his hope that McGee would continue to serve as an assistant in the bureau.[79]

Boas's response was predictable. He disliked Langley's choice and was dismayed to learn that the Smithsonian Institution and the United States National Museum would oversee and control the bureau's activities. Rather than simmer privately, Boas openly aired his objections. He contended that "subordination of the Bureau to museum interests" would gravely impair anthropological research and also retard the development of the United States National Museum.[80] Boas believed that the two institutions must remain separate. The bureau dealt with the "investigation of the life and customs of the North American Indians." The research conducted there encompassed studies of language, religion, customs and institutions. The museum, on the other hand, displayed only that part of Indian culture that could be illustrated by specimens.

With this difference in mind, Boas felt that the museum could not "develop systematically the whole field of anthropology," because "the primary objects of the museum forbid the systematic investigation of such subjects as mythology, primitive law and languages."[81] Arguing that the independence of the bureau from museum concerns must be assured, Boas described the danger of appointing one man to oversee two institutions. He concluded that the workload alone would overwhelm the "chief," resulting in "either inadequate supervision of both [institutions] or nominal control over the one or the other."[82] Explaining that anthropological work would suffer as a result of this policy, Boas strongly recommended that Langley reconsider his plan.

Boas also defended McGee, who had served under Powell for ten years and had been trained as his eventual successor. Boas argued that appointing any other man to the position would bring discontinuity to the bureau's organization. Without McGee in control, the stability of the bureau would be in jeopardy, and thus the whole future of its research activity would be called into question.[83] Fearing for the future independence of the bureau, Boas campaigned against Langley's decision. He contacted Daniel C. Gilman of the Carnegie Institute and Alexander G. Bell, one of the Smithsonian Institution's regents, urging that they exert pressure on Langley to reverse his decision.[84]

McGee himself protested Holmes's appointment. He called for Langley's immediate retirement, claiming to speak for many prominent American scientists. Believing that Langley was an obstacle to the best interests of the Smithsonian, McGee contacted a member of Congress concerning a possible congressional inquiry, should Langley refuse to resign.[85] Additionally, McGee wrote privately to Boas about Holmes's role in the affair. Suggesting that "Holmes has utterly gone back on every promise to me as well as every consideration of official decency, and adopted the policy of fair words and foul acts," McGee warned Boas that Holmes had the good of neither the bureau nor anthropology in mind.[86]

In light of Boas's earlier tangle with Holmes, McGee's attitude was most ironic. When Holmes received the appointment at the Field Columbian Museum, it was Boas who was resentful. McGee's role had been that of mediator. He had assured Boas that Holmes harbored no bad feelings toward him and that there was no deviousness involved in the appointment. This was not the case in McGee's current situation. Directly affected by the Langley decision, McGee viewed Holmes as the culprit in a larger conspiracy. Boas, however, did not play the role of mediator, since such a position ran counter to his personality. Outraged at the slight to McGee and still harboring animosity toward Holmes, Boas supported McGee and pressed for a judicious settlement of the problem.

The issue dragged on into the spring and summer of 1903. McGee, increasingly worried about his future, believed that Langley desired to close the bureau altogether. In this way the scientists attached to the bureau could be reassigned to the United States National Museum, thus increasing its stature. McGee hoped that Boas understood the gravity of the matter, and urged that he again contact Bell to protest the bureau's impending abolition. Again in ironic contrast to his earlier attitude, McGee revealed his true feelings about Holmes. He complained to Boas: "you have no idea how bad things have become; you saw Holmes' cloven foot at Chicago, but I see both of them and the forked tail as well."[87]

Boas did contact Bell a second time, and explained the situation with renewed vigor. Bell, obviously concerned about the problem, suggested that Langley appoint a committee to investigate the entire affair. Boas was invited to appear before that body, which was "investigating the affairs of the Bureau of Ethnology and attempting to give it 'sound administration.' "[88] McGee also met with the committee; convinced in his own mind that he would not receive satisfactory treatment at the bureau, he tendered his resignation.[89] Boas was disheartened by his action. He had hoped that McGee would continue to fight, both for his own position and for the bureau's autonomy. Nevertheless, he understood McGee's dismay.[90] McGee soon left Washington entirely to work at the upcoming world's fair and Louisiana Purchase Exposition in St. Louis.

Boas pressed ahead with his complaints. Although conceding that Holmes's work on prehistoric art and on the geological aspect of archaeology was significant, he believed that "his interest in that part of anthropology which deals with ideas alone is slight."[91] Boas's prejudice against amateur anthropologists was well-illustrated by this remark. And yet, McGee also was an amateur. Despite that, Boas thought that McGee's experience under Powell had made him invaluable to the further operation of the bureau. Moreover, he had not forgotten Holmes's role in the field museum affair. He believed Langley had reacted to the sad state of affairs within the bureau, which was caused by Powell's illness. "Powell was losing hold of his mental powers," and "the Bureau suffered accordingly." Instead of "giving relief by restricting Powell's influence," Langley "chose not to act, and to lay the blame for all that was wrong to McGee." Boas contended that Langley's own "failure to modify the anomalous administrative organization" of the bureau had retarded its development.[92]

Such protestations had no effect. Holmes became the chief of the bureau, which was then allied more closely with the United States National Museum, and McGee became involved with the Louisiana Purchase Exposition. Thus in the same year that he established himself as the founding father of the American Anthropological Association, McGee witnessed the beginning of a power struggle that ultimately forced him out of his affiliation with Washington-based anthropology.

Boas, although angered over the affair, did not sever his connection with the bureau. He continued his work as Honorary Philologist, no doubt with renewed confidence that anthropology's future rested with him and Columbia University.

His plan for the Anthropology Department at Columbia illustrated his positive feelings. His department's faculty had increased substantially. Marshall H. Saville was appointed professor of American archeology, and Clark Wissler and William Jones joined on as assistants.[93] With the enlargement of the faculty, Boas hoped for increased funding to expand his work. He had already developed the department's course offerings to include nine courses at Columbia, two at Barnard College and one extension course in the Teacher's College.

In looking to the future, he hoped for continual expansion in several distinct areas. He believed an assistant was needed to supervise activities in the laboratory of the American Museum of Natural History. Regarding linguistics and archaeology, he felt that both advanced and introductory courses were

vital for proper graduate training.[94] In general, he viewed the development
of his department as the logical result of a new emphasis on graduate education. In order to produce professional anthropologists, it was necessary to
offer a wide range of courses that, in combination, would embody all aspects
of anthropological endeavor.

Although matters ran smoothly at Columbia, Boas's dire predictions regarding the Bureau of American Ethnology soon came true. Holmes held up
information concerning Boas's linguistic work for the coming year. Boas
urged Holmes to push the plans immediately, so as to ensure that the work,
which had been in progress for several years, would not be jeopardized.[95]
Frustrated with the lack of progress made after his request, Boas decided to
seek immediate redress of his grievances by going over Holmes's head. In a
letter to Bell he outlined the inadequacies of the bureau, specifically men-
tioning the small staff as a critical factor.[96]

Pressing his case further, Boas contacted Charles D. Walcott of the Carnegie
Institute, the other major player in the Holmes drama in Chicago in 1894.
Boas informed Walcott that the bureau was not interested in advancing the
study of man, but rather cared only for simplistic investigations. Moreover,
Boas felt there was no "continuous policy" and complained that Langley
refused "to print linguistic material," which seriously impeded all ethnographic work.[97]

What disturbed Boas most of all was the bureau's hesitancy to continue
Indian research. He urged that work be "carried on with the greatest energy,
because all the Indian tribes, their languages and customs, are disappearing
with incredible rapidity."[98] He estimated that within five years much of the
information on Indians would be unavailable. Consequently, Boas suggested
the creation of an anthropological survey of the United States, to be established within the bureau. The proposed five-year project entailed research
into all races on the continent. In rough figures, Boas projected that government expenditures would begin at $87,000 for the first year, and would
culminate in a total outlay of $237,000.[99]

Government Indian policy would clearly reap the rewards of this research,
Boas argued, if anthropologists could determine the benefits of racial intermixture, the educational needs of Indian children, and the ways to help
smooth Indian "transition from savage to civilized life."[100] The survey could
also shed light on the "adaptation of the negro race," a problem with which
Boas was becoming increasingly concerned. Specifically, he was interested
in the "physical and mental character of the mulatto, and whether the development of the colored child is equal or inferior to that of the white
child."[101] Boas also hoped his project could investigate the European immigrant problem and the process of amalgamation.

The bureau did not accept the proposal, nor did the Carnegie Institute
which Boas had also contacted. The problems of blacks and immigrants were
not considered serious ones by government-supported science at this time,

so both areas of inquiry lay dormant. Boas, driven by both his liberal convictions and personal experience with prejudice, would soon strive to change this situation by taking up these research projects himself.

Without adequate funding, these new areas of research remained future considerations. Boas continued his work for the bureau on his *Handbook of North American Languages*, which would, ironically, also support his ideas about race, culture and language. Specifically concerned with the classification and structure of Indian languages, he increased his research staff significantly. John R. Swanton, a member of the Jesup expedition, dealt primarily with the Haida and Sioux dialects, while William Jones worked on the Algonquin Indians. Additionally, Boas hired J. N. B. Hewitt to do research on the Iroquois, H. H. St. Clair for the Shoshone, Roland B. Dixon for the Maidu, and Frank G. Speck for the Uchee. He also employed his former student Alfred Kroeber and field assistant James Teit, who worked with the Yokut and Salish languages respectively. Aside from coordinating these researchers, Boas personally attended to the languages of the Eskimo, Tsimshian, Kwakiutl and Chinook peoples.[102]

After a summer in Europe, Boas travelled to St. Louis to visit McGee. At the invitation of Simon Newcomb, McGee's father-in-law and chairman of the organizing committee of the St. Louis exposition, Boas delivered an address on anthropology's "progress during the last century." The address neatly summed up his theoretical progress since his arrival at Columbia, and illustrated his self-confidence in controlling the future direction of his science.[103] Boas availed himself of the opportunity to press his case for the development and training of professional anthropologists who could combine the various aspects of their science for the good of the nation.[104] He also cautioned that there were dangers inherent in any anthropological research based upon cultural comparison. He asserted that anthropologists must always correct the erroneous view that other cultures were inferior to their own.

Clearly Boas was already formulating the concept of culture that he would later develop in his classic book *The Mind of Primitive Man*. He summarized his position quite succinctly in the St. Louis address in discussing the significance of anthropological research:

Of greater educational importance is its power to make us understand the roots from which our civilization has sprung, that it impresses us with the relative value of all forms of culture, and thus serves as a check to an exaggerated valuation of the standpoint of our own period, which we are only too liable to consider the ultimate goal of human evolution, thus depriving ourselves of the benefits to be gained from the teachings of other cultures and hindering an objective criticism of our own work.[105]

Once again Boas was reacting to his own experiences with prejudice. He lashed out at the evolutionist stance that placed all ethnic and racial groups,

including his own, below white Anglo-Saxon Protestants on the evolutionary
ladder. Now secure in his position, both financially and intellectually, he
strengthened his public assault on evolutionary theory. He did so both because he believed it to be poor science and because it slandered his own
ethnic background.

The turn of the century was a hectic time for Boas. His responsibilities had
increased substantially as he branched out into many new areas. Despite his
seemingly frantic pace, he still retained his dedication to the further professionalization of anthropology. This was reflected in his teaching, research
and administrative duties. He also continued to view the activities at the
Bureau of American Ethnology with suspicion. This was partially the result
of McGee's belief that Langley and Holmes wanted to abolish the bureau
completely. McGee was especially critical of Holmes, whom he suggested
was "engaged in very dirty work," although these allegations remained un-
substantiated.[106] Walcott had informed Boas that there was no evidence to
support McGee's charges, and consequently Boas put the matter to rest.[107]
He continued to seek appropriations for Indian research from the bureau,
but no longer attempted to vindicate McGee by uncovering duplicity within
that department.

Boas remained friendly with McGee. As the St. Louis World's Fair came
to an end, Boas tried to help his friend find employment. He contacted Putnam concerning a position for McGee at the Field Museum. Aware of his
own poor relations with the museum and with George Dorsey, Boas asked
Putnam to intervene on McGee's behalf.[108] Suggesting that "a recommen-
dation on my part to Dorsey would be more likely to have a deterring effect than otherwise," Boas hoped that Putnam's opinion would be of more
positive value.[109] Much to his dismay, however, the museum did not hire
McGee.

The advent of the twentieth century marked a major transition in Boas's
life. The development of graduate training in anthropology at Columbia University and the establishment of the American Anthropological Association
signified the beginnings of professionalization and national recognition of
the study of man. Boas's increasing reputation was of further significance. No
longer burdened by the insecurity of his early life, he had continued to expand
his control and influence over his profession. The future of anthropological
development rested with Boas, rather than with the anthropologists of the
nation's capital. Perhaps foreseeing this inevitable event, the Anthropological
Society of Washington made Boas an honorary member in 1905. He looked
to the future optimistically. There would be pitfalls for him, as there had
been for McGee and others. If he could avoid the complexities and conflicts
inherent in the American scientific and academic community, his dominance
would be assured. The road ahead was hazardous, but Boas was prepared
to travel it.

## NOTES

1. John Michael Kennedy, "Philanthropy and Science in New York City: The American Museum of Natural History, 1868–1968," (Ph.D. diss., Yale University, 1968), pp. 134–37.
2. W. J McGee to Franz Boas, March 21, 1896, American Philosophical Society, Boas Correspondence. (Hereafter cited as APS/BC.)
3. Seth Low to Boas, May 7, 1896, APS/BC.
4. Kennedy, "Philanthropy and Science," p. 141.
5. Franz Boas, "The Limitations of the Comparative Method of Anthropology," *Science*, n. s. 4 (December 1896): 905.
6. Ibid.
7. Ibid.
8. Ibid., p. 906.
9. Ibid., p. 905.
10. Ibid., p. 908.
11. Marvin Harris, *The Rise of Anthropological Theory: A History of Theories of Culture* (New York: Thomas Y. Crowell, 1968), p. 259.
12. George W. Stocking, Jr., "Ideas and Institutions in American Anthropology: Thoughts Toward a History of the Interwar Years." In *Selected Papers from the American Anthropologist 1921–1945*, ed. Stocking (Washington, D.C.: American Anthropological Association, 1976), p. 3.
13. Ibid.
14. Ibid. Stocking merely hints at the ethnic dimension of Boas's attack on evolutionary theory. It is apparent, however, that Boas's ethnicity was a dominant motivating force that directly influenced many of his intellectual, scientific and political activities.
15. Leslie White, *The Ethnology and Ethnography of Franz Boas* (Austin: Texas Memorial Museum, 1963).
16. Harris, *Rise of Anthropological Theory*, p. 261.
17. Ibid.
18. Ibid., p. 262.
19. Ibid., p. 275.
20. Ibid., p. 278.
21. The debate concerning Boas's contributions to anthropological development is complex. Many of the criticisms were advanced after his death and will be treated in the concluding chapters.
22. Franz Boas, *The Publications of the Jesup North Pacific Expeditions* 1 (1898): 2.
23. Ibid., p. 5.
24. Ibid., p. 6.
25. Ibid., p. 12.
26. Boas to Marie Boas, August 16, 1900 in *The Ethnography of Franz Boas: Letters and Diaries of Franz Boas Written on the Northwest Coast from 1886 to 1931*, ed. Ronald Rohner (Chicago: University of Chicago Press, 1969), p. 261. (Hereafter letters from this work will be cited as RR/FB).

27. Memo, February 19, 1898, APS/BC.

28. J. Walter Fewkes, John W. Powell and Frank Baker to Boas, May 25, 1898, APS/BC.

29. Daniel G. Brinton to Boas, June 4, 1898, APS/BC.

30. Frederick Ward Putnam to Boas, June 8, 1898, APS/BC.

31. W J. McGee to Boas, June 10, 1898, APS/BC.

32. The editorial committee included: F. W. Hodge as secretary and managing editor, Frank Baker, Boas, Brinton, George Dawson, George Dorsey, Holmes, J. W. Powell and Putnam.

33. Weston Flint to Boas, November 25, 1898, APS/BC.

34. Seth Low to Boas, May 1, 1899, APS/BC. Up to this time Boas had been a lecturer in anthropology, connected to the psychology department. This promotion not only increased his stature but also indicated that anthropology as a science was now a viable academic subject, deserving its own administrative apparatus.

35. John R. Freeman, "University Anthropology: Early Departments in the United States" (paper read before the Kroeber Anthropological Society, April 25, 1964, Berkeley, California), pp. 3–5.

36. Ibid.

37. Curtis M. Kinsley, Jr., "Anthropology as Science and Politics: The Dilemmas of the Bureau of American Ethnology, 1879 to 1904," in *The Uses of Anthropology*, ed. Walter Goldschmidt, American Anthropological Association, 11, 1979, p. 15.

38. Ibid., p. 16.

39. Ibid.

40. Freeman, "University Anthropology," pp. 3–5.

41. Boas to Zelia Nuttall, May 16, 1901, APS/BC.

42. Boas to Frederick Ward Putnam, April 10, 1900, APS/BC.

43. Boas to Zelia Nuttall, May 16, 1901, APS/BC.

44. Ibid.

45. Freeman, "University Anthropology," p. 12.

46. Ibid., p. 13.

47. Ibid., p. 14.

48. Ibid., pp. 1–2.

49. J. Kirkpatrick Flack, *Desideratum in Washington: The Intellectual Community in the Capital City 1870–1900* (Cambridge: Schenkman Publishing, 1975), p. 163.

50. Ibid.

51. Boas to W. J. McGee, April 20, 1901, APS/BC.

52. S. P. Langley to Boas, May 23, 1901, APS/BC.

53. W J. McGee to Boas, January 4, 1902, APS/BC.

54. W J. McGee to Boas, January 21, 1902, APS/BC.

55. Ibid.

56. W J. McGee to Boas, October 30, 1896, APS/BC.

57. Boas to W J. McGee, January 25, 1902, APS/BC.

58. Franz Boas, "The Foundation of a National Anthropological Society," *Science*, n. s. 15 (May 1902): 805.

59. Boas to W J. McGee, January 25, 1902, APS/BC.

60. W. J. McGee to Boas, February 19, 1902, APS/BC.

61. Stocking makes an interesting point in this regard. Livingston Farrand had not responded to McGee's initial letter. When McGee wrote his February 19 circular,

which summarized the feelings of all those polled, he claimed that a majority favored an open policy. Farrand responded a week later, supporting the exclusive position. McGee replied to Farrand, explaining that he had assumed that that would be Farrand's position. Stocking, however, contends that McGee "chose to ignore this assumption" when tabulating the votes for open and closed membership policies. By so doing, McGee was able to obtain a victory for his position. George W. Stocking, Jr., "Franz Boas and the Founding of the American Anthropological Association," *American Anthropologist* 62 (1960): 3.

62. W J McGee to Boas, February 19, 1902, APS/BC.

63. Stocking, "Boas and the Founding," p. 4.

64. Boas to W J McGee, March 19, 1902, APS/BC.

65. Boas to W J McGee, March 25, 1902, APS/BC.

66. Stocking, "Boas and the Founding," p. 5.

67. Boas to W J McGee, March 26, 1902, APS/BC.

68. Stocking, "Boas and the Founding," p. 10.

69. Ibid.

70. George A. Dorsey to Boas, September 15, 1902, APS/BC.

71. Stocking, "Boas and the Founding," p. 6.

72. Ibid.

73. Mary O. Furner, *Advocacy and Objectivity: A Crisis in the Professionalization of American Social Science, 1865–1905* (Lexington: University Press of Kentucky, 1975), p. xxi.

74. Ibid., p. 313.

75. Furner deals specifically with economics, sociology and political science.

76. Robert Weibe, *The Search for Order, 1877–1920* (New York: Hill and Wang, 1967).

77. S. P. Langley to Boas, October 13, 1902, APS/BC.

78. Ibid.

79. Franz Boas, "The Bureau of American Ethnology," *Science*, n. s. 16, (1902): 828–29.

80. Ibid.

81. Ibid.

82. Ibid.

83. Ibid., p. 830.

84. Boas to Daniel C. Gilman, October 28, 1902; Boas to Alexander G. Bell, November 8, 1902, APS/BC.

85. W J McGee to Boas, November 27, 1902, APS/BC.

86. McGee to Boas, December 21, 1902, APS/BC.

87. McGee to Boas, June 16, 1903, APS/BC.

88. William H. Holmes to Boas, July 11, 1903, APS/BC.

89. McGee to Boas, August 1, 1903, APS/BC.

90. Boas to McGee, August 3, 1903, APS/BC.

91. Boas to Alexander G. Bell, August 7, 1903, APS/BC.

92. Ibid.

93. Boas to G. R. Carpenter, October 1903, APS/BC.

94. Boas to Nicholas Murray Butler, November 11, 1903, APS/BC.

95. Boas to William H. Holmes, November 20, 1903, APS/BC.

96. Boas to Alexander G. Bell, December 3, 1903, APS/BC.

97. Boas to Charles D. Walcott, December 7, 1903, APS/BC.

98. Franz Boas, "Organization of the Bureau of American Ethnology," December 1903, APS/BC.

99. Ibid.

100. Ibid.

101. Ibid.

102. William H. Holmes to Boas, May 25, 1904, APS/BC.

103. Franz Boas, "The History of Anthropology," *Science*, n. s. 20 (October 1904): 515. Address before the International Congress of Arts and Science, at the Louisiana Purchase Exposition, St. Louis, September 1904.

104. Ibid., pp. 523–24.

105. Ibid.

106. W J McGee to Boas, January 15, 1905, APS/BC.

107. Charles D. Walcott to Boas, February 27, 1905, APS/BC.

108. There are two possible reasons for this friction between Boas and Dorsey. During the debate over membership policy of the American Anthropological Association, they were on opposite sides. Dorsey, after incorporation, was delegated to break the news to Boas. Perhaps the meeting between them left a degree of bitterness that never faded. More likely, the animosity harks back to the Field Museum appointment in 1894. Dorsey went to work for the museum soon after the conflict. In need of some specimens and advice, he contacted Boas in New York. Boas refused to help, referring to the shabby treatment he had received by the Field Museum directors. This incident created a degree of resentment on Dorsey's part and helps explain Boas's comment to Putnam.

109. Boas to Frederick Ward Putnam, February 27, 1905, APS/BC.

# 4

# The Turn of the Century

With newfound optimism that the anthropological future belonged to the professional and that he himself would be instrumental in the study of man in America, Boas approached the turn of the century confidently. Moreover, his financial situation was stable; he had been promoted to a full professorship, and his plans for Columbia University's fledgling anthropology department and its connection with the American Museum of Natural History proceeded smoothly, at least initially. Yet the projected close association between the two institutions was soon jeopardized, and eventually shattered, by another skirmish in the raging battle between amateur and professional science.

The roots of the conflict were manifest four short years after Boas replaced Frederick Putnam as the curator of the museum's anthropological division. Putnam had resigned to divide his time more equitably between Harvard and the new museum established at the University of California. Boas's relationship with Morris K. Jesup, however, had already begun to deteriorate prior to this new appointment. In the fall of 1900, Jesup complained often about the delay in completing the results of the North Pacific Expedition. Boas attempted to mollify him by assuring him that the expedition was "known the world over" and was held in great esteem. Boas regretted that his many personal sacrifices and his dedication to the project had failed to meet with Jesup's approval.[1]

Soon after Boas's new appointment, tensions resurfaced. Although gratified by his promotion, Boas felt slighted at not receiving a raise in salary commensurate with his new status. For him this was clearly an issue of prestige rather than economics. Nevertheless, he protested vigorously to Jesup, explaining that his increased administrative duties disrupted his "scientific aspirations." Boas expected some sort of pay adjustment, but one was not immediately forthcoming.[2] This dispute, like the preceding one, faded quickly. It was replaced by a period of relative tranquility, marked by amicable relations between Boas and Jesup. In 1905, however, a major conflict began that ultimately led to Boas's resignation.

Jesup precipitated the controversy. An inspection of the ethnological collections of the museum had left him puzzled and displeased. He found Boas's system of labels and arrangements confusing and chaotic. Furthermore, he could not understand how the displays reflected the "life, habits, and customs of the people" under study. He demanded that Boas explain the system of classification.[3]

As if this were not sufficient grounds to raise Boas's ire, the director of the museum, Herman Carey Bumpus, also criticized Boas's future plans for the anthropological division. Suggesting that Boas's attitude toward "the work of the Museum as a whole" seemed "most unhealthful and dangerous," Bumpus used Jesup's own displeasure to launch his accusations.[4] Specifically, the director also condemned Boas's method of display. He referred to Clark Wissler's exhibit of the Blackfoot Indian collections as "most unsatisfactory" and ordered Boas to correct the installation so as to make it "intelligible, instructive, orderly and attractive."[5] Moreover, Bumpus demanded that Boas present for approval a general outline for the reconstruction before he began any actual work.

Boas took immediate exception to Bumpus's rebuke, believing it inappropriate for a museum director to criticize a curator's work. He explained to Jesup that he was "not inclined to accept the director's criticism of details, with which he is necessarily unfamiliar."[6] Boas also invited Jesup to tour the exhibition halls with him, so that Boas could explain the method of display.

The exhibition system reflected Boas's conception of the museum's purpose. He believed that the object of a large anthropological collection was to trace the history and progress of civilization "from the earliest forms up to the highest," by displaying diverse cultural artifacts.[7] He chose to emphasize man's relationship to nature, the development of industry, and patterns of customs and beliefs. This method, Boas explained, coincided with his own commitment to historical accuracy. Moreover, it was the exact system he had so laboriously defended in his exchange with evolutionists Otis Mason and John W. Powell.

Boas felt that his classification system was appropriate only for a large museum. As he explained to Jesup, small museums lacked both the space and resources to concentrate on such small details. For them, only general topics could realistically be addressed. However, a large museum afforded anthropologists the opportunity to delve into "more special questions, which are at the same time fundamental to an understanding of human history."[8] At the same time, a large museum's displays lacked the continuity and clarity found in smaller ones. "Without particular explanation of the subject matter of the exhibits," the layman would have difficulty understanding the displays, since each represented a different area of interest, designed for the specialist.[9] Boas believed that Jesup simply misunderstood the system's purpose. In defending his method of display, Boas hoped to convince Jesup that large museums served different purposes than small ones.

By so doing, Boas drove another wedge between amateur and professional anthropological interests. Theoretically, for Boas, a small museum directed itself to the general public, since it could present only small collections that remained simplistic both in scale and purpose. Juxtaposed to this, a large institution could appeal to more serious investigators because of the expanse of space and enormity of material. Concerning the American Museum of Natural History specifically, Boas sought to accommodate both the general interest in popular aspects of science and that of the specialist by offering two different series of collections. One, the more simplistic, would be assembled in a large hall and arranged in such a way as to be easily understandable to the general public. The other collection, bearing "upon special problems," would be constructed in a manner that would allow specialists an opportunity for detailed, complex analysis.[10]

What emerged from Boas's thinking was his firm commitment to the professional and his grudging recognition of the amateur. Hoping to appease the latter by offering a smattering of material upon which to whet their appetites, Boas tried to convince Jesup that large museums had responsibilities that transcended public entertainment. Wary of the popularization of science, a position consistent with his views on restricted membership in the American Anthropological Association, Boas warned Jesup that if the museum were devoted solely to the interests of the casual museum-goer, then people with specific needs or advanced education would have no opportunity or desire to study there.[11] Further, Boas feared that popularly oriented displays achieved "intelligibility" by "slurring over unknown and obscure points," which deluded the masses into believing that they had mastered scientific subjects after only brief contact with them.[12]

Jesup rejected Boas's explanation. Confessing that he lacked any scientific knowledge, Jesup admitted that his own "ignorance" prevented him from grasping Boas's reasoning. Moreover, Jesup, during his presidency, sought to expand the public's interest in his museum, both by increasing its physical size and by making the exhibits more accessible through later visiting hours. Consequently, he urged Boas to meet with him again so that they could devise a system of display that would truly appeal both to the masses and to those with special interests.[13]

Meanwhile, relations between Boas and Bumpus deteriorated. Boas asked the director for permission to solve the display problems on his own. If Bumpus felt the need to give final approval to every project proposed by a curator, then, according to Boas, he would require not scientists, but "persons without convictions" who would do as he wished.[14] Bumpus ignored the

request, but he did suspend indefinitely all Boas's future fieldwork and publication plans.[15] Boas, in a sniping memorandum, sarcastically informed the
director that he had begun the reconstruction of one of the exhibits. "The
change in the Peruvian Hall," Boas wrote, "which you ordered some time
ago, and countermanded in your letter, was begun and has been undone
again."[16]

The situation grew worse during a meeting between Boas, Jesup and Bumpus. Jesup reiterated his desire to have popular exhibits that would prove
entertaining for the general public. In support, Bumpus castigated Boas for
giving "an elaborate disquisition on complex scientific points instead of giving
points of view for popular exhibit."[17] In a statement that was assuredly enigmatic to Boas, Bumpus suggested that "the relation of man to nature and the
success of man in mastering nature are entirely irrelevant and unimportant
points in anthropology."[18]

From there the meeting degenerated into a series of defensive statements
and accusations. Boas criticized Bumpus's irrationality, lack of knowledge,
stubbornness and short-sighted attitude. He attempted to school Bumpus on
the various methods of museum display but found little ground on which to
fashion a compromise. In the end, Boas looked to Jesup for guidance. If the
president could not resolve the dilemma, Boas would have no choice but to
withdraw from all administrative duties.[19]

Less than a week after this meeting, Boas resigned his position as curator.[20]
He continued to work at the museum on Asiatic research and the Jesup
expedition, drawing a $4,000 salary.[21] Putnam, obviously upset upon hearing
the latest development, expressed sorrow at Boas's resignation. Claiming that
his great hopes for the museum's future were all shattered by the incident,
Putnam sympathized with Boas and took his side in the conflict.[22]

The controversy at the museum did not abate. Clark Wissler, Boas's colleague at Columbia, assumed the position of curator. Boas was upset by his
acceptance. Although he stated publicly that the museum would interfere
with Wissler's teaching obligations at Columbia, Boas reacted more out of
his own anger toward Jesup and Bumpus than from any real belief that Wissler
could not handle both tasks. Despite Boas's objections, Wissler became the
new curator of the anthropological division. Boas continued his research
projects, but his animosity remained. In defending his resignation, Boas compared the policy of the museum to that of a "great kindergarten in which
science, so far as the actual museum work goes, cuts only a very slight
figure."[23]

Despite this attitude, Boas did not completely sever his museum connections. Hoping to further the museum's research reputation, he proposed an
expansion of the Jesup North Pacific Expedition and a continuation of North
American research work. Specifically, he urged Jesup to make more funds
available to help substantiate many of the conjectures that grew out of the
original expedition. A more detailed investigation of Eskimo peoples in Alaska

and of the Indians of Vancouver Island would clear up problems that still remained regarding the origins of Indian tribes. Although Boas strongly believed that the Indians had originally migrated from Asia, his ever-present reluctance to generalize on the basis of less than complete research motivated this appeal to Jesup. In addition to his expanded research plans for the expedition, Boas suggested an increased commitment to research on the North American continent in general. He proposed to study the Indian tribes of California, and also hoped to complete the museum's study of the development of decorative art among the North American Indians.[24]

However, there was to be no peace as long as Boas and Bumpus found themselves under the same roof. In December of 1905, Bumpus renewed hostilities, informing Jesup that Boas refused to comply with his requests.[25] Boas was taken by surprise. He had no idea that Bumpus was displeased, and promised to smooth out any problems immediately.[26] Boas simply wished to be left alone to conduct his research. He abhorred interference with his scientific work and hoped that both the director and the president of the museum would allow him to proceed without interruption.[27]

His wish was not granted. Bumpus continued to meddle in his affairs by countermanding orders, transferring research material to other departments and refusing to discuss matters with Boas candidly. Consequently, Boas again complained to Jesup, who had himself grown tired of the childish bickering. Jesup issued an ultimatum, warning that if the two men could not work together in a "cordial and cooperative" fashion, then he would not renew Boas's contract after June. Although Jesup clearly regretted this prospect, he informed Boas that he had no other alternative.[28] Disheartened over this course of events, Boas resigned from the museum itself, effective July 1, 1906. He planned to complete work on the North Pacific Expedition but would do so from his office at Columbia, not from the museum.

The entire museum affair represented yet another struggle between amateur and professional science. The initial skirmish between the director and Boas, centering on modes of display, vividly illustrated this struggle. Bumpus's concern was general entertainment. Both he and Jesup hoped to create exhibits that would appeal to a mass audience. They tended toward popularization of science through their displays. Boas opposed this scheme. He acknowledged that every museum must provide a modicum of popularly oriented exhibits, which would help counteract the effects that "the saloon and the race track" had on the public.[29] He felt strongly, however, that large museums, such as the American Museum of Natural History, must also meet professional obligations. Consequently, although not abrogating his responsibility to the general public, Boas favored a dual method of display that was reflective of the scholar's needs as well.

This system emanated from Boas's own dedication to professional anthropology. He had previously warned against any popularization of science with regard to membership policies in the American Anthropological Association.

He realized, however, that in a museum setting some concession to popular science was necessary. His specific disagreement with Bumpus and Jesup centered on his concern for the scholar, who was neglected in a system catering only to the public. Boas hoped to achieve a balance where all interests were represented. Jesup was not opposed to this plan in theory, but he offered little constructive help. Bumpus, on the other hand, was openly hostile, perhaps feeling threatened by Boas's scientific prowess. In any event, the early conflict turned on the question of a museum's professional versus popular responsibilities.

The second controversy emanated directly from the first. The animosity between Bumpus and Boas had remained, stirred by both personal animosity and professional envy. Bumpus perceived his adversary to be an aspiring, highly educated scientist who was attempting to usurp control of the museum. Boas viewed Bumpus's interference as amateurish and irresponsible. Clearly, from Boas's point of view, Bumpus did not have the best interests of science in mind. Of course, Boas's problem with people in positions of authority over him also played a part. As his own status grew, he became less willing to accept criticism, feeling that he had earned respect after many years of struggle and uncertainty. His own experience with anti-Semitism had also toughened him, teaching him to stand firm against any personal or professional attack.

Boas's resignation called into question the museum's commitment to professional anthropology. Jesup's short-sightedness no doubt convinced Boas more firmly than ever that Columbia University would remain his sole power base and the best hope for anthropology's future growth.

The museum's reputation fared poorly as a result of the battle. Even before Boas's resignation, George Dorsey of the Field Museum, a man not usually found on Boas's side, had visited the museum and was appalled by its "radically wrong" administrative operation. He blamed "criminally dangerous" storage facilities and Bumpus's vast ignorance as major weaknesses. In an unsolicited comment to Boas after his departure, Dorsey assured him that he would soon have his revenge.[30] The museum's future was not bright.[31] The entire museum episode lingered in Boas's mind. A year after his resignation, he continued to express himself publicly regarding the general purposes of museums. He was no doubt motivated by his recent problems and felt the need to defend his own actions.

The end of Boas's connection with the American Museum of Natural History allowed him the opportunity to redirect some of his energies. He became increasingly active in the Germanistic Society in New York, which he had helped found. The society sponsored lectures by German scholars to help promote in America "a knowledge of German civilization . . . as manifested in art, science, religion, and the economic condition of the people."[32]

Moreover, despite his resignation from the museum, Boas continued to direct the publications of the Jesup expedition. In the spring of 1906, prior to his departure from the museum, plans for the completion of the Jesup volumes were in flux. Boas was convinced that Bumpus intended to interfere with the written work being done by Waldemar Jochelson and Waldemar Bogoras. If Bumpus could prove that the two Russian scientists had received too much money for too little publishable material, Boas felt the director could demand a decrease in the museum's expenditures. To avoid such a possibility, Boas urged both men to send as much material as possible to justify continued funding.

Meanwhile, Boas sought to reach a new understanding with Jesup that would permit him to conclude the publication project outside of the museum itself, where he would be immune to Bumpus's meddling. Boas wished to enter into a contract with Jesup, in which he would receive payment upon delivery of the manuscript material. Boas put himself at "the mercy" of his contributors, feeling safer with this arrangement than one that involved Bumpus. Yet he knew the perils as well. As he explained to Bogoras: "if you do not deliver to us the manuscripts which are required according to the published plan, I am going to have considerable financial losses."[33]

The arrangement was most disagreeable to Boas. He abhorred the fact that Jesup and Bumpus treated "scientific work purely as a matter of business," but he had strong reasons for not abandoning the project.[34] He feared that he would receive much personal criticism if he did not finish the work. Jesup and Bumpus would surely lay the blame on him, making him the scapegoat and suggesting that Boas cared more for his "personal vanity" than for the advancement of science.[35] Consequently, Boas negotiated with Jesup. Although willing to complete the project, he refused to have any further face to face contact with Bumpus, for whom he felt "nothing but contempt."[36] Boas and Jesup finally agreed to terms and signed a contract for the completion of the published material.[37]

Even after the compromise, problems plagued the project. Boas had continued difficulty obtaining the published work from his Russian colleagues. The fact that Jochelson was in London and Bogoras in St. Petersburg contributed significantly to the problem, as did the mails, which often delayed the manuscripts. Largely, however, the authors were to blame. They were less than committed to finishing their work rapidly, which caused Boas great anxiety. The project lingered on until Europe went to war in 1914. At that time all work ceased, not to be resumed until World War I had ended. Boas, meanwhile, continued to do what little he could concerning the published material. He remained in written contact with Bumpus regarding his progress. The two men corresponded in an extremely formal manner, although it was obvious by the tone of his letters that Boas had no respect for the museum director and that he remained convinced that all worthwhile anthropological research at the museum had ended.

Although not seriously concerned about the museum's future, Boas was worried about the general quality of scientific activity in New York. He believed that the breakdown of all serious research work at the museum created a void in the city. Consequently, he developed a plan to promote anthropological investigation. He proposed the establishment of a fund "which would enable the instructors and advanced students of the Department at Columbia to undertake research work in various parts of the world."[38] This would not only foster increased scientific activity within the city, but would also advance the national reputation of his own department.

Boas expressed his concern to Oswald Garrison Villard, editor of the *New York Evening Post*, who had followed the controversy at the American Museum of Natural History and had met with Boas on previous occasions. Villard appeared equally concerned about the status of intellectual activity in New York and fully supported Boas's efforts.

In hopes of rectifying the current situation, Boas not only offered his plan for Columbia, but also sought to publicize the museum's shortcomings. He felt that a wide disparity existed between the progress enjoyed by commercial enterprise and the pitiful status of scientific activity in New York City. Compared to the treatment science received in Paris, London, Berlin and Chicago, New York seemed backward.

Two principal factors contributed to this condition. Lack of sufficient financial support limited Columbia University's ability to expand the scope of science. If the university had funds equal to those given the University of Chicago, the problem would not exist. The other weakness, of course, lay within the American Museum of Natural History, which catered "primarily to the spectacular needs of the public."[39] Only by a reversal of current practices could the museum aid in improving the city's dismal scientific status.[40]

Once again, Boas's stance on professionalism was evident during this campaign. Science must address itself more to scholarly pursuits than to public entertainment. As he had explained previously, the museum could accommodate both the professional scientist and the layman. That it chose only to attract the latter lay at the root of the problem. Jesup's death in the spring of 1908 did not noticeably change the situation. His successor, Henry Fairfield Osborn, did not impress Boas. Believing Osborn's "scientific horizon" to be "limited," Boas saw no hope for the advancement of anthropological research at the museum.[41] Any attempt to promote scientific work in New York would have to originate elsewhere.

As if anticipating this, Boas proposed a further expansion of his department. In 1906 he had contacted Nicholas Murray Butler, Columbia's president, concerning the university's role in the International School of American Archaeology in Mexico City. Boas requested that Columbia, along with other leading American institutions, send instructors there on a rotating basis.[42] This connection could only serve to widen the reputation of Columbia's department of anthropology, and would also enhance Butler's position as a leader in the promotion of international scientific activity.

Aside from the Mexican school, Boas also envisioned expansion from within the department. By 1907, several highly regarded graduate students were in training at Columbia. Edward Sapir, Frank Speck, Robert Lowie and Alexander Goldenweiser studied under Boas in this period. Their future contributions to the study of man affirm the excellence of Boas's instruction. Yet Boas was not satisfied with the department, nor with his students' preparation. He frequently required them to repeat courses until he was satisfied with their performance. He felt many anthropological problems remained unexplored. It was necessary, in his opinion, to train each graduate student in all facets of research. Furthermore, he desired the construction of laboratory facilities for the students in physical anthropology, "preferably in connection with the biologic work of the University."[43] He also hoped that the "scope of special training in ethnography" could be broadened to include the study of Africa and southeastern Asia.[44] In this way Columbia could continue to dominate anthropological development in the United States.

Although hard at work on a local level, Boas never lost sight of the national aspects of his science. In the spring of 1906, at the request of Andrew White, Boas expressed his views concerning the man most qualified to succeed S. P. Langley as secretary of the Smithsonian Institution. The invitation provided Boas with one last chance to attack the policies that had driven WJ McGee from Washington. Boas suggested that the Smithsonian must give up direct control of the various bureaus under its rule. If scientific bureaus maintained their own administrative offices, there would be more progress. Not only could the Smithsonian take up new areas of research, but the bureaus themselves would run more efficiently. Boas hoped the new secretary would be a man "equally interested in mental science, in biology, and in physical science." Further, he would have to be willing to promote "the best interest of science," even if that entailed giving up control over the vast bureaucracy that had been established at the Smithsonian.[45]

Langley had failed to meet this standard. In Boas's mind, two men fit the criteria for effective leadership. One was Henry E. Donaldson, Boas's former colleague at Clark and current head of Philadelphia's Wistar Institute. The other was James McKean Cattell, the former chairman of Columbia's anthropology and psychology department. Both individuals, Boas felt, were capable of injecting new life into the Smithsonian. Both would certainly contribute to the progress of science. Yet, the regents of the Smithsonian passed over both men, choosing instead Charles Doolittle Walcott.[46] The appointment did not displease Boas, but the choice would have serious future ramifications for him.

In 1907 Boas was elected vice president and chairman of Section H of the American Association for the Advancement of Science. The previous year a committee consisting of Boas, Cattell, William Holmes and Alfred Kroeber had changed the section's designation from "Section of Anthropology" to "Section of Anthropology and Psychology." Boas, representing Section H and the American Ethnological Society, then joined a small group of anthropol-

ogists in drafting a plan for the future direction of the science.[47] The group
addressed the Carnegie Institute pinpointing the "researches that should be
undertaken for the furtherance of anthropological sciences."[48] One crucial
area for future study was South America, where racial and cultural development was of "fundamental importance" for anthropology in general. The
group proposed specific avenues of investigation with an estimated annual
appropriation of $20,000. Although the institute did not agree to fund the
study, Boas came away from the deliberations firmly convinced that such a
study was essential.

Aside from these grandiose attempts to expand anthropology on both local
and national levels, smaller events also spurred Boas to action. The illness
of Albert S. Gatschet, an employee at the Bureau of American Ethnology,
concerned him deeply. Gatschet had done significant work on Indian ethnology, specifically with the Miami Indians of Indiana. Soon after the turn of
the century, however, he began to suffer from degeneration of the brain,
which abruptly halted his scientific activity. In response, the Smithsonian gave
him a leave of absence without pay.[49] Boas found this callous action repre-
hensible. He petitioned members of the Smithsonian, the Carnegie Institute
and Congress for redress. Through his efforts, and those of Putnam and John
Swanton, the executive committee of the Carnegie Foundation for the Advancement of Teaching voted a retiring fund of $1,000 per annum to Gatschet,
who died the following year.[50]

In the spring of 1907, the Bureau of American Ethnology prepared to
publish Boas's first volume of the *Handbook of North American Languages*,
although the book did not appear for four more years.[51] Additionally, the
University of Chicago invited Boas to leave Columbia for a head professorship
in anthropology.[52] Ironically, it was Chicago that had decided not to hire Boas
following the Clark imbroglio in 1892. At that time Boas lacked financial
security and would, in all likelihood, have accepted an offer. By 1907 he was
no longer struggling. His position at Columbia was secure. In fact, Boas had
gone ahead with plans to build a home in Grantwood, New Jersey, to which
he and his family would move from their rented home on Manhattan's upper
West Side. He rejected Chicago's offer, no doubt with some measure of
satisfaction.

In April, Columbia held a ceremony honoring Boas. His friends presented
him with an anniversary volume to commemorate twenty-five years since he
had received his doctorate at Kiel. Boas felt "embarrassed by the honor."[53]
He humbly acknowledged that anthropology, being a new science, yielded
"ample returns" for anyone who studied it and that as a result "science
achievement is easy."[54] Despite his modesty, Columbia University and anthropologists in general recognized Boas's commitment to his profession.
The Smithsonian Institution was no exception. Secretary Walcott designated
Boas as the institute's representative to the 1908 Congress of Americanists to
be held in Vienna.[55]

Despite such accolades, Boas soon found it necessary to defend his reputation from slander. During an informal meeting with George Dorsey, Boas began speculating on Walcott's decision not to appoint him as the new director of the Bureau of American Ethnology. Dorsey responded to Boas's query by explaining that Walcott and Holmes believed that several years ago some illegal activity had taken place within the bureau. Specifically, they questioned Boas's involvement in the sale of some manuscripts to McGee. Walcott had told Dorsey that the transaction "would not bear the light" of an investigation. Dorsey inferred from these remarks that the incident had created uneasiness toward Boas and cost him the appointment.

Boas immediately defended himself. He not only explained the entire transaction to Dorsey, he also sought to clear up the matter with Walcott directly.[56] He asked that Walcott send him specifics of the alleged financial irregularities.[57]

Walcott denied that he had ever called Boas's integrity into question. He simply believed that Boas was "not a good financial manager," judging from his work with the *American Anthropologist*. Walcott also explained that the manuscript transaction stemmed from McGee paying Boas in advance for the delivery of written work. Walcott felt this was questionable "from a government officer's standpoint," but in no way impugned Boas's honesty.[58] He regarded Boas as "one of the ablest, if not the ablest American ethnologist."[59]

Not content with this explanation, and unmoved by the flattery, Boas sought legal advice. He considered a slander suit against Walcott, and even contacted Dorsey to determine if he would testify in court.[60] To Boas the accusations made by Walcott related directly to the Field Columbia Museum conflict of 1894. Walcott had engineered Holmes's appointment in Chicago in order to make room for John W. Powell at the bureau. Since Boas was in the way, Walcott maneuvered the appointment clandestinely. McGee alone had attempted to console Boas. When Powell died and Langley passed over McGee in choosing a successor, Boas reentered the picture. He demanded that McGee receive his deserved position. Boas felt that those two incidents prejudiced Walcott. As Boas saw it, "I was in his way in Chicago, and then I stood by McGee, who is disliked by a great many of the Washington people."[61] Thus Boas was aware that he had alienated himself from both Walcott and Holmes, who now were perhaps the two most powerful men in the Washington scientific community.

Since Walcott's accusations also impinged on McGee's reputation, Boas contacted his old friend, who was working in the Department of Agriculture. Apparently McGee had anticipated the situation all along and had prepared himself. He informed Boas that Langley was to blame. Walcott, according to this scenario, did not understand the situation, and had "accepted second-hand information rather than documents which should be in his custody."[62] McGee charged that Langley had made accusations "deliberately and maliciously in a surreptitious manner with the object of discrediting the Bureau and the leading experts connected with it."[63]

This was part of Langley's attempt to close down the bureau completely.

McGee believed that Langley was "jealous of Powell's superior ability and prestige" and thus sought to discredit the bureau immediately after Powell's death. Walcott, in McGee's view, simply did not know the facts. Langley covered up the investigation into the bureau's activities, and the new secretary never saw the report. Consequently, Walcott relied on false information provided by Langley. Although this seemingly pointed to Walcott's innocence, McGee still did not trust him. He characterized him as "devoid of sympathy with the sciences" in which Boas was interested, and felt he knew as much about anthropology "as the babe born blind knows of the solar spectrum."[64]

Walcott, meanwhile, attempted to smooth over relations with Boas. He reiterated that Boas's honor was not at issue.[65] Boas remained skeptical, especially when Dorsey added fuel to the fire by informing Boas that Holmes and Walcott had "trumped up the matter" as an excuse for not offering him the directorship of the bureau. Upon learning this, Boas demanded a public retraction from Walcott, which he did not receive.[66]

Dorsey also intervened on Boas's behalf, but Walcott stonewalled. Privately, Boas hoped that the secretary would settle the matter by offering him the directorship of the bureau. Although Boas would decline such an offer, the invitation, he felt, would vindicate him completely.[67] Walcott obviously had no plans to make such a move, which led Boas to exonerate himself publicly. Unwilling "to be whitewashed by a few polite phrases," Boas published all the correspondence between Walcott and himself.[68] He mailed packets to anyone who "may have heard about this affair," including the regents of the Smithsonian and members of Congress who served on the Smithsonian's various committees.[69]

The tactic did not prove worthwhile. Putnam sided with Boas and believed that Walcott should apologize. Most of the Smithsonian regents did not respond. McGee, however, decided that he too must demand a retraction of the unproven allegations. He requested either a public apology from Walcott or permission to print the correspondence that would prove his innocence.[70] Walcott declined. Frustrated by this continued intransigence, McGee inquired whether Walcott lacked "the courage and sense of honor required to submit to arbitration the sequestered records bearing on the matter."[71] Apparently Walcott lacked both, for he made no reply.

The incident ended with neither Boas nor McGee obtaining public apologies. Boas emerged from the conflict with his reputation intact. Walcott's letters acknowledged that there was no question regarding his honesty. McGee, however, did not fare as well. The allegations of financial bungling still marred the Powell-McGee administration of the bureau.

Walcott's motive in implicating Boas was unclear. Possibly, as Boas suggested, the secretary of the Smithsonian resented him since the Field Museum incident, as well as for his later defense of McGee. On the other hand, as Dorsey believed, Walcott and Holmes may have invented the charges as a way of keeping Boas from gaining power at the bureau. This was most plausible. The entire event emanated from the jealousies that continued to plague the anthropological community. Walcott and Holmes had good reason to fear Boas's power. By the turn of the century he had acquired a formidable reputation. Moreover, professional anthropologists in general increasingly threatened amateurs' status. Walcott attempted to hold Boas's power in check, at least in the nation's capital.

Whatever the motivation, Boas overreacted. He overestimated the damage Walcott could inflict. By publicly circulating the letters, Boas made more people aware of the case than was necessary. Yet his personality allowed him no alternative. Just as he refused to ignore scientific errors, so too was he unwilling to refrain from defending his reputation. The incident died down quickly, with Boas continuing his work as honorary philologist and maintaining an amiable relationship with both Walcott and Holmes. However, neither Boas nor the secretary forgot the affair.

Overall, the early 1900s were a time of increased stability for Boas. Although separated from the American Museum of Natural History, he had a secure future at Columbia. His additional connections with the Smithsonian Institution, the American Association for the Advancement of Science and the American Ethnological Society all attested to his national prominence. The twentieth century, however, brought significant new problems to American society. Afro-Americans continued to experience the cruelty of racial prejudice. Increased immigration from Europe led to xenophobia and consequent hostility on the part of native Americans. These attitudes fostered talk of immigration restriction. Boas viewed these attitudes with alarm, both because they looked to science for support and because they exuded virulent racism. Rather than act out the role of passive observer, he took up the challenge, armed with the implements of his science.

## NOTES

1. Franz Boas to Morris K. Jesup, October 25, 1900, American Philosophical Society, Boas Correspondence. (Hereafter cited as APS/BC.)
2. Boas to Jesup, March 21, 1901, APS/BC.
3. Jesup to Boas, April 28, 1905, APS/BC.
4. Hermon C. Bumpus to Boas, April 28, 1905, APS/BC.
5. Ibid.
6. Boas to Jesup, April 29, 1905, APS/BC.
7. Boas to Jesup, April 29, 1905, APS/BC.
8. Ibid.
9. Ibid.
10. Ibid.
11. Ibid.
12. Franz Boas, "Some Principles of Museum Administration," *Science*, n. s. 25 (June 1907): 922–23.
13. Morris K. Jesup to Boas, May 2, 1905, APS/BC.

14. Boas to Hermon C. Bumpus, May 5, 1905, APS/BC.

15. Bumpus to Boas, May 6, 1905, APS/BC.

16. Boas to Bumpus, May 6, 1905, APS/BC.

17. "Notes of Interview with Mr. Jesup and Professor Bumpus," May 17, 1905, APS/BC.

18. Ibid.

19. Ibid.

20. Boas to Morris K. Jesup, May 23, 1905, APS/BC.

21. Jesup to Boas, May 24, 1905, APS/BC.

22. Frederick W. Putnam to Boas, May 29, 1905, APS/BC.

23. Boas to Alfred C. Haddon, June 25, 1905, APS/BC.

24. Boas to Jesup, November 25, 1905, APS/BC.

25. Jesup to Boas, December 20, 1905, APS/BC.

26. Boas to Jesup, December 21, 1905, APS/BC.

27. Boas to Abraham Jacobi, January 24, 1906, APS/BC.

28. Jesup to Boas, February 2, 1906, APS/BC.

29. Boas, "Principles of Museum Administration," pp. 921–22.

30. "Conversation with Dorsey in my office at museum," May 14, 1906, APS/BC.

31. Curiously, John Michael Kennedy ignored this entire affair in his doctoral dissertation, "Philanthropy and Science in New York City: The American Museum of Natural History, 1868–1968" (Ph.D. diss., Yale University, 1968). He erroneously reported that Boas resigned his position at the museum in 1903 due to a conflict with Jesup over the North Pacific Expedition. Kennedy also suggested that Putnam, although taking Jesup's side in the affair, resigned at the same time. This has no basis in fact. Kennedy failed to note Putnam's resignation in 1901 and Boas's promotion to the curator post. He also ignored the conflict between Bumpus and Boas. The fact that Kennedy found the roots of Boas's departure in a disagreement over the Jesup expedition is ironic, since that project became the only link Boas retained with the museum after he resigned in July 1906.

32. Boas to W. T. Hewett, November 17, 1905, APS/BC.

33. Boas to Waldemar Bogoras, May 25, 1906, APS/BC. This would occur because each published book included written material from all the authors concerned. If one failed to deliver his manuscript, the museum, according to the terms of the contract, could withhold all funding.

34. Boas to Bogoras, June 2, 1906, APS/BC.

35. Ibid.

36. Ibid.

37. Boas to Bogoras, June 8, 1906, APS/BC.

38. Boas to Archer M. Huntington, April 6, 1907, APS/BC.

39. Boas to Oswald G. Villard, December 9, 1907, APS/BC.

40. Ibid.

41. Boas to Berthold Laufer, March 11, 1908, APS/BC.

42. Boas to Nicholas M. Butler, December 8, 1906, APS/BC.

43. Franz Boas, "The Department of Anthropology," *Columbia University Quarterly* 10 (1908): 307.

44. Ibid.

45. Boas to Andrew D. White, March 22, 1906, APS/BC.

46. Otis T. Mason to Boas, January 30, 1907, APS/BC.

47. The group included Putnam, representing the Archaeological Institute of America; Roland Dixon of the American Folk-Lore Society; William Holmes of the Anthropological Society of Washington; and Alfred Kroeber of the American Anthropological Association.

48. Boas et al., to R. S. Woodward, April 3, 1907, APS/BC.

49. Boas to Alexander G. Bell, July 31, 1906, APS/BC.

50. Henry Pritchett to Boas, August 1906, APS/BC.

51. William H. Holmes to Boas, March 26, 1907, APS/BC.

52. George A. Dorsey to Boas, March 26, 1907, APS/BC.

53. Boas to Livingston Farrand, April 19, 1907, APS/BC.

54. Franz Boas, "Response to Address by the President of Columbia University on the Occasion of the Formal Presentation of the Boas Anniversary Volume, at a Meeting of the University Council," *American Anthropologist* 9 (1907): 647.

55. "Memorandum from Charles D. Walcott," January 22, 1908, APS/BC.

56. George A. Dorsey to Charles D. Walcott, July 25, 1909, APS/BC.

57. Boas to Walcott, July 10, 1909, APS/BC.

58. Walcott to Boas, August 8, 1909, APS/BC.

59. Ibid.

60. Boas to George A. Dorsey, August 17, 1909, APS/BC.

61. Boas to Abraham Jacobi, September 2, 1909, APS/BC.

62. W J McGee to Boas, September 26, 1909, APS/BC.

63. McGee to Boas, October 11, 1909, APS/BC.

64. Ibid. Ironically, McGee has also been criticized for his anthropological ignorance. Marvin Harris in *The Rise of Anthropological Theory: A History of Theories of Culture* (New York: Thomas Y. Crowell, 1968), described McGee as "an inexhaustible mine of every error of substance and theory that it was possible to commit on the basis of the most vulgar prejudices masquerading as scientific expertise" (255). Although Boas considered McGee an amateur, there is no indication in his correspondence that he agreed with this appraisal. It seems, however, that their friendship was not based on mutual exchange of scientific information, but rather was derived from the fact that they had come to each other's aid in times of crisis.

65. Charles D. Walcott to Boas, October 15, 1909, APS/BC.

66. Boas to Charles D. Walcott, November 8, 1909, APS/BC.

67. Boas made this clear in a letter to Jeremiah Jenks; Boas to Jeremiah Jenks, January 20, 1910, APS/BC.

68. Boas to Jenks, January 14, 1910, APS/BC.

69. Boas to Nelson S. Spencer, December 20, 1908, APS/BC.

70. W J McGee to Charles D. Walcott, January 26, 1910, APS/BC.

71. McGee to Walcott, April 28, 1910, APS/BC.

# 5
# The Struggle for Racial Equality

As the twentieth century began, Boas became increasingly disturbed over the rising wave of racial prejudice displayed in white attitudes toward blacks. His thought and activity became highly significant for the nascent Afro-American civil rights movement, and his contributions remained important as the movement progressed.

This was so precisely because the active phase of that struggle for equality, commencing after the Supreme Court's 1954 *Brown v. Board of Education* decision, drew so heavily on the past. The philosophies and opinions of black leaders such as W. E. B. Du Bois, Booker T. Washington, Marcus Garvey, and Asa Philip Randolph were the wellsprings out of which the movement grew. Black leaders utilized these ideologies in developing the tactics necessary to combat segregation and discrimination in the economic, social and political aspects of American life. Boas's insight into the dilemma of American race relations and his activities during the early years of the twentieth century had a crucial impact on the transition in intellectual thought that occurred between the *Plessy v. Ferguson* decision of 1896 and *Brown* fifty-eight years later. His race theory became the foundation on which other social scientists would build a counterattack against pseudoscience. Boas's involvement, moreover, is of particular interest because his motivation stemmed in large measure from his own ethnicity and personal experience with persecution. His activities underscore an important link between antiblack and anti-Semitic prejudices, while at the same time calling attention to the role of Jews in the early civil rights movement.

Boas, in typical fashion, first attempted to solve the race problem through further research. He proposed a plan to establish an anthropological survey under the auspices of the Bureau of American Ethnology as an initial step in studying the problem. His concern grew, especially after the bureau decided not to fund the survey.

Clearly, Boas had valid reasons to worry. Disfranchisement of black voters and the development of peonage practices both testified to the Afro-American's inferior treatment. The civil rights cases of 1883 all but invalidated the 1875 Civil Rights Act. With the Supreme Court's *Plessy v. Ferguson* decision, all hope vanished for full black participation in American life; Jim Crow became acceptable. By the 1890s blacks had attained no more than "demi-freedom."[1] Political, economic and social avenues were closed to them.

Many scientists of the period justified the poor treatment blacks received. White supremacists relied on scientific findings to prove their allegations of black inferiority and hence bolster their belief that blacks deserved second-class citizenship. Such reasoning was not new. Prior to the Civil War, slaveholders had used the findings of scientists such as Josiah Nott and Samuel George Morton to justify keeping blacks in servitude. By the late nineteenth century, physicians began to point out the major differences between white and black physiques. They "vehemently dismissed the possibility of race improvement" for blacks, based on their health and constitution.[2]

Physicians were not the only men of science to become involved in the discussions of black inferiority. Daniel G. Brinton, Professor of American Linguistics and Archeology at the University of Pennsylvania and a staunch advocate of professional anthropology, held that blacks were generally inferior physiologically. Nathaniel Southgate Shaler, Professor of Geology at Harvard University, supported these views. He postulated that "the Negro was 'nearer to the anthropoid or pre-human ancestry of men' than any of the other races" and that this proximity explained both the race's present status and its future limitations.[3] The statistician Frederick L. Hoffman's findings were also influential. His 1896 essay, "Race Traits and Tendencies of the American Negro," claimed that blacks, because of poor constitutional construction, tended to be more seriously and more frequently afflicted by disease than whites.[4]

In this context, the problem of race mixture became a frequently discussed topic. Extensive studies of black sexual organs, so long a source of fascination for some white Americans, claimed to prove the dangers inherent in miscegenation between black men and white women. Brinton, for example, warned that miscegenation "brought an 'indelible degradation' to the descendants of the white partner in such a marriage."[5] Moreover, offspring of such a pairing could not adjust successfully to the American climate. Joseph LaConte turned the argument of black physical inferiority on its head. He suggested that weaker white strains should mix with blacks to ensure the latter's survival. Without this influx of strong Teutonic blood, LeConte warned, the black race faced certain extinction.[6]

In sum, most nineteenth-century scientists saw little hope for the black

American. Being of weaker stock than whites, blacks had little chance of survival. The contributory factors were alleged physiological deficiencies, especially the lack of adequate brain power. Many scientists suggested that "only the hothouse environment of slavery had preserved the race from the rigors of natural laws."[7] Slavery, from this perspective, had perpetuated the black race in America, not weakened it.[8]

Boas challenged these scientific assumptions for several interrelated reasons. His liberal ideology was aroused by the inhumanity surrounding racism. Reacting against American racial hatred and hopeful that blacks could one day share in the true meaning of democracy and the American dream, Boas was motivated by goals similar to reformers like Oswald G. Villard, Joel E. Spingarn and Mary White Ovington, who expressed concern over racial prejudice and attempted to combat it. The establishment of the National Association for the Advancement of Colored People was a step in this direction; Boas supported the association and its demands for equal treatment for blacks.

Boas's concern for scientific accuracy was of equal importance in shaping his racial views.[9] He could not tolerate generalizations or scientific opinions drawn on faulty data. The pseudoscientific support given to theories of black inferiority ran against his emphasis on meticulous research. Accordingly, he sought to prove these theories wrong, not so much to champion the cause of blacks as to purify science and its application. In this respect his involvement in the plight of black America "sprang from a scientist's desire to rid his discipline of prevailing amateurism and to substitute the rigorous methods of science for facile generalization."[10]

Although these two factors were significant in Boas's decision to become active in black protest, another factor was of critical importance as well. Boas's own experience in Germany played a role in his sensitivity to racial discrimination. His encounters with anti-Semitism had angered him. They had already caused him to flee his homeland. In America, although anti-Semitism existed, he was free to do as he pleased. Blacks, he perceived, were not, and he identified with their situation.[11] Moreover, he still considered himself a foreigner in America, subject to both overt and covert forms of prejudice.[12] During a 1906 commencement address at Atlanta University, Boas compared the black situation in America to the one faced by Jews in Europe. His 1921 article, "The Problem of the American Negro," made the same point; in it Boas specifically drew an analogy between antiblack and anti-Semitic feelings. Neither prejudice, he reflected, would disappear from the American scene until the black and the Jew disappeared as distinct types.

Boas understood that racism lay deeply within the American psyche. Accordingly, throughout his attack on bigotry he sought to pit "science and rational thought against the irrational authority of tradition."[13] He hoped to challenge American xenophobia and racism by juxtaposing science, at once logical and persuasive, with the emotion-laden utterances of prejudice. This approach would not only crush the illogical antiblack hatred that flourished in America, but would also destroy the undergirding of anti-Semitism. In this sense, "Boas's science was not only self-justifying, but to a very great degree self-centered."[14] He hoped to better his own condition as well as that of blacks.

Other factors also pushed Boas in this direction. His "great affection for the primitives he studied" carried over into his decision to help black Americans.[15] Boas valued every human culture regardless of its place on the scale of civilization. For him, each distinct culture, no matter how primitive, had made substantial contributions to human history and progress. His argument for cultural relativism meshed with his own sense of historical particularism, and clashed with traditional prejudices directed at cultures not at the pinnacle of civilized society. Historical circumstances, not mental ability, determined a culture's progress.

Respect for the relative nature of culture was part of Boas's contribution to anthropological thought and was an important element pushing him to a defense of Afro-Americans and immigrants in America. So too was his desire to use his research "in the interest of freedom."[16] His theory had "evolved in a political milieu," and he often employed anthropology "to modify" those circumstances.[17]

Finally, Boas's acquaintance with history influenced his treatment of the African experience and the debilitating effects of slavery. Upon understanding the background of the race problem and America's responsibility for robbing Africans of their culture, Boas could do no less than attempt to rectify the situation. For him, the study of man was more than a passive enterprise; it often became an active attempt to improve upon the condition of mankind.

Boas's crusade for black equality must be viewed against the background of the broader attack on the intellectual underpinnings of nineteenth-century evolutionary theory. Boas, as was obvious in his debate with Otis Mason and John Wesley Powell, was one of several influential thinkers who fashioned a critique of that theory. John R. Swanton, for example, in his studies of American Indian tribes, dissented vigorously from the hierarchical ranking of races. He condemned evolutionists who "took the ground that that was highest developed which approached nearest to the standards of European civilization, that to which they themselves belonged." Arguing that over time Darwin's "original idea" had been subject "to certain misconstructions," Swanton believed it "unwarrantable" and "entirely out of place" to use evolutionary theory to determine the relative worth of civilizations.[18] W. E. B. Du Bois, in his sociology program at Atlanta University, also attacked the evolutionary model by conducting studies that demonstrated black cultural contributions, both in America and Africa, and that belied the stereotypical image of Afro-Americans as "primitive."

As early as 1894, Boas spoke out against racial prejudice. In his vice-presidential address before the American Association for the Advancement of Science, he argued that race did not determine an individual's intelligence.

Scientists could not prejudge a black man's mental ability, for example, on the basis of his color alone.[19] The statistics Boas collected showed a wide range of mental capacities within each race. Consequently, each race possessed a complex spectrum of differing mental abilities. No generalizations applied to all individuals within any racial group; each race comprised at least some intelligent individuals and some who were mentally backward. Boas further suggested that some members of the black race were equal to or more intelligent than members of other races.[20]

This assertion that human faculty was not racially determined became one of Boas's favorite arguments in combating allegations of black inferiority. He often combined this argument with discussions of slavery's injurious effects and the vitality of African culture. In a 1904 article, "What the Negro has Done in Africa," he revealed a defense of blacks to which he would return frequently. Discussions of racial capabilities confined to the American experience were unjust because slavery had so oppressed Afro-Americans. It was, he said, "hardly fair to form a judgement of the whole race by considering what it has done under trying conditions."[21] He suggested the necessity of viewing African cultural achievement as an essential part of the black heritage. Consequently, he sought to compare "the achievements of the African tribes with those of the tribes of the New World, and even with those of the tribes of northern Europe at a period before they had come under the influence of Mediterranean culture."[22]

These comparisons painted a favorable picture of blacks. African communities were models of "thrift and industry," according to Boas. Africans tilled their fields with iron and wooden implements, raised and bred domestic animals, and possessed such skills as wood carving and iron-smithing. Besides these achievements, Boas found a strong "legal trend of mind" among African people. "No other race," he explained, "on a similar level of culture has developed as strict methods of legal procedure as the negro has. Many of his legal forms remind us strongly of those of medieval Europe."[23]

Boas then turned to the problem of assimilation. He rejected scientific claims that blacks could not adapt to the American environment. Again using a comparative framework, he cited the ease with which the Mohammedans were able to educate and influence Africans. Juxtaposing their success to whites' failure in this regard, he suggested that different methods of introducing culture were responsible. Whites sent only "the products of their manufactures and a few of their representatives into the negro country," while the Mohammedans infiltrated the culture and sought amalgamation through practices such as polygamy.[24] Their success indicated the ability of blacks to assimilate and thus disproved American theories of black inferiority regarding acculturation.

Citing the history of the medieval kingdoms of Ghana and Songhai, Boas mustered further evidence of African cultural achievement. He described the power possessed by African kings and the justice with which they presided over their subjects. In conclusion, he examined the significance of the African past for the present condition of blacks in America. He explained: "The achievements of the negro in Africa, therefore, justify us in maintaining that the race is capable of social and political achievements; that it will produce here, as it has done in Africa, its great men; and that it will contribute its part to the welfare of the community."[25]

Yet, though Boas was committed to equal opportunity for the races, he was not a full-fledged egalitarian. He was haunted by the belief that "the Negro race, on average, was slightly (but inherently) inferior to the white in mental ability."[26] Although he frequently stated that individual variations within each race were more important than interracial comparisons, he did not suggest that the races were fully equal. He instead put forward the hypothesis that slavery had left an indelible mark on Afro-Americans, which prohibited the freedom necessary for cultural development.[27]

Although he clearly dismissed the notion of equality of the races in his own lifetime, Boas believed that parity would be achieved in the future. Once blacks were given the freedom to experience the same historical and environmental conditions that whites enjoyed in America, the gap between the races, he believed, would diminish. Boas was therefore adamant in his belief that blacks deserved equal treatment and opportunity. In this sense Boas was a racial egalitarian. He did not stress equality in the present, but argued, rather, for the equipotential of the races.

Accordingly, Boas frequently lectured black audiences on the need to press for "full opportunities" to exercise their abilities. At Atlanta University in 1906, Boas urged the graduating class not to despair. He advised black youths on how to meet whites who were convinced of black inferiority:

To those who stoutly maintain a material inferiority of the Negro race and who would dampen your ardor by their claims, you may confidently reply that the burden of proof rests with them, that the past history of your race does not sustain their statement, but rather gives you encouragement. The physicial inferiority of the Negro race, if it exists at all, is insignificant when compared to the wide range of individual variability in each race.[28]

Boas went on to invoke his comparison with Jews, stressing that blacks would have to prove themselves in America to gain acceptance, just as the Jews had done in the face of all detractors. He reminded his audience that "in every single case in history the process of adaptation has been one of exceeding slowness."[29] Blacks must not be discouraged.

In closing, Boas presented the graduating seniors with what seemed to be an awesome responsibility. He stressed that "any failure of one of your race, and particularly any fault of one of you who have enjoyed the advantages of education, will be interpreted only too readily as a relapse into the old ways of an inferior race. If, therefore, you want to overcome the old antagonism, you have to be on your watch all the time. Your moral standards must be of the highest."[30]

Boas's discussion of anti-Semitism heightened the significance of the Atlanta speech. Not only did it reflect his own experiences with prejudice, it also foreshadowed the development of a new, controversial aspect of his thought on American racial problems, which would not be fully developed until after World War I. At that time he began serious consideration of interracial marriage as a method of easing racial friction.

In a speech given at the second National Negro Conference in 1910, and reprinted as "The Real Race Problem" in the NAACP's *The Crisis*, Boas first expressed an interest in the mixture of the two races. He claimed that unions between blacks and whites did not necessarily lead to an infusion of black blood as white supremacists feared; the result depended on the character of the sexual union. Intercourse between a black male and a white female would infuse black blood into the offspring, but the reverse pairing would not. Since sexual relations occurred between white men and black women more frequently than between black men and white women, Boas explained that the overall effect of intermixture would be to "whiten" more offspring than it would "darken." As a result, the "relative proportion of Negro blood in the following mixed generation becomes less," and therefore, "a gradually increasing similarity of the two racial types may develop."

Exploring American race prejudice with this thought in mind, Boas concluded that "our race problems will become less intense, the less the difference in type between different groups of our people." In essence, Boas argued that intermixture would ease racial tension. He saw the "inexorable conditions" of American life leading toward the inevitable "disappearance of the most distinctive type of Negro."[31] This would obviously result in the alleviation of race prejudice.

Boas did not actively encourage racial intermixture. He merely pointed out that racist fears of an increase in black blood were misplaced. Proceeding uncharacteristically from a questionable scientific base, Boas argued that far from posing a threat to the country, intermixture was a source of hope. Nonetheless, his overall pessimism regarding America's future remained. Traditional prejudices being what they were, only an elimination of distinct differences of color would lead white Americans to accept blacks as equals. It would take such a long-term transition to reduce racial hatred.

The race problem in America intensified after World War I. The reemergence of the Ku Klux Klan and the bitter Red Summer of 1919 heightened racial prejudice. The clashes between whites and blacks in major cities exacerbated tensions throughout the country. Observing these events from his vantage point at Columbia University, Boas felt the future was bleak. Prejudice did not abate; his efforts since the 1890s had achieved little. Yet Boas could not surrender. His commitment to professionalism forced him to challenge the inappropriate applications of science; his liberal ideology motivated him to press on no matter what the odds; and his own ethnicity was a constant prod.

His 1921 article "The Problem of the American Negro," published in the *Yale Review*, must be seen against the background of a country that had only recently emerged from a destructive and inconclusive war. Boas retraced much that was familiar to those who knew his work. He questioned the significance of intelligence tests because of their disregard of the effects of social environment, and again employed his African comparison, in which cultural achievements were taken as proof of black ability. What was new in Boas's treatment was his perception of the race problem in America. He now stressed the social aspect of race prejudice. He believed that bigotry was founded on "the tendency of the human mind to merge the individual with the class to which he belongs, and to ascribe to him all the characteristics of his class." Hence, when whites encountered a poor black they tended to believe that all blacks were similar. Boas felt that the "self-respecting negro" would be unable "to overcome the prejudices that merge him into a type" and would come to resent his inability to be seen as an individual. Economic conflict between the races was also a factor, but similar to other conflicts, it "presupposed the social recognition of the classes."[32]

The general answer to the question of how to ease racial tension seemed obvious to Boas. Whites must begin to view blacks as individuals rather than as members of a class. Although the goal seemed simple, the procedure remained complex. As Boas explained, "the natural habit of protecting our-selves against a supposedly hostile foreign group determines our life in great matters as well as in small details."[33] Accordingly, Boas saw no cause for optimism. The race problem in America would remain. Some strong-minded individuals would "free themselves from race prejudice," but the weak would not follow their example.

And yet, he was hopeful. If blacks and whites could lessen the racial differences between them, then they could lessen the consciousness that fostered prejudice. Hence, intermixture was the answer. It would "decrease the contrast between extreme racial forms" and eventually "would lead to a lessening of the consciousness of race distinction."[34] Consequently, Boas thought American society should not restrict marriages between white men and black women. In fact, he advocated all types of intermixture, since he saw no scientific reason to prohibit them. According to Boas, miscegenation had occurred in America since blacks were first brought to the continent, and the modern attempts to prevent it lacked justification. So he concluded that "it would seem that man being what he is, the negro problem will not disappear in America until the negro blood has been so diluted that it will no longer be recognized, just as anti-Semitism will not disappear until the last vestige of the Jew as Jew has disappeared."[35]

In view of Boas's usual concern for scientific accuracy and meticulous research, his advocacy of intermixture based on limited evidence was curious.

Perhaps his frustration at the seemingly immutable nature of American society led him to this controversial position. More probably, however, his own emotional experience with anti-Semitism weakened his usually rigorous scientific standards and led him to adopt the pessimistic position that all traces of "non-American" cultures must be eliminated for prejudice to cease. Boas believed that Americans would not tolerate anyone who failed to fit totally into their traditional way of life. Consequently, in order for the persecution of Afro-Americans to end, Boas believed the color difference must first disappear.

Beyond the questionable scientific accuracy of Boas's work on intermixture and the likelihood that emotion rather than reason influenced his own thinking, there remains a basic contradiction in Boas's civil rights strategy. He encouraged blacks to be proud of their distinctive heritage and for whites to respect it, and yet at the same time he suggested that only intermixture, by eliminating the differences between whites and blacks, would alleviate racial tensions. Surely such a theory was repugnant to those who stressed the importance of black pride and racial awareness.

Boas moved away from this controversial position after one of his students, Melville Herskovits, demonstrated in his research on the African past "a tendency toward 'the darkening of the whole colored population.' " Convinced that intermixture would not after all provide a biological solution to American racism, Boas "was forced to rely on the hope that by the conscious control of the cultural process itself mankind might yet eliminate racial prejudice—through education and the creation, especially among children, of social groups in which other principles of cohesion would override race."[36]

Accordingly, Boas sought to inform public opinion on all levels. He wanted to undertake scientific research on the capabilities of blacks in America. He was distressed by claims of black inferiority based on the early arrest of development of the black child. Finding the evidence supporting this theory to be insufficient, he sought to take up the problem himself.[37] He required financial support to carry out his research, however, and tried to secure funds from several New York organizations. He hoped to determine whether "an earlier arrest of mental and physical development" occurred in black children than in white ones, and if social causes rather than "anatomical and physiological conditions" were responsible. Moreover, Boas wished to study the position of the mulatto in relation to both the black and white races, specifically questioning whether the mulatto was an intermediate type or a reversion to either race.[38] No money was forthcoming for the projects, however, and Boas was forced to postpone his research plans.

Not content simply to offer strategies for black advancement and equality, Boas, beginning early in his career, attacked those individuals who justified racial prejudice. He reacted violently to the publication of Robert Bennett Bean's article, "The Negro Brain," which appeared in *Century Magazine* in 1906. Bean, an anatomist at the University of Virginia, suggested that the smaller size of the negro brain limited mental development among blacks. He concluded that unless blacks crossbred with other races, they could hope for little advancement.[39] Although offering this theory with certainty, Bean presented no data to support his beliefs; he claimed that a more scientific treatment of the same subject was in preparation.

This was exactly the type of thing that led Boas to fear the popularization of science. He found both the unscientific nature of the article and its conclusions offensive. In a letter to Richard Watson Gilder, the magazine's editor, Boas expressed dismay that the article had appeared without the publication of the corroborating data. Furthermore, he sought the opportunity to challenge Bean's theory publicly, once the data were published. He warned that "the mere fact that a paper of this kind should have found a place in a journal of the reputation of *The Century* will give strong support to those who deny to the negro equal rights; and from this point of view I think the advance publication of the paper is not just to the cause of the negro."[40]

The pseudoscientific pronouncements of men such as Bean disturbed Boas deeply, and he searched for a way to present to the public valid evidence on black achievement. Convinced that an understanding of black progress in Africa could only improve blacks' position in the United States, Boas tried to establish an African museum that would present to the public, "by means of exhibits and by means of publications, the best products of African civilization."[41] The museum would also sponsor a scientific study of that civilization. Further, in a second division of the institution, scientists would study the anatomy of Afro-Americans. Specifically, Boas hoped to work on "differing types of organization of the brain, and the laws of growth and of development of the negro race."[42] The knowledge gleaned from this study would be of use in determining general policy regarding black Americans. A final division of the proposed museum would collect statistical data on blacks.

Boas acknowledged the enormous expense involved in such an enterprise. He estimated that the building alone would cost $500,000, with an additional $40,000 immediately required for "exhibits, publications, and investigations."[43] Nevertheless, he recognized the pressing need for such an establishment. By informing the public of the black race's cultural achievements, he hoped to replace prejudice based on ignorance with an acceptance of equal rights for Afro-Americans.

To accomplish this goal, Boas wrote to the Carnegie Institute and to John D. Rockefeller, describing his plans in detail. He suggested that American attitudes toward blacks "might be materially modified if we had a better knowledge of what the Negro has really done and accomplished in his own native country." Boas urged support for his museum, believing that not only would it change white attitudes, it would also be a source of pride for all black Americans. He suggested that there was a "strong feeling of despondency among the best classes of the Negro" in the United States, which he attributed to their own perceptions of the "economic, mental, and moral inferiority of the race" in this country. The museum could rectify this problem by giving black Americans "the knowledge of the strength of their parental race in their native surrounding," which would have a "wholesome and highly stimulating effect."[44] By casting the problem in crisis terms, Boas hoped to receive economic support. He indicated the growing sense of tension between blacks and whites in the country, and presented his plan as a viable solution. But the foundation heads did not agree, and the African Museum remained a dream.

In typical style, Boas did not become discouraged by rejection. He continued to air his protests of race prejudice and looked for new ways to combat the problem. He gave a series of public lectures in New York City designed to explore the complexities of the race question and to demonstrate that no proof of racial inferiority existed. Much like his planned African museum, the lecture series was aimed to enlighten white Americans about the capabilities of blacks.[45]

In a further attempt to popularize his contention that blacks deserved equal treatment, Boas published an article in *Van Norden's Magazine* on "The Anthropological Position of the Negro." Although opposed in principle to submitting scholarly work to such a publication, he hoped that the magazine's popular format and attention to current affairs would help him reach a general audience. Intent on counteracting the pseudoscientific theory advanced by Bean, Boas dealt with the size and weight of the brain. He concluded that in a survey of 100 whites and 100 blacks, "the bulk of the members of the two races" possessed equal brain size. Believing that Bean had proceeded unscientifically, Boas asserted that "the anatomical differences between the two races are minute."[46]

Boas's commitment to scientific accuracy, however, forced him to acknowledge the possibility that the white race possessed "a slightly greater ability" in intelligence. He attributed this to the somewhat larger size of the white brain, but immediately cautioned that this was not a scientific certainty. In fact, he pointed out that no scientist had yet proved that brain size affected mental capacity. Boas attributed the poor position of the Afro-American to social conditions. He drew his familiar contrast between African cultural achievement and the legacy of slavery. The American experience, not mental deficiency, was responsible for the lack of black cultural progress in the United States. According to Boas there was "no scientific proof, that will stand honest criticism, which would prove the inferiority of the negro race."[47]

In closing, Boas placed the blame for racial tensions on all white Americans. If blacks could achieve a high level of culture in Africa but not in the United States, Boas suggested, then Americans were at fault. They had created slavery and the unfavorable conditions into which blacks were transported. Accordingly, it was, in Boas's mind, "our duty as men, as well as for the weal of our commonwealth, to restore to the negro what he has lost, and to raise him above the level of what he was before he came into contact with European civilization in Africa."[48]

Boas also attempted to popularize his views in *Century Magazine*, which, despite his protest concerning Bean's article, continued to publish similar accounts of black inferiority. Believing the magazine owed blacks "a presentation of a more favorable aspect of their achievements," Boas proposed an article on African culture based on photographs of African works of art that had been collected by various European museums.[49] Since Boas had planned a summer journey to Europe, he intended to collect these documents and prepare an essay to accompany them.

Gilder accepted Boas's offer, providing that the article took a "popular approach." Accordingly, Boas's essay, "The Industries of the African Negro," accompanied by nineteen photographs illustrating specimens of African manufactures, carefully avoided scientific discussion and attempted to present a popular history of African achievement.[50]

Despite this effort on Boas's part, Gilder rejected the article.

Convinced more than ever of the need to speak out against "the idea of an inferiority of the negro race," and frustrated by this rejection, Boas sent his manuscript to the Hampton Institute.[51] H. B. Frissell, editor of the institute's journal, the *Southern Workman*, was delighted with the article and agreed to publish it. Boas refused to accept any money for his work, making it a gift to Hampton Normal and Agricultural Institute.

The piece, which appeared in 1909, focused on African cultural achievement as an index of black abilities. Americans, Boas claimed, failed to "lay much stress upon the evil influences connected with the removal of the Negro from Africa to the shores of our continent." But slavery had created a break with the African's historic past. According to Boas, "this loss of connection with the historic past is without a doubt one of the most degrading influences in human culture." Unlike the African village experience, which offered the individual a sense of belonging and responsibility, slavery in America required blacks to perform work that had no relation to their "inner life" and gave them no satisfaction. Enslavement robbed the Afro-American of his identification with his culture. Thus blacks in America appeared stupid and lazy, and from this appearance emerged the myth of black inferiority, which still held sway in the twentieth century. By pointing to "African industry and artistic work of high merit," Boas hoped whites would begin to realize that "the failure of the American Negro to manifest himself in any of these directions is due, not to native inability, but to the degrading conditions under which he has been placed for generations."[52]

Boas's public utterances established him as a champion in the fight for black rights. Other reformers who were involved in the nascent civil rights movement asked his opinion regarding scientific theories connected to the black problem. For instance, Oswald Garrison Villard, whose "call" gave birth to the NAACP in 1909, met with Boas in New York on several occasions to discuss strategies for black equal rights. In 1907, Isidor Singer, the editor of the Singer Publishing Company of New York, sought Boas's help for what appeared to be an undertaking of tremendous importance in promoting a better understanding of Afro-Americans. Having read Boas's article in *Van Norden's*, Singer recognized the sincerity behind Boas's commitment to blacks and wanted to enlist his aid in publishing an *Encyclopedia of the Negro Race*. Singer was well qualified for the endeavor, for this was not his initial venture in the area of ethnic studies. In 1905 he had completed a twelve-volume *Jewish Encyclopedia*, which had been well-received. To launch this new enterprise, Singer had already written to Booker T. Washington, who expressed strong interest in the project and was "ready to assume the editor-in-chief-ship, with assistance from Mary Church Terrell."[53] In writing to Boas, Singer hoped to gain another ally for the project. He asked Boas to consider working in either an editorial or advisory capacity.

Boas strongly approved of the plan. His enthusiastic reply prompted Singer to suggest that Washington and Boas serve as coeditors of the encyclopedia. Washington could deal with "the practical questions making up the Negro Problem," and Boas with "the scientific ones." Boas again responded by offering his approval of the venture, but made no mention of accepting editorial responsibility. Singer nonetheless formally launched his enterprise in November. He received the endorsement of Andrew Carnegie, which he interpreted as an act assuring the project's success. He again offered Boas an editorial position, hoping that the commencement of actual work would lure Boas to make a decision.[54]

Meanwhile, Singer received additional offers of assistance. Daniel Murray of the Library of Congress, who had collected some 8,000 biographical sketches of prominent blacks throughout the world, made his researches available to Singer. James Bryce, the British ambassador in Washington, also wrote Singer, offering both praise and advice. He suggested that the encyclopedia focus on blacks all over the world, since race prejudice was not confined to the United States alone. Boas, however, remained uncommitted. Finally, on February 8, 1908, he met with Singer and Washington at the Hotel Manhattan. At the conclusion of that meeting Boas strangely accepted a position as editor.[55]

Announcement of the project elicited a favorable response. Many black and white colleges endorsed the encyclopedia and agreed to purchase the volumes. David Starr Jordan believed the endeavor would be "most valuable" and would "tend to give dignity to the position of a misunderstood group of Americans." James H. Linford, president of Brigham Young College, also supported the effort. Believing that lynchings and mobbings were based on misinformation and misunderstanding between the races, he hoped Singer's plan would help alleviate the problem by lessening ignorance.[56]

Despite such enthusiastic support, Singer never published the encyclopedia. The reasons are obscure. Perhaps the same lack of financial support that had aborted Boas's African museum was responsible. Nevertheless, Boas's cooperation in the project illustrated his desire to champion the struggle for black equal rights.

Boas's preoccupation with black rights carried over into his teaching as well. His undergraduate anthropology courses at Columbia dealt extensively with the differences in achievement between blacks in Africa and in the United States. He concentrated on the "physical characteristics of the Negro Race as compared to others, the ethnological characteristics of the Negro Race in Africa, and the effect of forcible importation of the Negro into America." Additionally, he treated "the economic and psychological influences" that "determine the relations between the Negro Race and the white Race in America" and "the development of the Negro Race since the abolition of slavery" in the United States.[57] Boas also advocated the adoption of a "black studies" curriculum at Columbia, which would serve to enlighten students about African culture. The design of the courses was similar in its instructive value to Boas's proposed African museum.

In addition to scholarly publications and academic attempts to solve the race problem, Boas translated his professional work into political activity. He attended the first National Negro Conference in 1909, which led to the establishment of the NAACP, and was invited to speak at the second meeting held the following year. There, he shared the podium with Albert Bushnell Hart of Harvard, Ida Wells and Mary Church Terrell, and publicly discussed intermixture for the first time.[58] In 1911 he joined the Greenwich House Committee on Social Investigations, and wrote the foreward to Mary White Ovington's study of blacks in New York. Again he spoke of black equal rights, condemning segregation and the development of racial prejudice as "the gravest obstacle to the progress of the Negro race."[59]

He also continued to attack the racist doctrines supposedly supported by scientific evidence. R. W. Shufeldt, a Washington, D.C., physician, requested Boas's comments on a book condemning miscegenation. Shufeldt's earlier work, *The Negro, a Menace to American Civilization* (1907), advocated the emasculation of all blacks in the United States to prevent intermixture and the consequent destruction of the white race. Rather than comment on a theory so obviously repugnant to him, Boas simply informed Shufeldt that he was not "at all convinced that the miscegenation of the races is a bad thing from a biological point of view," and suggested that the author would not appreciate his opinion.[60]

Other letters and requests often elicited caustic replies. When asked whether the offspring of intermixture could produce children, Boas sarcastically responded in a one-line letter, "mulattoes are fertile."[61] These questions, however, must have troubled him greatly. His efforts to publicize the erroneous assertions of black inferiority were prompted by such ignorance. Yet white supremacy continued to flourish with much "scientific" support.

Perhaps in a further effort to educate the public, Boas included his views on the Afro-American problem in his 1911 study, *The Mind of Primitive Man*. Although the book presented Boas's general theories on racial development and had serious ramifications for America's immigration problems, it also contained a reference to the black situation. Boas stated that blacks could progress on an equal level with all other races, if given the opportunity. Thus, people who advanced theories of black inferiority spoke from ignorance. A glance at the past history of Africa, Boas suggested, presented positive proof that the races were equal.

Blacks themselves were not aware of their race's achievements. Boas followed the lead of W. E. B. Du Bois in attempting to rectify this situation. He hoped "to devise some means of bringing home to the negroes the great achievements of their race."[62] Aside from his own published work, public lectures and support for organizations devoted to equal rights, Boas hunted for other avenues to air his beliefs. He became interested in the collection of black folktales and folksongs, again in an attempt to learn more of African cultural life.

Many of his students continued his efforts in this area. Melville Herskovits expanded upon Boas's research on African cultural achievements. His work, *The Myth of the Negro Past*, rested on the assumption that pre-American patterns of black life must be examined to understand the complexities of the American race problem. Ruth Benedict's *Race: Science and Politics* and Ashley Montagu's *Man's Most Dangerous Myth: The Fallacy of Race* renewed Boas's battle against both prejudice and those racists who misused science in its support. Zora Neale Hurston, in her study *Mules and Men*, in her work on folklore, and in her poetry, concentrated on black culture and the interplay of the African and American experiences.[63]

Boas's family was affected by his crusade against racism. Perhaps no remark better illustrated Boas's feelings on race prejudice in America than one made by his daughter Franziska. When asked whether her father would have allowed her to marry a black man, she responded that "theoretically he didn't mind," but he would have warned her of the social problems they would encounter.[64]

Boas's fight for black rights spanned half his life. From his 1894 address to the American Association for the Advancement of Science to his death in 1942, he remained deeply concerned about racism. He came to the defense of blacks in large measure because he had undergone similar discrimination. Feeling that a scientific investigation of race prejudice centered on Jews would leave him open to the charge of subjectivity, Boas used the Afro-American as a substitute. When he challenged pseudoscientific theory alleging black inferiority, he was reacting to his personal experience. Jews had progressed in all areas of American life, yet anti-Semitism remained alive, fanned by the emotional fires of traditional prejudice. Boas had experienced this firsthand in his dealings with the Wasp scientific community, which sought to exclude him. By focusing on blacks, he could lay siege to the underpinnings of all forms of racist thought while maintaining scientific objectivity. He surmised that if he could abolish racism as it pertained to blacks, Jews would also benefit. If he could convince the public that no race was pure and that each made valuable contributions to civilization, perhaps both Jim Crow and anti-Semitism would fall.

To some extent Boas was guilty of ethnic chauvinism. By his own example and his pronouncements, he demonstrated that Jews had progressed under persecution. He did not make the same claims for blacks. Realizing that mainstream American society was not impressed with the contributions of minority groups, he sought to focus on racism itself, using blacks as a surrogate for his real concern. This is not to imply, however, that Boas was unconcerned about black problems in America. Clearly he saw the two forms of prejudice as interrelated problems. Yet when it became an issue of cultural contribution, his ethnic identification caused an emotional reaction that belied his reputation as a cold, objective scientist. Ironically, it was this very reality that he wished to avoid by concentrating on blacks rather than Jews.

In this regard, Boas may not have been alone. Many Jewish intellectuals, including Joel E. Spingarn, Eric Reuter and Julius Rosenwald, became involved in the race issue and the black struggle for equality. Their legacy even carried over into the active phase of the civil rights movement, after the *Brown* decision. Clearly, they saw black and Jewish problems as twin evils. For them, "the collaboration was extremely beneficial. By assisting in the crusade to prove that Afro-Americans could be decent, conformist, cultured human beings, the civil rights Jews were, in a sense, spared some of the necessity of directly rebutting anti-semitic stereotypes." Perhaps, as Boas had done, they attempted to avoid charges of bias and subjectivity by focusing on blacks alone, convinced that if they were successful in eradicating prejudice on one front, it would crumble on the other as well.[65]

Whatever Boas's motivation, his participation was significant. He developed some of the arguments that the modern civil rights movement would use. He stressed "the impact on the Negro of a hostile social environment, his need for race pride, the contributions of Africa to culture and civilization, the essential equality for the races, and the insignificance of some racial differences in the face of large individual variations."[66]

Boas's primary contributions to the struggle for black equal rights lay in his theory of the equipotential of the races, his study of African culture and his participation in civil rights activities. More than any other anthropologist, he was responsible for a fundamental shift in science away from social Darwinism to support of equal rights. No longer could pseudoscientists monopolize science to prove their theories of black inferiority. His reasoned assault on racism, and his defense of Afro-Americans, were characteristic of the nexus between Boas's social activism and his professional work.

A host of intellectuals, both inside the anthropological profession and in the general scientific community, were influenced by Boas's stance. Many were drawn to Boas during the 1920s because of his reputation as a scholar and the logic of his views. The sociologists St. Clair Drake and Horace Cayton, in *Black Metropolis*, and Charles S. Johnson, in *Growing Up in the Black Belt*, used Boas's emphasis on environment in analyzing the social conditions of black life. Otto Klineberg, in *Negro Intelligence and Selective Migration*, reinforced the environmentalist position that surroundings rather than heredity determined mental ability.

As the United States moved through the 1930s to its showdown with Nazi race theory, many more Americans saw the contradiction between their country's opposition to Hitler and its own quiet acquiescence to Jim Crow. Gunnar Myrdal's classic study, *An American Dilemma*, highlighted the discrepancy between the American ideal and America's actual race relations. Myrdal paid indirect tribute to Boas by restating his belief that prejudice emanated from ignorance and fear rather than from proved inequality. In doing so, Myrdal, along with many others, including some of Boas's former students, further chipped away at racist American science.

Perhaps the finest compliment paid to Boas came, paradoxically, from one of his chief detractors. Carleton Putnam, well known for his white supremacist attitudes, demonstrated Boas's legacy succinctly and gave him major credit for affecting the Supreme Court's *Brown* ruling: "In the *Brown* case, *in a footnote* to its opinion, the Supreme Court referred to various sociological tracts and at the end of the note added, 'see generally Myrdal, *An American Dilemma.*' This reference, however oblique, was an effective way of saying 'see generally Boas and his disciples,' for Myrdal's *American Dilemma* was Boas from beginning to end."[67]

Boas's critical contribution, then, lay in providing a new way of thinking, without which America could not have traveled the long road from *Plessy v. Ferguson* to *Brown v. Board of Education*. W. E. B. Du Bois best expressed Boas's significance when he recalled:

Franz Boas came to Atlanta University where I was teaching history in 1906 and said to a graduating class: You need not be ashamed of your African past; and then he recounted the history of black kingdoms south of the Sahara for a thousand years. I was too astonished to speak. All of this I had never heard and I came then and afterwards to realize how the silence and neglect of science can let truth utterly disappear or even be unconsciously distorted.[68]

Obsessed with the injustice of American race relations and with his own experience with discrimination, Boas dedicated himself to the task of weaning "people from a complacent yielding to prejudice."[69]

## NOTES

1. Morton Keller, *Affairs of State: Public Life in Late Nineteenth-Century America* (Cambridge, Mass.: Belknap Press, 1977), p. 152.

2. John S. Haller, *Outcasts from Evolution: Scientific Attitudes of Racial Inferiority, 1859–1900* (New York: McGraw-Hill, 1975), p. 68.

3. Ibid., p. 178.

4. Ibid., pp. 60–63.

5. Ibid., pp. 114–19.

6. Ibid., pp. 160–63; Winthrop D. Jordan in *White Over Black: American Attitudes Toward the Negro, 1550–1812* (Chapel Hill: University of North Carolina Press, 1968) devotes an entire chapter to white attitudes toward black sexuality both during and after slavery, and discusses why white myths concerning black sexual prowess arose.

7. Ibid., p. 209.

8. Ulrich B. Phillips espoused this view in 1918 and again in 1922, with the publication of his two most noted works: *Life and Labor in the Old South* and *American Negro Slavery*. From this perspective, slavery educated blacks and prepared them for life in America. In no sense was the institution evil or debilitating. Without it, Phillips believed, Africans could not have survived.

9. Edward H. Beardsley, in his article, "The American Scientist as Social Activist: Franz Boas, Burt G. Wilder and the Fight for Racial Justice, 1900–1915," *ISIS* (March 1973), pp. 50–66, sees the concern over scientific accuracy as Boas's major driving force. Although this certainly helps explain Boas's commitment to black equality, I believe his own ethnicity is the most significant factor.

10. Edward H. Beardsley, "The American Scientist as Social Activist: Franz Boas, Burt G. Wilder, and the Fight for Racial Justice, 1900–1915," *ISIS* (March 1973): 54–55.

11. Melville Herskovits, in *Franz Boas: The Science of Man in the Making*, also finds anti-Semitism as a motivating force in Boas's decision to fight for equal rights for blacks, although he does not clarify how this concern is linked to other forces in compelling Boas to act.

12. George Stocking in "Anthropology as Kulturkampf: Science and Politics in the Career of Franz Boas" relates one pertinent example. During Boas's tenure on the faculty at Clark University, he was the object of nativistic wrath. This resulted from his study of children in the Worcester area, specifically related to the measurements he took of "naked schoolchildren." The *Worcester Daily Telegram* made reference to Boas's "duel-scarred face" and left the impression that his "alien status and menacing appearance" indicated that he was up to no good. See Stocking, "Anthropology as Kulturkamp," *The Uses of Anthropology*, ed. Walter Goldschmidt (Washington, D.C.: American Anthropological Association, 1979), p. 35.

13. Stocking, "Anthropology as Kulturkampf," p. 34.

14. Ibid.

15. Beardsley, "The American Scientist as Social Activist," p. 55.

16. Ibid.

17. Stocking, "Anthropology as Kulturkampf," p. 33.

18. John R. Swanton, "Some Anthropological Misconceptions," *American Anthropologist* 19 (1917): 461. See also Swanton, "The Social Organization of American Tribes," *American Anthropologist* 7 (1905): 663–73.

19. Franz Boas, "Human Faculty as Determined by Race," *Proceedings of the American Association for the Advancement of Science* 43 (September 1894): 301–327.

20. Ibid.

21. Franz Boas, "What the Negro Has Done in Africa," *The Ethical Record* 5 (1904): 106.

22. Ibid.

23. Ibid.

24. Ibid., p. 108.

25. Ibid., p. 109.

26. Beardsley, "The American Scientist as Social Activist," p. 51.

27. Boas was not alone in believing that Afro-Americans had not achieved a high level of culture in the United States. Most of the early civil rights leaders, including Booker T. Washington and W. E. B. Du Bois, shared this belief. They too viewed this situation as the logical manifestation of slavery and the post-emancipation practices of Jim Crow, which retarded black freedom. The revisionist view of slavery, which points to a vibrant slave culture, calls this position into question.

28. Franz Boas, "Commencement Address at Atlanta University," *Atlanta University Leaflet*, no. 19, May 31, 1906.

29. Ibid.

30. Ibid.

31. Franz Boas, "The Real Race Problem," *The Crisis* 1 (1910): 25.

32. Franz Boas, "The Problem of the American Negro," *Yale Review* 10 (1921): 392.

33. Ibid., p. 394.

34. Ibid.

35. Ibid., p. 395.

36. Stocking, "Anthropology as Kulturkampf," p. 43.

37. Franz Boas to Edward T. Devine, October 21, 1905, American Philosophical Society, Boas Correspondence. (Hereafter cited as APS/BC.)

38. Boas to Vladimir G. Simkhovitch, March 15, 1906, APS/BC.

39. Robert Bennett Bean, "The Negro Brain," *Century Magazine* 72 (1906): 778–79.

40. Boas to Richard Watson Gilder, September 18, 1906, APS/BC.

41. Boas to Felix Adler, October 30, 1906, APS/BC.

42. Ibid.

43. Ibid.

44. Boas to Starr Murphy, November 23, 1906; Boas to Andrew Carnegie, November 30, 1906, APS/BC.

45. Boas to George A. Plimpton, May 10, 1907, APS/BC.

46. Franz Boas, "The Anthropological Position of the Negro," *Van Norden's Magazine* (April 1907): 42.

47. Ibid., p. 47.

48. Ibid.

49. Boas to Richard Watson Gilder, May 22, 1907, APS/BC.

50. Gilder to Boas, May 31, 1907; Boas to Gilder, September 7, 1907, APS/BC.

51. Boas to H. B. Frissell, September 27, 1907, APS/BC.

52. Franz Boas, "The Industries of African Negroes," *Southern Workman* 38 (1909): 217–19, 229.

53. Isidor Singer to Boas, March 29, 1907, APS/BC.

54. Singer to Boas, July 18, 1907; Boas to Singer, August 9, 1907; Singer to Boas, November 2, 1907, APS/BC.

55. Daniel Murray to Singer, November 9, 1907; James Bryce to Singer, November

9, 1907; Boas to Singer, February 8, 1908, APS/BC. The reasons for both his initial reluctance to become an editor and his later acceptance remain unclear.

56. David Starr Jordan to Singer, February 11, 1908; James H. Linford to Singer, February 17, 1908, APS/BC.

57. "Test for Course in Anthropology," 1907, APS/BC.

58. Oswald Garrison Villard to Boas, March 16, 1910; Boas to Villard, March 17, 1910; Villard to Boas, March 25, 1910, APS/BC.

59. Franz Boas, foreword to Mary White Ovington's *Half a Man: The Status of the Negro in New York* (New York: Longman Green, 1911), pp. viii–ix.

60. R. W. Shufeldt to Boas, September 23, 1914; Boas to R. W. Shufeldt, September 29, 1914, APS/BC.

61. A. J. Griffin to Boas, February 6, 1915; Boas to A. J. Griffin, February 9, 1915, APS/BC.

62. Boas to George Peabody, June 13, 1918, APS/BC.

63. For an excellent study of Zora Neale Hurston, see Robert E. Hemenway, *Zora Neale Hurston: A Literary Biography* (Urbana: University of Illinois Press, 1977).

64. "The Reminiscences of Franziska Boas," Oral History Research Office, Columbia University, 1972, p. 70.

65. David Levering Lewis, "Parallels and Divergences: Assimilationist Strategies of Afro-American and Jewish Elites from 1910 to the Early 1930s," *Journal of American History* 71 (December 1984): 564. Lewis includes Boas in his analysis but does not suggest that Boas used blacks as a surrogate to avoid charges of scientific bias. In his view, the Jews involved in Afro-American civil rights activities linked better treatment for blacks with better treatment for Jews. They simply preferred to battle for black rights rather than have to deal with the ugly "stereotypes" associated with anti-Semitism. According to Lewis, these individuals fought anti-Semitism "by remote control" (555). There is clearly an element of this in Boas's thinking as well. However, his previous personal dealings with anti-Semitism and his desire to remain scientifically objective are crucial additional factors that account for his extensive involvement in the struggle for black equality.

66. Beardsley, "The American Scientist as Social Activist," p. 65.

67. Carleton Putnam, *Race and Reality: A Search for Solutions* (Washington, D.C.: Public Affairs Press, 1967), p. 70.

68. W. E. B. Du Bois, *Black Folk: Then and Now* (1939; Milwood, New York: Kraus-Thomson Organization, 1975), p. vii.

69. Herskovits, *Franz Boas*, p. 106.

# 6

# The Confrontation with Nativism

Blacks were not the sole victims of American racial prejudice. Newly arriving white immigrant groups also sent shock waves through the native population, producing fears that the purity of Anglo-Saxon stock was endangered. Although these nativistic sentiments existed before the Civil War—most forcibly expressed by the Know-Nothing Party—the late 1880s and 1890s marked a significant rise in anti-immigrant feelings. This particular xenophobic outburst resulted from the changing nature of immigration patterns.

In the early years of the nineteenth century, the majority of new arrivals came from northern and western Europe. Immigrating in response to labor needs and in small enough numbers to allow for facile assimilation, these new Americans met with little hostility. By 1880, however, the situation had changed. The majority of immigrants now came from southern and eastern European nations, and arrived with neither a promise of employment nor the ability to speak English. Additionally, labor violence associated with the Haymarket Riot of 1886 made native Americans anxious. They feared that the new arrivals sought the overthrow of American democratic institutions. Nativism emerged in response to this paranoia. This "massive late nineteenth-century immigration from southern and eastern Europe evoked responses that differed more in degree than in kind from the sentiment against Orientals."[1]

Similar to antiblack agitators, nativists utilized science to bolster their assumptions. Nathaniel S. Shaler, outspoken in his belief in black inferiority, suggested that immigrant groups could not assimilate into American society. He contended that the "'inferior races' remained outcasts from the evolutionary struggle, restricted from participation because of innate racial characteristics that were unresponsive to environmental influences."[2] In this manner, the struggle for survival became a critical weapon in the nativist argument.

John Fiske strongly exemplified this mode of thought. He suggested that "smaller-brained races were 'almost wholly incapable of progress, even under the guidance of higher races.' " Believing these races to be only "somewhat more teachable than any brute animals," Fiske saw certain immigrant groups bound for extinction when challenged by the evolutionary struggle.[3] He articulated beliefs synonymous with those espoused by Herbert Spencer. The "lesser races," in the Spencerian paradigm, fared poorly in the social Darwinian struggle for survival.

Many prominent Americans shared Spencer's beliefs. Theodore Roosevelt and Henry Cabot Lodge, for example, viewed the increased wave of immigration with alarm. In their minds, the racial purity of America could not withstand the onslaught of foreigners. Concerned over the structure of American society, these individuals sought "to limit opportunity" in the United States to the Caucasian who "embodied the highest level of adaptability, inventiveness, and democratic principles."[4] At the same time, these "American Spencerians" attempted to restrict the immigration of allegedly inferior people, suggesting that they were not worthy of participation in the American dream.

These theories closely resembled those advanced by European race thinkers. Count J. A. de Gobineau of France, considered the father of racist thought, hypothesized the "existence of a higher, Teutonic type of man who belonged to a superior master race."[5] Terms such as Aryan and Nordic were used to describe this Anglo-Saxon type. Houston Stewart Chamberlain, in his 1897 book, *Foundations of the Nineteenth Century*, stressed that the terms Teuton, Aryan and Anglo-Saxon all represented the same racial group. They comprised a superior race, whose hegemony existed not only over blacks and orientals, but also over other white "non-aryan" peoples.[6]

Other race-conscious Americans found further uses for science in attempting to prove the inferiority of the immigrant. The eugenics movement, the brainchild of Sir Francis Galton, attracted many racists in the United States. Talk of race suicide and the need for breeding pure stocks became common around the turn of the century. Charles B. Davenport achieved much notoriety as America's leading eugenicist.[7] By 1907, he had convinced the American Breeder's Association to consider eugenic studies in addition to its regular investigation into plant and animal breeding.[8] Viewing the immigration problem from a biological perspective, Davenport and his fellow eugenicists strongly believed that "admitting 'degenerate breeding stock' seemed one of the worst sins the nation could commit against itself."[9] It was not surprising that many immigration restrictionists emerged from the ranks of the eugenics movement.

Thus, nativistic sentiments heightened around the turn of the century. Science once again was employed to support race prejudice. This combination of theories and fears led many native Americans to question the policy of unrestricted immigration. As economic conditions deteriorated in the 1890s, nativism increased. Labor strikes added to the rising xenophobia. Supported by scientific opinions, this mounting paranoia led inevitably to increased racial hatred. The various scientific theories "interacted to support a racio-cultural hierarchy in terms of which civilized men, the highest products of social evolution, were large-brained white men."[10] It followed then that many native Americans began to condemn immigration, especially that which brought individuals from southern and eastern Europe to the United States. Those people were not of the Aryan stock that racists revered. Unlike northern and western European immigrants, these newcomers were not infused with "Teutonic blood." This made them not only inferior, but also a threat to America's global supremacy.

Few Americans were more concerned with the immigration problem than Franz Boas. The misuse of science to support allegations of racial inferiority troubled him, and his liberal beliefs again pushed him squarely into confrontation with those who favored immigration restriction. Further, since Boas was himself an immigrant, personal feelings once again figured prominently in his attitude. The same forces were at work in Boas's defense of immigration as in his attack on theories of black inferiority.

Boas reacted initially to the misapplication of science, claiming that scientists who relied on the cephalic index and drew conclusions solely from it were generalizing from insufficient evidence.[11] This was not to say that Boas objected to using the index. He found it a valuable tool, if used cautiously. What he objected to were "anthropologists who limited their work to the mechanical application of measurements, particularly of single measurements, and who try to trace the relationships of races by such means."[12] In Boas's mind, the index did not permit any broad generalizations. Physical anthropology could not solve the riddle of racial makeup by itself. Ethnology and linguistics, the other major anthropological branches, must also play a role in determining the early history of mankind.

And yet, ironically, the cephalic index became of one of Boas's most formidable weapons. He was not, however, "willing simply to go around measuring heads and computing cephalic indices."[13] As early as 1899, he had stressed the need to explore the biological significance of the index. He concluded that it did not "express any important anatomic relation," although it did provide some useful information.[14] For instance, the circumference of the head was the most accurate means of judging cranial size in living human beings. Boas felt such measurements were necessary in any investigation into racial differences, but by no means could they be used to determine mental ability or to rank races on any hierarchical scale.[15]

Head form studies became increasingly important to Boas. By the turn of the century, scientists debated the viability of Gregor Mendel's heredity theories. Boas sought to determine if offspring represented a blending of parental types, or whether there was, as Mendel had predicted, a reversion to a dominant parent. Boas's early work in this area persuaded him that Mendel's theories were plausible, although he remained skeptical. At any rate, Boas's concern with heredity led him to further exploration in physical anthropology.

This was not his initial venture into the physical aspects of anthropology. He had begun gathering physical measurements while under the influence of G. Stanley Hall at Clark. At that time, however, he was less concerned with racial problems than with "the influences of environment upon growth."[16] Nevertheless, those early studies gave him invaluable experience that he later brought to his defense of immigration.

The federal government also became seriously concerned with the immigrant problem, although seemingly for different reasons than Boas. Despite unwillingness to fund research into the causes of black-white tensions, Congress established a commission in 1907 to investigate all aspects of the immigration question. Three senators, three representatives and three presidential appointees composed a congressional committee, chaired by Vermont senator William P. Dillingham.[17] The key member of the Dillingham Immigration Commission was Cornell University economist Jeremiah Jenks, a presidential appointee whose restrictionist sentiments reflected the general bias of most members of the group.[18]

Ironically, it was Jenks to whom Boas turned. Recognizing the changing composition of the immigrant population and the criticisms raised concerning the influx of eastern and southern European types, Boas proposed to study the process of amalgamation. He wished to utilize current anthropological methods in gathering information that would shed light on "the selection that takes place by immigration; the modifications that develop in the children of the immigrants born in this country; and the effect of intermarriages."[19] Additionally, he hoped to determine what impact the American environment had on immigrants, specifically focusing on "the assimilation or stability of type and the changes in the characteristics of the development of the individual."[20] The answers to these questions, Boas hoped, would pinpoint the extent to which the new immigrant groups were able to assimilate into American society.

In conducting the study, Boas planned to gather extensive measurements of both native and immigrant groups, concentrating on the "stature, weight, circumference of chest and strength of muscle" of each group.[21] Boas decided to conduct his research in the environs of New York City, intending to collect data among immigrants arriving at Ellis Island, individuals leaving the country, schoolchildren and members of the resident population.

The plan required substantial funding, which Boas estimated at approximately $20,000. This sum would include salaries for a superintendent to prepare the final report, an assistant superintendent, twenty observers to conduct the measurements, and the necessary statistical and clerical staff to handle logistical problems.[22] Boas assured the Dillingham Commission that such a study would prove whether or not southern and eastern Europeans could assimilate successfully.

Jenks optimistically brought Boas's plan to the attention of his committee. The only potential problem he foresaw was that one committee member believed the research had "too little connection with the sociological" nature of the commission.[23] Boas wasted little time in correcting that assumption, explaining that the principal problem was to determine the extent to which different races assimilated in America, and "how far the social changes that take place among them are sufficiently intensive to subject them to the influences" of America's social and physical environment.[24] Boas argued that the physical examination he proposed would be an invaluable supplement to the commission's report, since it would illustrate the "actual effect of the new environment upon the physique of the immigrants."[25]

The commission was hesitant to allow Boas to proceed, largely because several members believed that the measurements would not be conclusive, and accordingly were not worth such a large expenditure.[26] Following this setback, Boas proposed a preliminary report that would address the question of assimilation and outline what instruments, forms and other essentials would be mandatory to complete the observations.[27] He also expressed a willingness to conduct some preliminary measurements at Ellis Island in order to determine the amount of time and expense this required. He promised that the total outlay for such a draft would not exceed $1,000.[28] Boas felt the experiment would illustrate the type of material he could make available to the commission and would hopefully persuade the recalcitrant members to accept the larger scheme.

The Dillingham Commission approved the preliminary plan, and Boas quickly arranged to begin measurements at Ellis Island. He also enlisted the aid of New York City public schools, since he believed the study of children was a vital component of his research. Some school directors hesitated to give Boas permission. Perhaps they feared rumors of sexual abuse, which had surfaced in Worcester, Massachusetts when Boas began his work in physical anthropology. Nevertheless, many people offered to help. City College of New York and many area high schools allowed Boas to gather data. His work also attracted the attention of New York's Educational Alliance, settlement workers and the Children's Aid Society.[29]

Boas conducted research throughout the summer of 1908, and submitted the final draft of the preliminary report in September. Although acknowledging that the data were not broad enough for generalizations, Boas explained that the results indicated that significant changes took place among the offspring of immigrants. The children whose parents immigrated earliest were taller and heavier than those of other groups. Furthermore, their mental development had been more rapid, allowing for smooth progress through the public schools.[30] Boas also suggested "that different changes of considerable magnitude" were occurring, and that a more complete inquiry could conceivably lead to unanticipated conclusions.[31]

Boas succeeded in selling the full-scale investigation. The Dillingham Commission acted favorably upon the request, based on the preliminary findings. Now charged with a tremendous scientific undertaking, Boas moved ahead enthusiastically. Throughout 1909 he directed research into various areas of the immigrant experience. His data collectors amassed thousands of measurements of recent immigrants, schoolchildren and white native Americans. In addition to this new material, Boas also incorporated his earlier measurements of schoolchildren in Toronto, Worcester and Oakland, for which the commission paid him a modest $300.[32]

By early 1910, Boas learned that the commission would expire in December of that year. Consequently, he sought outside support from the Smithsonian Institution to continue the research. Charles Walcott turned down his request, which came as no surprise to Boas, who informed Jenks that the Smithsonian frequently hesitated to help scientists resolve questions of considerable importance.[33] With the appropriation about to expire and no other source of support available, Boas began preparing his results in the fall of 1910. He presented his final report to Senator Dillingham, whose committee accepted it officially on June 8, 1911.

*Changes in Bodily Form of Descendants of Immigrants* represented a substantial contribution to the immigrant problem that confronted America. It focused largely on body form, "the most stable characteristic of any given race or type."[34] The report revealed statistics collected from various ethnic groups, including East European Jews, southern Italians, Bohemians, Hungarians and Scots. Relying on earlier studies conducted by Benjamin A. Gould on Civil War soldiers and by H. P. Bowditch on Boston schoolchildren, the report accepted the premise that under favorable environmental conditions a race's physical development might improve. Although neither of these earlier investigations proved that hypothesis, Boas hoped to determine "whether the American environment had a favorable or unfavorable effect upon the descendants of immigrants."[35]

In determining stages of development, Boas analyzed stature, weight, and general physiological development. He amassed data on "the length and width of the head, width of the face measured between the zygomatic arches, color of hair, eyes and skin" in order to draw composite racial pictures of each immigrant group.[36]

The most significant measurement for Boas was the cephalic index, or form of the head, which anthropologists had long considered one of the "most stable and permanent characteristics of human races."[37] Boas's study, however, challenged that belief. Eastern European Jews, normally possessing a round head (85 on the cephalic index), produced more long-headed offspring in America (roughly 81). Conversely, southern Italians, who displayed long heads in Italy (78), produced children with shorter heads in America (80).

In both cases head forms approached a more unified type in the United States. These changes proved that "not even those characteristics of a race which have proved to be most permanent in their old home remain the same under new surroundings."[38] Boas further suggested that if head form changed, the entire bodily and mental makeup of the immigrants might also be altered. Accordingly, he argued that contrary to earlier scientific opinion, the evidence demonstrated "a great plasticity of human types."[39]

Boas also postulated that duration of residence was a critical element in determining head form, because the "influence of the American environment upon the descendants of immigrants increased" the longer the parents resided in America before giving birth to their children.[40] Consequently, the longer the duration between arrival in the United States and the birth of the child, the greater would be the difference in type between the descendant and parents. Boas also found that differences in type between the American-born descendants of immigrant parents were not restricted to early childhood. Variations persisted throughout the individual's life.

Moreover, the effects of urban living differed depending on the immigrant group involved. East European Jews developed favorably in the urban American environment, even in the most congested parts of the city, while Italian offspring appeared to grow weaker in stature. Boas offered no plausible explanation for this occurrence, and advocated more detailed research in that area.[41]

Throughout the report it was clear that Boas had anticipated his critics. In several instances he suggested possible weaknesses of the investigation, only to destroy the straw men he had created. For example, in discussing differences in head form, Boas expected challengers to argue that "changes among the Hebrews might indicate merely that the American method of cradling was used more frequently the longer the family had resided" in America. In this instance "the position of the child on the back" produced short-headedness, "and the position on the side" resulted in long-headedness.[42] Although unable to disprove that theory, Boas pointed to "weighty considerations" that would argue against it. Specifically, he explained:

If we assume that among the Hebrews the children born abroad have a lesser length of head than those born here, because they are swathed and lie more permanently on their backs than the American-born children who can move about freely, we must conclude that there is a certain compensatory decrease in the other diameters of the head of the American-born. Since this compensation is distributed in all directions, its amount in any one direction will be very small.... If, therefore, in one case the greater freedom of position of the child increases the length of the head, it is difficult to see why, among the Bohemians, the same causes should decrease both horizontal diameters of the head, and why, among the Sicilians, the length should decrease and the width increase.[43]

As usual Boas urged people not to draw generalizations from his investigation. He cautioned that he was not arguing that all European types made a transition to an American type solely as a consequence of environmental forces. Much more study could conceivably answer such a question, but he refused to speculate. He was equally reluctant to argue that the changes would lead to a uniform, general type, since the question could not be addressed until the variations were complete (meaning that some types were still in transition and he could not speculate on their final form).

Personally, Boas did not consider a uniform type possible. He suggested that "the proof of the plasticity of types does not imply that the plasticity is unlimited."[44] Consequently, although the facts supported the view that the American-born descendants of immigrants did change, resembling an American type, Boas did not propose that such transformation was infinite. Nor did he feel that American surroundings were uniquely responsible. Any environmental change could produce variations in the human form. The various immigrant groups would not all merge over time into a uniquely American type. They would, however, lose their distinct European characteristics and become closer to a generalized American type.

A final aspect of the report dealt with heredity. Boas began the study still uncertain about the validity of Mendelian law. However, by employing the values of the cephalic index, he determined that "children do not form a blend between their parents but revert either to one type or to the other."[45] These findings convinced Boas that Mendel was correct.

The head form study had significant anthropological repercussions. Boas's most important discovery was the instability of the human form, which contradicted all previous knowledge. This finding also reconciled the dichotomy between the roles that heredity and environment played in influencing the development of an individual. Rather than being mutually exclusive, these elements, in Boas's view, were "complementary forces in shaping the human organism."[46]

Furthermore, the study armed supporters of racial equality with some potent scientific ammunition. Prior to Boas's effort, "physical anthropology was heir to polygenism and parent to the obscurantism of the type concept."[47] Science, in other words, had supported the racists alone. The Boas study marked a definite watershed. It was now possible to employ science in defense of equality rather than only in opposition.[48] Perhaps recognizing the extent to which Boas had aided the cause of racial justice, the editors of the journal, *The Survey*, considered *Changes in Bodily Form of Descendants of Immigrants* "the most distinctive contribution of the Immigration Commission."[49]

This, of course, did not dismiss the many critics, who quickly pointed out the report's shortcomings. Some believed that Boas had erred in suggesting the existence of an American type into which European types could develop, although Boas had taken great pains to explain that he was not convinced that such a unique type existed or that plasticity was unlimited. Nevertheless, the furor surrounding the melting pot concept caused a strong reaction on the part of opponents of theories of immigrant assimilation. Other detractors found more specific errors, ranging from a lack of consistency in observation among the research assistants to a criticism of the small number of cases involved. Others questioned the accuracy of the cephalic index itself, or held that many of the individuals measured were "not of pure descent," and thus skewed the survey.[50]

The most pertinent criticism, voiced long after Boas had died, was that the report lacked "any systematic sampling technique."[51] Various immigrant groups were measured with no specific or planned breakdown. Additionally, the changes Boas found were statistically very small. Stature changed by "only a half to one inch" and "one to two millimeters in head length and breadth" (ibid.). Boas, of course, realized the "smallness of the changes observed," which led him specifically to argue against both a unique American type created solely by environment and unlimited plasticity of the human form. These methodological and theoretical criticisms were most valid. However, they did not detract from the report's main contribution to the development of physical anthropology, which was to strike a "death-blow to belief in the fixity of head form."[52]

Boas's report differed substantially from the other forty volumes that constituted the published findings of the Dillingham Immigration Commission. The inquiry as a whole "confidently endorsed the conventional view of America's recent immigrants."[53] The pattern of new immigration was found to be far different from the old. Southern and eastern Europeans appeared weak, inferior and threatening to American racial supremacy. Government policy, if based solely on the commission's report, would no doubt mandate restriction. Twentieth-century immigration was widely viewed as "a prime cause of social ills," and clearly, the Dillingham Commission supported this position.[54] Boas's study was the sole exception. It found no proof that immigration was detrimental to the country, arguing instead that the melting pot worked, at least to some extent.

That Boas's report was out of harmony with the rest of the commission's findings was obvious. Significantly, it was also the only study not originally planned by the committee. Boas had approached Jenks initially to propose the project. This factor explained the divergent results. Boas had attempted to obtain objective, scientific information for a commission that not only had a predetermined attitude toward immigration, but had been warned by Theodore Roosevelt not to rely on "too many professors" who might prove that immigration was not a threat to the country.[55]

The issues of prejudice, mental ability and assimilation were never far from Boas's mind. His activity on behalf of victims of American racial bias preoccupied him during the early part of the twentieth century, and as was the case with Afro-Americans, his concern for immigrants increased as talk of restriction and xenophobia grew. To this end, Boas chose the themes of race and culture as subject matter for two lecture series he gave, the first at Boston's Lowell Institute in 1910 and the second at the National University of Mexico the following year. Published in 1913, they together formed Boas's most widely read and perhaps most famous work, *The Mind of Primitive Man*.

For those familiar with Boas's earlier work, the volume represented a revised, updated version of the major strains of his thought, which he had expressed in previous publications.[56] Yet the book itself became more than a collection of past work. It not only presented a seething indictment of American racial bigotry, it offered scientist and layman alike an opportunity to understand the way in which science supported equality. Perhaps no greater accolade was conferred on the book and its author than when it was rumored that Adolf Hitler ordered the revised 1936 version removed from German libraries and publicly burned.[57]

Boas hoped at the outset to dethrone the white Anglo-Saxon Protestant type from its mythical position at the pinnacle of the evolutionary schema. To do this, he challenged two assumptions: that human faculty was racially determined, and that anatomical and physiological differences had any influence on mental process. He rejected the former assertion by harking back to his own address in 1894 before the American Association for the Advancement of Science. For the latter he turned to the research conducted by Karl Pearson, whose extensive studies proved that the "characteristics of the osseous, muscular, visceral, or circulating system, have practically no direct relation to the mental ability of man."[58] Boas also refuted the myth that there was a correlation between the size of the brain and mental ability, explaining that brain function depended on nerve cells and fibers, which did not increase with the size of the brain.

The volume also recapitulated much of the immigration study conclusions, suggesting that environment directly influenced bodily form. Plasticity of form existed, but clearly within certain boundaries. As its title suggested, the volume treated primitive civilizations, examining the differences found between more and less advanced groups comprised of members of the same race. Boas attributed varying behavioral patterns among these peoples to their relative degree of domestication. The more advanced a civilization had become, the more it affected its members' actions. This was not to say, however, that primitives were inferior in ability or in action. As Boas always cautioned, a race's faculty could not be measured by the cultural progress it had made. Humans simply became more domesticated as their civilization advanced.[59]

Boas also reaffirmed his acceptance of Mendelian heredity. As he had done in his head form study, he argued that heredity and environment both influenced development. Moreover, "the differences between different types of man" were "small as compared to the range of variation in each type."[60] Boas condemned theories of racial inferiority as unscientific, if they were based upon such differences. He believed that all races possessed similar mental abilities, and stressed that all races could achieve a level of culture equal to that of white native Americans.[61]

The fact that races were found at different points on the scale from primitive to civilized had little bearing on the intelligence of that particular race. Cultural stages were "dependent upon historical causes, regardless of race," and thus, there could be no close relationship between race and culture.[62] Primitive man was different than, but not inferior to, civilized man. Primitives tended to act on emotional associations, while civilized groups relied more on intellectual reflections. Boas felt this was not due to ability, but rather grew out of the current stage of each culture. In fact, in many instances, Boas discovered that both primitive and civilized man acted because of a shared respect for custom.

Having proved that there was no association between race and culture, Boas applied his findings to America's racial situation. His final chapter, entitled "Race Problems in the United States," discussed immigration, blacks and the destructive aspects of race prejudice. Tackling the often-voiced criticism that America was destined to become a "mongrel nation" due to the mixture of different European types, Boas challenged the view that any country contained pure stocks. He recounted the movements of various peoples throughout Europe.[63] The emphasis on history, so much a part of Boas's science, was significant. He concluded that both "the assumption of the existence of a pure type in any part of Europe, and of a process of mongrelization in America" were fallacious.[64]

Boas urged Americans to be "most cautious" in their reasoning, and to "refrain from all sensational formulations" of the immigrant problem, which would unjustifiably threaten the welfare of millions.[65] In a query typical of Boas the scientist, he pondered whether it would "not be a safer course to investigate the truth or fallacy of each theory rather than excite the public mind by indulgence in the fancies of our speculation."[66]

*The Mind of Primitive Man* attacked prejudice on all fronts. Boas hoped that his book would teach Americans "a greater tolerance of forms of civilization different" from their own, and that they would "learn to look upon foreign races with greater sympathy," acknowledging that each could make a contribution to the nation if they were given "a fair opportunity."[67]

The book was well-received, especially among American intellectuals. Randolph Bourne praised it for "the light it shed on race prejudice." He felt that Boas had advanced the struggle for the "Brotherhood of man, which religion has failed to achieve."[68] Boas's own students also held the study in high regard. Leslie Spier most notably exemplified this tendency, calling the book "a Magna Carta of race equality." It was Boas, according to Spier, "who wrote quietus to any 'scientific' pronunciamentos on 'higher' and 'lower' races."[69] Additionally, *The Mind of Primitive Man* became the bible of antiracists everywhere. Employing science on behalf of racial equality, the book undercut much of the scholarly support on which racists based their theories.

Beyond the volume's popularity, its significance was immeasurable. It clarified much of Boas's thinking on race and culture and placed it in a unified corpus. Without specifically coining the phrase, the work advanced Boas's concept of cultural relativism. The book demonstrated how "in human culture, the plurality of forms represents an overlay of the unities which exist in the endowments, needs and aspirations of all men."[70] That Boas found no fundamental differences in the thought processes of primitive and civilized man illustrated his belief in the importance of history. Mental ability did not affect cultural progress. Historical factors were the crucial determinant of civilizations' advance. This theory not only emphasized equality among races but also pointed to the value of historical particularism in the study of man.

The publication marked a new stage of Boas's thought regarding cultural laws. He "had given up the possibility that significant developmental uniformities involving whole congeries of institutions would be found."[71] *The Mind of Primitive Man* contained evidence of this shift, since in the book "the absence of uniform developmental sequences" was "clearly and explicitly related to an absence of a determinative order between the various parts of culture and between culture and the natural environment."[72] Boas had rejected parallel evolution. All aspects of a culture could have developed independently. Hence the search for cultural laws was a search in vain.

The work's final importance lay in its explication of Boas's concept of race. Rather than classifying humans into four races, Boas suggested a twofold system. One principal type was the Mongoloid, of which the Caucasoid was a subtype. The other type was the Negroid, which also included the Australoid.[73] *The Mind of Primitive Man* reserved the use of the "term 'race' for groups of men whose unity was strictly biological, groups defined in terms of inherited physical characteristics."[74] This view differed from the older method of "employing race as one of a number of more or less interchangeable terms all of which implied some degree of hereditary socio-biological unity."[75] Significantly, Boas eliminated cultural differences as a determinant of race. Although the older theory defined a race in both physical and cultural terms, Boas found no proof to support that conjecture. By abolishing the connection between race and culture, he discovered two major races that differed only in physical attributes.

Boas never concluded, however, that there were no mental differences between the races. Although his credentials as a race champion often obfuscated this fact, he continued to stress their "equipotentiality as carriers of culture."[76] Yet, at one and the same time he defended the cultural contributions of all civilizations, and castigated "modern civilization" for ignoring them. This "external reference point was one of the leitmotifs of Boas's career, and it tended to carry with it a double standard of cultural evaluation: a universalistic one in terms of which he criticized the society in which he lived and a relativistic one in terms of which he defended the cultural alternative."[77]

*The Mind of Primitive Man* summed up most of Boas's thought on race and culture, which he had first publicly discussed in 1894. The volume elaborated upon "conclusions already reached." Boas had "reaffirmed the psychic unity of mankind" in a nonevolutionary context.[78] He had also brought to public attention his belief that all races shared the potential for equal mental ability.

The same nexus of forces that lay behind Boas's defense of Afro-Americans led him in this direction. He reacted violently to nativism and immigration restriction because they impinged on his egalitarian notions of individual and human freedom. His concern for scientific accuracy also shaped his views in this regard. Finally, he had experienced immigration firsthand. Although he had not arrived at Ellis Island on a ship overcrowded with newcomers, Boas considered himself an immigrant. He identified with the trials confronting them. His work for the Dillingham Commission and his discussions in *The Mind of Primitive Man* reflected his concern for people less fortunate than himself. Those who experienced the hardships of immigration, he felt, deserved better. Coupled with this identification was his ever-present experience with anti-Semitism. Not surprisingly, many anti-immigrant theorists were anti-Semitic as well. Consequently, Boas viewed the immigrant problem as another way of combating the discrimination he had himself encountered.

Although his campaign against prejudice dominated his activity into the second decade of the twentieth century, Boas did extend the scope of his other ethnological work. The publication of the Jesup expedition material, for example, continued to plague him. The American Museum of Natural History delayed payments for completed manuscripts, forcing Boas to complain once again to Hermon Bumpus. At this time Boas also realized that the amount of material was too vast for the projected twelve-volume study.

He met with the museum's new president, Henry Fairfield Osborn, early in 1909 to discuss the feasibility of the project's expansion. Osborn vetoed the idea, but allowed Boas the option of printing the remaining research data privately.[79] Accordingly, Boas set up a new series of works at Columbia to handle the overflow from the Jesup project. However, the administrative haggling surrounding the museum venture continued. By April 1910, ten volumes of the expedition reports had been published.[80] The remaining work dragged on, interrupted in 1914 by World War I.

Boas also participated in the founding of the International School of American Archaeology and Ethnology in Mexico City. He assisted in drawing up the initial plans for the institution in 1910, and remained actively involved in the early years of the school's existence. He travelled to Mexico frequently and became the director of the facility for the 1911–12 academic year. The school ran into problems, however, following the revolution in Mexico in 1912, which by the following year had forced Woodrow Wilson to order all Americans out of Mexico. The school fell on hard times as a result.

Nevertheless, the venture was successful. Operated jointly by Boas of Columbia, Alfred Tozzer and Roland Dixon of Harvard, J. Alden Mason of the University of Pennsylvania and several scientists from abroad, the institution uncovered much new material related to past Mexican civilizations. Further, the array of eminent scholars at the school provided invaluable training for new ethnologists.

It was during one of his early visits to Mexico that Boas experienced the first repercussions of his earlier conflict with Charles Walcott. Boas learned that certain individuals had made disparaging remarks about his character, which emanated from Walcott's public utterances concerning Boas's managerial inadequacies. The slander, as Boas was to discover, came from Edgar L. Hewett, director of the Archaeological Institute of America, who, at a meeting late in 1910, had informed several of his colleagues, most notably Francis Kelsey of Ann Arbor, Michigan, that Boas had "swindled" funds from the Smithsonian in payment for some manuscript material.

Boas contacted his lawyer at once to investigate the situation. He also communicated with Roland Dixon, who discovered that Kelsey and Hewett were closely associated and were displeased that Boas had hesitated to support the Archaeological Institute of America. Dixon believed they resented Boas for this, and were attempting to strike back at him. Alfred Tozzer, Dixon's colleague and Boas's close friend, also overheard Hewett's derogatory remarks. He informed Boas that Hewett had described him as "being under a heavy cloud" regarding the Walcott affair, and had said that Walcott had affidavits that would dishonor Boas. The affair grew complicated as a number of people traded rumors concerning Hewett's allegations and their validity.[81]

Finally, to settle the matter, Boas again resorted to publishing the relevant correspondence privately in the fall of 1911. The pamphlet contained an open letter to Hewett that briefly recited the history of the issue and demanded that Hewett acknowledge his role in making the accusations, which up to that time he had denied. Boas further warned him that he would not hesitate to test "the questions between us in the courts" if he did not settle the affair immediately.

Additionally, Boas included in his publication a 1909 letter of resignation that he had written to the Archaeological Institute of America, since he was convinced that this incident lay at the root of Hewett's remarks. Boas had disassociated himself from the institute because it emphasized public entertainment more than science, and because he objected to the administrative methods of the controlling council.[82] Since Hewett was the director of the institute, most of Boas's criticisms had been aimed directly at him. It was apparent that Hewett had counterattacked, intent on damaging Boas's reputation.

Hewett did not respond to the open letter. Boas contemplated litigation, but decided against it. Instead he attempted to forget the entire affair. The letters he published depicted Hewett as a poor scientist, an incompetent administrator and a coward. The incident did Boas little harm, but it again illustrated his obsessive need to vindicate himself at all costs. Whether the attack was personal in nature or concerning scientific theory, Boas always sought to defend his position, either directly or through a surrogate group, as in the case of blacks. It seemed vital that he protect the reputation and dignity he had worked so hard to build. Significant also in this case was the fact that Boas's commitment to professional science precipitated the crisis. Had he not resigned from the institute due to its inherent amateurism, the incident would not have occurred.

Despite this feeble attempt to damage Boas, his reputation grew. In 1911, the long-awaited first volume of the *Handbook of American Indian Languages* appeared. The work was the "culmination of a quarter-century of linguistic work."[83] It included research conducted as long ago as Boas's field trips under the auspices of the British Association for the Advancement of Science. The *Handbook* illustrated the great variety of Indian languages, and stressed Boas's belief that the languages were not based on a "simple psychological principle."[84]

In his introduction to the *Handbook*, Boas articulated his ideas concerning the nexus between language, culture and race. He repudiated previous attempts by scientists such as Blumenbach, Cuvier, Huxley and Gobineau to classify mankind into subdivisions based on "anatomical form, language and culture," emphasizing the chaos and contradictions inherent in such efforts. For Boas, both language and culture could change substantially without requiring a transformation in physical type; or conversely, physical type could change as a result of mixture without any impact on language or culture.[85] From his own extensive investigations into language, he deduced that "every classification of mankind must be more or less artificial," and that historical influences had the strongest impact on language development.

Consistent with his belief that all cultures could produce similar levels of civilization if exposed to identical historical circumstances, Boas argued forcefully in the introduction to the *Handbook* that language was yet another example supporting his theory. Primitive man, for example, did not develop language appropriate to discourse on abstract ideas because his interests focused instead on "occupations of his daily life."[86] If the need arose for such philosophical discussion, Boas was certain that appropriate language would be forthcoming. In his introduction, he made it abundantly clear that all "traits of human thought, which are known to influence the history of science and which play a more or less important role in the general history of civilization, occur with equal frequency in the thoughts of primitive man."[87]

The influence of Boas's thought on the field of linguistics, and of his insistence on relativism, was profound. "He refused to impose on primitive tongues the familiar forms and categories of the two great families of language, insisting that every tongue must be studied according to its own structure."[88] His theories in the area of language, his linkage of culture to "linguistic form" and his own field research contributed mightily to the "rapid emergence of comparative linguistics."[89] Moreover, at a time when his funding requests to study racial and ethnic problems were routinely denied, his linguistic theories provided an alternate avenue for attacking racism and prejudice.

Boas's preoccupation with the affairs of science did not blind him to the need for social reform. The Progressive era clearly influenced him during these years. His protest against race prejudice was one major indicator of his progressive tendencies. He also supported women's suffrage, on the grounds that "in our modern social conditions woman is to a very great extent economically independent," thus, "there is no reason for withholding from her the privileges enjoyed by men."[90]

Nor did Boas forget his friends. In 1915 he mourned the death of Frederick Putnam, who had been instrumental in aiding him during his early years in America; Boas delivered a glowing tribute to him in the pages of *Science*. Two years before, Boas had eulogized his other old friend, W J McGee. He also continued to advise former students. Edward Sapir, who had received his doctorate in 1909, worked with Boas on ethnological material and contributed to the *Handbook of American Indian Languages*. A. A. Goldenweiser, at Boas's suggestion, joined Columbia University as a lecturer in anthropology. Moreover, at this time, Boas was in the process of training one of his most prominent graduate students, Ruth Benedict, who began taking courses with him in 1913.

In February of 1915, at the request of Sapir, Boas took up the cause of the Kwakiutl Indians, whose potlatch ceremony was in jeopardy. The federal government considered the ritual dangerous and proposed laws to control it. Boas considered the plan unwise, informing the government that abolition of the potlatch would be a great hardship to the Indians, both economically and culturally. He equated its abolition with declaring that all paper money in the United States was suddenly worthless. Furthermore, eliminating the ceremony would degrade the Indians and bring about a loss of incentive for social advancement.[91] Boas suggested that the government not restrict Indian practices simply because a particular custom was alien to American culture.

Boas's protest in this matter illustrated well his concern for all minorities in the United States and his increasing willingness to use his science to influence public policy. His outspoken belief that all cultures possessed equal mental capacity ran throughout the pre–World War I period. He was committed to improving American society at a time when many reformers shared his vision. Yet Boas was one of only a handful of progressives who spoke out for racial equality.[92]

By 1915 Boas had established his reputation atop the anthropological profession and had reached out to use his science to shape American life. Yet, challenges lay ahead that threatened to topple him from that pinnacle. The coming of the Great War was a time of uncertainty for him. Once again his enthusiasm and outspoken attitudes led him into controversy, and it remained to be seen if he could survive the fears and anxieties of a country at war.

## NOTES

1. Morton Keller, *Affairs of State: Public Life in Late Nineteenth-Century America* (Cambridge, Mass.: Belknap Press, 1977), p. 445.

2. John S. Haller, *Outcasts from Evolution: Scientific Attitudes of Racial Inferiority, 1859–1900* (New York: McGraw-Hill, 1975), p. 187.

3. Ibid., p. 134.

4. Ibid., p. 152.

5. Russel B. Nye, *This Almost Chosen People: Essays in the History of American Ideas* (East Lansing: Michigan State University Press, 1966), p. 339.

6. Ibid.

7. John Higham, *Strangers in the Land: Patterns of American Nativism, 1860–1925* (New York: Atheneum, 1963), p. 151.

8. Ibid.

9. Ibid.

10. George W. Stocking, Jr., ed., *Race, Culture, and Evolution: Essays in the History of Anthropology* (New York: Free Press, 1968), p. 122.

11. The cephalic index was created by Paul Broca. It represented a measurement of "the breadth of the head above the ears expressed in percentage of its length from forehead to back." John Haller in *Outcasts from Evolution* explains: "assuming that the length is 100, the width is expressed as a fraction of it. As the head became proportionally broader—that is, the more fully rounded, viewed from the top down—the cephalic index increases. When it rises from 80, the head is called brachycephalic, when it falls below 75, the term dolichocephalic is applied to it. Indexes between 75 and 80 are characterized as mesocephalic" (14).

12. Franz Boas, "Some Recent Criticisms of Physical Anthropology," *American Anthropologist* 1 (new series) (1899): 103.

13. Stocking, *Race, Culture, and Evolution*, p. 181.

14. Franz Boas, "The Cephalic Index," *American Anthropologist*, n.s. 1 (1899): 461.

15. Ibid.

16. Stocking, *Race, Culture, and Evolution*, pp. 165–66.

17. The other senate members were Henry Cabot Lodge; Asbury Latimer, who died on February 20, 1908; Anselm J. McLaurin, appointed to succeed Latimer; and Le Roy Percy, who replaced McLaurin upon his death on December 22, 1909. The representatives were Benjamin F. Howell, William S. Bennet and John L. Burnett. Additionally, President Theodore Roosevelt appointed Charles P. Neill, Jeremiah W. Jenks and William R. Wheeler.

18. Thomas Kessner, *The Golden Door: Italian and Jewish Immigrant Mobility in New York City, 1880–1915* (New York: Oxford University Press, 1977), pp. 24–25.

19. Franz Boas to Jeremiah Jenks, March 23, 1908, American Philosophical Society, Boas Correspondence. (Hereafter cited as APS/BC.)

20. Ibid.

21. Ibid.

22. Ibid.

23. Jenks to Boas, April 14, 1908, APS/BC.

24. Boas to Jenks, April 15, 1908, APS/BC.

25. Ibid.

26. Jenks to Boas, April 29, 1908, APS/BC.

27. Boas to Jenks, May 2, 1908, APS/BC.

28. Ibid.

29. Boas to Jenks, June 9, 1908, APS/BC.

30. Boas to Jenks, September 3, 1908, APS/BC.

31. Ibid.

32. Jenks to Boas, June 15, 1909, APS/BC.

33. Boas to Jenks, March 21, 1910, APS/BC. Despite Walcott's decision and Boas's critical remarks, there is no evidence to suggest that either man's actions emanated from their conflict of the previous year.

34. Franz Boas, *Changes in Bodily Form of Descendants of Immigrants*, Reports of the Immigration Commission, Senate Documents, 61st Congress, 2nd session, 1909–1910, vol. 64 (Washington, D.C.: Government Printing Office, 1911), p. 1.

35. Ibid., p. 2.

36. Ibid., pp. 2–3.

37. Boas's own description of the cephalic index, as employed in his investigation, is as follows: "The head form may conveniently be expressed by a number indicating the transversal diameter (or width of the head) in per cents of the diameter measured from forehead to the back of the head (or the length of the head). When the head is elongated (that is, narrow when seen from the front, and long when seen in profile), this number will be low; when it is rounded (that is, wide when seen from the front, and short when seen in profile), this number will be high" (5).

38. Boas, *Changes in Bodily Form*, p. 5.

39. Ibid.

40. Ibid., p. 7.

41. Ibid., pp. 62–64.

42. Ibid., p. 70.

43. Ibid., pp. 70–71.

44. Ibid., p. 76.

45. Ibid., p. 77.

46. Melville J. Herskovits, *Franz Boas: The Science of Man in the Making* (New York: Charles Scribner's Sons, 1953), p. 42.

47. Stocking, *Race, Culture, and Evolution*, p. 194.

48. Ibid.

49. Higham, *Strangers in the Land*, p. 125n.

50. Melville J. Herskovits, "Franz Boas as Physical Anthropologist," *American Anthropologist* 45 (September 1943): 47.

51. J. M. Tanner, "Boas' Contributions to Knowledge of Human Growth and Form," *American Anthropologist* 61 (October 1959): 102.

52. Ibid., p. 107.

53. Kessner, *Golden Door*, p. 25.

54. Keller, *Affairs of State*, p. 447.

55. Kessner in *The Golden Door* notes that all the commission members were restrictionists.

56. Specifically Boas referred to the following sources: "Human Faculty as deter-

mined by Race" (1894); "The Limitations of the Comparative Method of Anthropology" (1896); "The Mind of Primitive Man" (1904); "Race Problems in America" (1909); "Psychological Problems in Anthropology" (1910); the introduction to the *Handbook of American Indian Languages*; and some results of *Changes in Bodily Form of Descendants of Immigrants*.

57. Melville Herskovits, introduction to Franz Boas, *The Mind of Primitive Man* (1913; New York: Macmillan, 1938), p. 6. It is difficult to ascertain whether or not this rumor had any basis in fact.

58. Franz Boas, *The Mind of Primitive Man* (New York: Macmillan, 1913), p. 24.

59. Ibid., pp. 30–75.

60. Ibid., p. 94.

61. Ibid., p. 123.

62. Ibid., p. 249.

63. Ibid., pp. 256–57.

64. Ibid., p. 260.

65. Ibid., p. 263.

66. Ibid., p. 264.

67. Ibid., p. 278.

68. Louis Filler, *randolph bourne* (New York: Citadel Press, 1943), p. 35.

69. Leslie Spier, "Some Central Elements in the Legacy," *American Anthropologist* 61 (October 1959): 147.

70. Herskovits, introduction to Boas, *Primitive Man*, pp. 10–11.

71. Marvin Harris, *The Rise of Anthropological Theory: A History of Theories of Culture* (New York: Thomas Y. Crowell, 1968), p. 278.

72. Ibid., p. 279.

73. Herskovits, *Franz Boas*, p. 30.

74. George W. Stocking, Jr., "American Social Scientists and Race Theory: 1890–1915" (Ph.D. diss., University of Pennsylvania, 1960), p. 188.

75. Ibid.

76. Ibid., p. 591.

77. George W. Stocking, Jr. "Anthropology as Kulturkampf: Science and Politics in the Career of Franz Boas," in *The Uses of Anthropology*, ed. Walter Goldschmidt, (Washington, D.C.: American Anthropologist Association, 1979), p. 47.

78. Stocking, "American Social Scientists", pp. 555–56.

79. Henry Fairfield Osborn to Boas, March 19, 1909, APS/BC.

80. Boas to Waldemar Bogoras, May 22, 1909, APS/BC; Boas to F. V. Skiff, April 2, 1910, APS/BC.

81. Boas to Nelson Spencer, December 2, 1910; Roland B. Dixon to Boas, February 1, 1911; Francis Kelsey to Spencer, February 22, 1911; Dixon to Boas, February 24, 1911; Boas to Spencer, March 27, 1911; Alfred Tozzer to Boas, May 29, 1911, APS/BC.

82. Private pamphlet published by Boas, November 13, 1911, APS/BC.

83. George W. Stocking Jr., ed., *The Shaping of American Anthropology, 1883–1911: A Franz Boas Reader* (New York: Basic Books, 1974), p. 157.

84. Ibid., p. 159.

85. Franz Boas, *Introduction to Handbook of American Indian Languages* (1911; Lincoln: University of Nebraska Press, 1966), p. 5.

86. Ibid., p. 60.

87. Ibid., p. 68.

88. Abram Kardiner and Edward Preble, *They Studied Man* (New York: World Publishing, 1961), p. 137.

89. Ibid.

90. Boas to Senator James A. C. Johnson, January 10, 1913, APS/BC.

91. Boas to Edward Sapir, February 18, 1915, APS/BC.

92. Robert L. Allen in his work, *Reluctant Reformers: The Impact of Racism on American Social Reform Movements* (Washington, D.C.: Howard University Press, 1974), acknowledges that Boas was one of the few reform-minded people of the era who did not shy away from the problem of racism.

# 7
# Trial by War

The outbreak of war in Europe in 1914 profoundly affected the American scientific and academic communities. The initial frustration caused by Wilsonian neutrality and his eventual declaration of war created many problems. Academic freedom became an expendable right during the conflict, not only in university circles, but in scientific organizations as well. Boas was soon trapped by this situation: the nature of his grievances and the candor with which he expressed them sent tremors throughout anthropological circles.

Boas took immediate interest in the European war. Rejecting assertions that the conflict was a race war, he contended that the passions of nationalism were to blame.[1] He pointed out that "an aggressive intolerance" of nations had grown up within each country, which could be resolved peaceably by the creation of a "federation of nations."[2] Boas criticized the modern peace movement for advocating arbitration of disagreements. He hoped, instead, that all nations would endorse his federation concept, since it would curtail competing nationalisms and make war unnecessary. The idea, at least in Boas's mind, was not utopian, but marked a logical progression in the growth of modern nations.[3]

Boas's plan remained a vision, while the war became a terrible reality. He predicted that a German defeat would unleash a hatred capable of stirring up "her nationalism for centuries to come." However, a victory would create an arrogance that would be equally damaging.[4] Although taking Germany's side, Boas never condoned the fighting. He felt patriotism was the principal problem, since it limited one's vision by excluding the contributions that other cultures had made to civilization's advance. As *The Mind of Primitive Man* had made explicit, all cultures played a role in mankind's progress. Patriotism, which ignored other nations, represented a biased, uninformed world view. "German arrogance, French lust for revenge and English envy" all contributed to the conflict.[5]

American neutrality became Boas's obsession during the early war years. He urged Americans to refrain from taking sides, and hoped to quell nationalistic fervor. As he explained to his son:

There is one lesson for all of us: one should kill false patriotism.... This is true of all things, from the small to the great ones: family pride, party hatred, etc. All this originates from the fact that we always consider the little group to which we belong better than the whole world, and therefore we always want the best for it. Instead, we should do the best we can for our own group and always appreciate what other people achieve also.[6]

By the spring of 1915, Boas became "dreadfully depressed" by the war's "long continuance and the apparent impossibility of bringing the affair to an end."[7] Additionally, pro-Allied sentiments within the United States increasingly concerned him. In an attempt to move the country back into a more neutral posture, Boas began a public assault on partisanship. He condemned the American policy of shipping arms to the Allies. He stressed that neutrality was vital not only for American security, but also for the realization of world peace. Boas wrote his senators urging a change in the arms policy, and he supported a petition to prevent arms shipments to all warring nations.[8] The sale of arms to the Allies would require countermeasures by the Central Powers, which would then prolong the fighting.

Boas believed further that the American policy was contradictory, since on the one hand it professed an abhorrence of war and yet on the other it profited "by supplying the means with which war is conducted."[9] Boas argued that the United States had a moral obligation to remain totally neutral; he stressed that the termination of arms sales would underscore this impartiality. He concluded that because Americans believed themselves to be the "staunchest supporters of the movement for universal peace," it was their duty "to live up to their expressed convictions and to put an end to a traffic that belies their loud professions."[10]

Boas also became increasingly worried about Anglophile sentiment in the country. Careless anti-German rhetoric, he felt, had already led to the establishment of a German-American party. Such partisanship could only draw America closer to war. Accordingly, he pleaded publicly for a curtailment of pro-Allied sentiments, so that pro-German sympathizers would not grow more vocal. He desperately wanted America to remain at peace "with the nations of the world."[11] Yet Boas was convinced that America had harmed Germany. The arm shipments to the Allies, Boas felt, were cause enough for war between the United States and the Central Powers. He was bewildered by American favoritism of the Allies, and depicted Germany as an injured victim.

These public utterances evoked a series of responses that well exemplified the xenophobic tensions extant in America. Boas was criticized for portraying Germany as a victim in the conflict. The Reverend William Morgan, for example, scolded: "My dear Professor, while you are teaching others, pray stop a moment and try to teach yourself. Don't whisper threats of what your nation may do to us after the war; but consider how we ought to revoke your naturalization and ship you all back to the Vaterland, which you gladly left."[12]

Undeterred, Boas continued his assault on violations of neutrality. He argued that America had no right to impose its ideals upon other nations. Germany, Austria and the other nations could solve their problems without the "benefactions" of the United States. "The very standpoint that we are right and they are wrong," he wrote, "is opposed to the fundamental idea that nations have distinctive individualities, which are expressed in their modes of life, thought, and feeling."[13]

Many individuals agreed with Boas's opinions and thanked him for his contribution. Others were less laudatory. Arthur Walker of Columbia University regretted Boas's remarks, especially in light of their affiliation on the same faculty. Walker asked Boas how he could support Germany, whose own repressive policies had forced Boas to come to America.[14] E. W. Bulkley, fashioning himself an American patriot, castigated Boas for alleging that the United States was an aggressor nation. Bulkley demanded that Boas delineate specific instances in which Americans had "endeavored to impose their ideals upon other nations."[15]

Rather than dissuading him, personal criticisms incited Boas to further action. As America moved closer to the Allies, his protest intensified. He saw Wilson obeying "the letter of international law" regarding Germany, while ignoring all rules when supplying England and France.[16] He believed that all the combatants were equally responsible for the war, and condemned nationalistic desires for territorial acquisition. He suggested that America should steer clear of partisanship, lest it abandon the democratic principles and social justice for which it stood.[17]

The presidential campaign of 1916 underscored Wilson's contradictory position. Although he had "enthusiastically" voted for Wilson in 1912, Boas could not do so again. Wilson had manipulated Congress and had interfered in the internal affairs of Mexico, while "pretending to consider Mexico a sovereign state."[18] Regarding the European war, Boas accused Wilson of failing "to protect the interests" of the United States. Instead of guarding American rights as neutrals against all attacks, Wilson had "chosen to select certain rights which he will protect, others which he will disregard."[19] Boas was further annoyed by the administration's curtailment of civil liberties for those people who protested against America's war policy. Accordingly, he supported Charles Evans Hughes for the presidency in 1916. Hughes's "sense of justice" would prevent him from creating "internal discord," and he would "protect the interests of the country."[20] Boas's vote, however, was more a negative reaction against Wilson than an endorsement of Hughes.

By late 1916 Boas was extremely disillusioned. The "craze for prepared-ness" had reached scientific organizations and affected their operations. The National Academy of Science devoted much of its time to war preparation, and at least one university denied a teaching position to a professor because he was pro-German.[21] Boas pleaded with Wilson to keep America out of the war, and proposed that the question of American intervention be submitted to the people in a referendum.[22] He insisted that Wilson was leading the nation to the brink of hostilities, and cautioned that Americans "must retrace [their] steps" to maintain peace.[23]

Tensions throughout the nation heightened the following spring. The re-pressive climate of opinion was nowhere better illustrated than at Columbia University. On March 5 the board of trustees passed a resolution establishing a committee to investigate the political sentiments of the faculty as a whole. The faculty revolted. Elsie Clews Parsons, alumnus of Columbia and former trustee of Barnard College, depicted the university as "efficiently 'prussian-ized' by such a declaration," and called the trustees' violation of academic freedom "a grotesque . . . bit of almost incredible buffoonery."[24]

Boas also protested, exclaiming that the "stupid resolution . . . cannot intim-idate us."[25] He publicly delineated his political views to his classes, discussing six principles that determined his attitude:

1. The foremost duty of every individual and every country is to serve the interests of mankind.
2. While the nearest duty of each state is to its citizens, no State has the right to perform acts the evil effects of which upon mankind outweigh the benefits accruing to the citizens of the State.
3. It is nobler to suffer intimidation than to act unjustly. For this reason we should be slow to maintain our rights by force when patience promises redress by peaceful means.
4. War is justifiable only in self-defense and for the maintenance of great principles acknowledged by the consensus of opinion of the best of mankind.
5. There are higher duties than patriotism, as at presently generally conceived.
6. I wish to see the United States of America the exponent of the highest ideals of the State as a servant of mankind.[26]

Not only did he read these principles to his students, he also submitted them to the *New York Evening Mail* for publication. To Boas they represented a forceful argument against American involvement. This projected editorial, however, was not published. Wilson's declaration of war on April 2, 1917, and Congress's ratification four days later dashed Boas's hopes for continued American neutrality.[27]

In response to the declaration of war, the Germanistic Society, under the direction of Nicholas Murray Butler, suspended all its activities, much to Boas's dismay. He believed the high ideals of the society should not be jeopardized by political differences, and thus dissented from the decision.[28] Yet, Boas did not continue to protest publicly. Although he privately voiced his opposition to American intervention, he wrote no editorials condemning Wilsonian policy once America entered the conflict. As a pacificist, however, he frequently used the press to beg for a cessation of fighting.[29] He also sought to mitigate the negative German stereotypes held by most Americans. Beyond this he did not go.

Nevertheless, America's involvement in the war significantly influenced Boas. The repression and abandonment of civil liberties that followed intervention affected several people with whom he was closely associated. James McKean Cattell, Boas's friend and former chairman of Columbia's combined anthropology and psychology department, became enmeshed in a major controversy. On August 3, 1917, Cattell addressed a letter to the members of Congress, urging them "to support a measure against sending conscripts to fight in Europe against their will."[30] Cattell held that military conscription was unconstitutional if conducted without "the consent of the people," and that "the President and the present Congress were not elected to send conscripts to Europe."[31]

Columbia president Nicholas Murray Butler and the board of trustees thought Cattell's remarks were "in opposition to the enforcement of the laws of the United States" and thus constituted an "act of sedition and treason." Accordingly, they sought his dismissal from Columbia. Cattell, however, believed the affair afforded Butler the opportunity for which he had long been waiting. In a detailed letter to the American Association of University Professors, Cattell explicitly described the personal friction that had existed between Butler and himself. The accusation of treason was nothing more than a trumped-up excuse for Butler to rid himself of an implacable enemy.

The real reasons for Cattell's dismissal, whatever they may have been, did not concern Boas. He reacted violently to an apparent abridgement of academic freedom. Cattell had been fired after publicly opposing the government's wartime policy. In a manner reminiscent of his attempt to vindicate the reputation of W J McGee in 1902, Boas campaigned strenuously against Columbia's actions. He contacted Butler to protest the dismissal. Although explaining that he personally disapproved of "the personal character and vehemence" of Cattell's attack on Butler, Boas praised Cattell's scientific contributions, and urged that Columbia reconsider its stand. Attributing the controversy to the excitement of the times, Boas stressed the need for rationality.[32]

Boas did not hide his differences from Cattell. While admiring his "courage and independence," Boas made it clear that he did not totally agree with "his opinions or method."[33] Nevertheless, he promised to continue to fight for Cattell's right to free speech, and stepped up his campaign when Cattell resigned the editorship of *Science*. To Boas this constituted a grievous injury to scientific endeavor in the United States. Accordingly, he contacted many of his colleagues in the scientific community, including Henry Donaldson,

William Welch, Jacques Loeb, Robert Millikan and Edward Grant Conklin, in the hopes that they would assist in preventing the resignation.[34] Welch responded immediately, urging Cattell to stay on at *Science*.[35] Loeb and Conklin reacted with equal fervor, petitioning Columbia in protest of such a clear violation of academic freedom.[36] Despite the protests, Cattell was discharged and in the fall of 1921 was still embroiled in controversy regarding both his pension and his personal disagreements with Butler.[37]

The case was emblematic of wartime hysteria within the academic community. The sacred right of freedom of speech became expendable in the face of the blind patriotism that Boas loathed. Such repression, moreover, was not confined to universities. Boas's involvement in the case of Leo J. Frachtenberg revealed similar nationalistic sentiments within scientific organizations.

Frachtenberg had received his doctorate in anthropology at Columbia under Boas's tutelage. From there he secured employment at the Smithsonian Institution as a Special Ethnologist in the Bureau of American Ethnology, and also assisted Boas with the ongoing *Handbook of American Indian Languages* project. In the fall of 1917, however, Charles Walcott dismissed him from his position for "utterances derogatory to the Government of the United States."[38] Shocked at the firing, Frachtenberg contacted Walcott immediately and begged for an appointment to clarify his position. He assured Walcott that he had made no statements derogatory toward the United States. He confessed only to "grumbling against the rising cost of living and Congress' unwillingness to curb these rises," but denied doing anything more serious. Accordingly, he hoped Walcott would reconsider and not turn him out "penniless and jobless," ever to be viewed as a traitor to his country.[39]

Boas came to Frachtenberg's defense after learning that he had made no seditious remarks, but had merely championed Germany's cause prior to American involvement.[40] Frachtenberg believed he had been framed by A. A. Michelson, who first exaggerated his statements and then passed them on to Walcott.[41] Boas also learned that the Justice Department had no grounds on which to prosecute Frachtenberg for disloyalty, and that the entire affair rested with Walcott. Accordingly, Boas enlisted the support of Elsie Parsons, who was well-connected in Washington circles. Boas hoped Walcott would drop the matter both "for the sake of justice and for the sake of science."[42]

The incident dragged on throughout the remainder of the year, with Frachtenberg professing his innocence and great love for America. Boas, ashamed of Frachtenberg for falling "all over himself to prove his loyalty," nevertheless recognized the dangers implicit in Walcott's actions.[43] He objected to "the despotic way of managing so-called scientific institutions and the outrageous dismissal of men without any hearing."[44] As in the Cattell case, the defense of individual freedom was of paramount importance to Boas.

Late in January 1918 Walcott finally met with Frachtenberg, but still maintained that his remarks were "derogatory." Although acknowledging that "it was without disloyal or treasonable intent," Walcott believed "such utterances are inimical to the public welfare, especially in wartime, whether intentional or unintentional."[45] Consequently, he considered Frachtenberg's "usefulness as an employee of the Bureau of American Ethnology" seriously impaired and refused to retain his services.[46] Frachtenberg, discouraged by the outcome, found employment in February 1919 as a factory superintendent.

The affair had a strong impact on Boas, who became convinced that individual freedom no longer existed in America. Scientists and academics, blinded by patriotism, behaved irrationally. His disillusionment was profound, yet uncharacteristically he did not speak out publicly against the war during America's involvement. Rather, he turned his attention to other pursuits. He renewed his interest in establishing cooperation between Columbia and the American Museum of Natural History. In conjunction with this effort, he was involved in the establishment of the Museum of the American Indian, consulting with and advising the museum's director, George Heye. Additionally, Boas created the *International Journal of American Linguistics* in 1917, which he edited until his death.[47]

Nonetheless, the war's repercussions continued to affect him. The Cattell controversy underscored the power held by Columbia's trustees and the corresponding weakness of the faculty. This realization was heightened when the university cut Alexander Goldenweiser's salary in a blatant attempt to force his resignation. Boas believed the incident was personal, but remained powerless to stop it.[48] He did, however, secure Goldenweiser a position as lecturer in anthropology at the New School for Social Research.[49] This incident persuaded him further that Columbia was "developing into a model of bureaucratic machinery, the equal of which it would be hard to find in any part of the world."[50] He was "disgusted with the whole situation," in which the trustees controlled everything and the faculty remained powerless. Boas was convinced that the trustees viewed the university as "a kind of club, the welfare of which [was] in charge of the Trustees, who have to watch carefully over the character, opinions, and deeds of the men who have joined."[51]

In response to this overwhelming control, Boas sought to limit the powers and privileges of the board of trustees. He proposed the establishment of joint faculty-trustee committees to deal with both financial and technical problems on a more equitable basis.[52] He also challenged a college's right to restrain an instructor from free expression. Beyond the constitutional issue of free speech, Boas felt a teacher must control what was taught, "so that there may be an opportunity for the young to receive impressions from different points of view."[53]

Students, too, needed the liberty to pursue their course of study. Boas believed that "the rigid administrative organization of departments of instruction" restricted academic freedom of choice.[54] Faculties created artificial barriers by establishing course requirements that limited students' intellectual growth. Boas envisioned a more open policy within the university structure to allow for greater freedom and diversity in attaining knowledge.[55]

This concern over intellectual freedom at Columbia soon blossomed into an increasing skepticism toward the concept of American democracy itself. Boas reacted to the abridgement of civil liberties in the nation and began to view democracy as a negative force that prohibited freedom of dissent. The disparity between true democracy and the version practiced in America led him closer to socialism. As he suggested, "nobody who knows the conditions of life of the rich and the poor could claim that we offer equal opportunities for all."[56] It was not surprising that Boas publicly stated his intention of voting for the socialist platform in the 1918 off-year election. Perceiving the "rehabilitation of our civic liberties" as the fundamental issue, he chose socialism because it advocated the "repeal of those laws that have resulted in an abridgement of the freedom of speech and of the press, of the right of the people peaceably to assemble and to petition the government for a redress of grievances."[57]

The armistice of November 1918 ended Boas's public silence on governmental policy. Significantly, he had actively protested prior to American intervention but remained mute during the actual involvement. Once peace was declared he again expressed his strong views, this time concerning the nature of the peace treaty. His interest in the Versailles negotiations was heightened by his appointment by the governor of New York as an honorary delegate to the Atlantic Congress, which was to convene in February 1919 to promote the League of Nations.[58]

Boas was disillusioned with the Versailles proposals because they were designed to "throw the people of Germany into bondage."[59] He repeatedly expressed the opinion that Germany was not solely responsible for the conflict and hence should not bear the full burden of reparations. Borrowing Woodrow Wilson's own slogan, Boas argued that if America "fought the war to end war," it should "see to it that the conditions of peace do not contain the germs of future wars."[60] He cajoled his senators to reject a treaty that both imposed a vindictive settlement on the Central Powers and took Germany's colonies away, distributing them as mandates among the Allies. Instead, Boas supported the British Labour party plan, which advocated "international protection of the colonies of all countries against exploitation and of their governments in the interest of the natives and of humanity."[61]

What troubled Boas about the peace had also bothered him prior to American intervention. He viewed nationalism as an aggressive, limiting philosophy that worked against peaceful coexistence. Love of country should not "exclude admiration of foreign modes of life," but such was the case.[62] Respect for all people was necessary for future progress. The vengeful Versailles settlement, a product of unbridled nationalistic fervor, was an obstacle to world peace.

The limitations placed on civil liberties in wartime America also reflected this zealous nationalism. Boas condemned the limitations as a "sign of weakness."[63] The League of Nations could only succeed, Boas believed, if nationalism could be destroyed. A league based on imperialism would not survive, so long as citizens of any nation were placed under the control of another. For Boas, "equality of rights of members of mankind, regardless of nationality," had to be the basis for any international organization, if peace was to endure.[64] Boas's scientific findings shaped these anti-imperialistic political beliefs. In his mind, the success of the League of Nations rested on the recognition of equal mental abilities among all races. Without this vital element, the federation could not survive. Boas, the scientist-statesman, predicted far better than most politicians.

However, his scientific scruples and strict sense of professional ethics embroiled him in a major controversy late in the decade. The roots of the incident dated back to the summer of 1917, when Boas's friend, Berthold Laufer, had harmlessly informed him of the status of the Field Museum's staff. James Alden Mason, an ethnologist connected to the museum and one of Boas's own colleagues in Mexico, had received a summons from the War Department and a leave of absence from the museum. Mason had explained that he was engaged in some archaeological work for the government, but Laufer remained convinced that he was on "a political mission," because he had "no commission or authority for any work in Mexico from the Field Museum."[65] Boas refused to believe Laufer, because Mason was a respected scientist who would not undertake a "secret political mission," especially since he was greatly obligated to Mexico. Accordingly, Boas gave Mason the benefit of the doubt.[66] Apparently reassured by Boas's attitude, Laufer adopted a similar stance.[67]

For two and a half years the issue lay dormant. It reemerged dramatically on December 20, 1919 (the Versailles Conference had taken place earlier that year), when the *Nation* published an open letter written by Boas. Initially Boas had hoped that *Science* would print it, but due to political problems of his own, Cattell declined, although he agreed with the article's sentiment.[68] The editorial, "Scientists as Spies," shocked the anthropological community not only by suggesting that American democracy was a poor "fiction," but also by alleging that a number of scientists had "prostituted science by using it as a cover for their activities as spies."[69]

Arguing that a scientist's life should be dedicated to "the service of truth," Boas found the incident an "unpardonable offense" and refused to continue to recognize the individuals as scientists. He had discovered, accidentally, that four anthropologists, "while employed as government agents, introduced themselves to foreign governments as representatives of scientific institutions in the United States." Though all claimed to be conducting research, they were in fact acting as spies. Not only did they do the "greatest possible disservice to scientific inquiry" by their actions, they also "raised a new barrier against the development of international friendly cooperation."[70]

The editorial brought immediate response and rebuke. Charles Walcott stripped Boas of his position as honorary philologist in the Bureau of American Ethnology, which he had held since May 1901.[71] But the Smithsonian secretary did not stop there. Motivated largely by his own sense of patriotism, which first surfaced in the Frachtenberg affair, Walcott now carried a double burden. His son had been killed in action during the war.[72] This increased his already intolerant attitude toward those who protested America's role in the war. General nativistic hysteria, associated with the "One Hundred Per Cent Americanism" that infected the country, further exacerbated the situation. As if these factors were not sufficient, the entire history of disagreement between Walcott and Boas, dating back to the 1894 Chicago appointment, intensified Walcott's resentment.

Accordingly, Walcott attempted to oust Boas from several major scientific organizations. He personally directed a campaign to remove Boas from the National Academy of Sciences and from Columbia University, although in neither case was he even remotely successful. Academy members such as Edward Grant Conklin were mildly distressed by the editorial, but felt that Boas did not deserve punishment.[73] George Ellery Hale seemed more disturbed by the incident, in light of Boas's pending membership on the National Research Council, but he also found the incident too minor to warrant direct action.[74]

Stronger sentiments emanated from the halls of the American Museum of Natural History, where Henry Fairfield Osborn lashed out at Boas in a polemic replete with anti-Semitic overtones. He castigated Boas for "his lack of appreciation of Mr. Jesup and his unwillingness to do anything in return for the wonderful service he had rendered him."[75] Influenced more by past disagreements between Boas and the museum than by the *Nation* editorial, Osborn absurdly concluded that Boas occupied a "comparatively obscure and uninfluential position" with "few students and few followers."[76] Michael Pupin, a physics professor at Columbia, also condemned Boas as "an objectionable public nuisance." Yearning for a return to the "good old days of absolutism where the means were always at hand for ridding oneself of such a nuisance as Franz Boas," Pupin well illustrated the hysteria infecting both the incident and the nation at large.[77] His remarks also reflected the irrational attitude that permeated American science during the Great War.

These bitter accusations and derogatory comments did not perceptibly tarnish Boas's stature. In addition to his break with the Smithsonian, the Anthropological Society of Washington called his actions "inconsiderate to the best interests of his American colleagues."[78] The American Anthropological Association passed a resolution calling the editorial "unjustified," stating that it did not represent the association's views, and it removed Boas from its governing council.[79] These repercussions were mild, however, when compared to what transpired within the National Research Council.

Established in response to the war preparedness frenzy that swept America in 1916, the council included a division on anthropology, which during the war years leaned heavily toward physical anthropology. Among its members were "several racialist anthropologists" and "two leading eugenicists." After the war, the council intended to restructure the committee on anthropology by widening its scope to deal with "the pressing problem of the racial composition of the American population, studied in close cooperation with psychology, biology, and neurology."[80]

Boas was nominated to the delegation for the council, as one of the representatives from the American Anthropological Association, and he attended the initial planning meeting in November.[81] In the aftermath of the *Nation* editorial and the reaction within the American Anthropological Association, he withdrew his name from the council's nominations committee. Clearly Boas did not intend this as an admission of any wrongdoing; in fact, he forcefully reminded the council that the use of scientists as spies was unjustifiable and against the best interests of both anthropology and the country at large.[82]

The entire imbroglio exemplified the chaotic nature of American science during the war. Patriotism, as Boas had feared, blinded many intelligent individuals. However, the strong reaction against him came principally from Washington anthropologists, whose long-standing fear of his increasing power no doubt helped define their position. In many instances the protests against the editorial were simply vehicles to attack a man whose power had caused much envy and status anxiety among lesser members of America's scientific community.

Certainly it appeared that Boas's "spies" accusation was valid. Walcott himself acknowledged that he "knew of the activities of most of the men" singled out by Boas, and said he approved of their "counteracting German propaganda in the countries in which they were working."[83] Further proof came from J. Alden Mason, who confessed to Boas that he had acted undercover for the government, not out of personal desire but simply to assist the nation in time of war.[84]

Walcott's personal war-related problems, the former friction between Boas and himself and the general tensions of the postwar period combined to intensify reaction to the editorial. Moreover, Boas's rise to a position of power within American anthropology had created considerable jealousy among other scientists, exemplified in the responses of men such as Osborn and Pupin. Feeling threatened by the ascendancy of professional ethnologists who sought to refocus anthropology along cultural lines, these individuals felt a natural antipathy toward Boas. Coupled with this was their own increasing status anxiety. They felt threatened in their work by a new breed of scientist, and saw their societal position as Wasps in danger at the hands of a Jewish immigrant, who both argued that no race was superior to another and appeared to be living proof that such was the case. Accordingly, they reacted strongly not over the substance of the editorial but over the larger threat

Boas posed to their professional lives and to their social status. As such, the "spies" incident served as a microcosm of a large rift within the anthropological community and of fundamental changes in American society.[85] It also contributed to Boas's understanding that American anti-Semitism thrived.

Both the war and the frenzy that followed it disillusioned Boas, but neither destroyed him. Unlike many other Columbia professors, he was not fired. The fact that he had remained relatively silent during America's actual involvement in the war undoubtedly accounted for this. Or, perhaps, as Boas's daughter has suggested, "Butler liked to have opposition in his backyard."[86] In any case, Boas did not suffer Cattell's fate. He remained at Columbia. Yet the war took a personal toll. Boas became disturbed with America, where democracy seemed illusory. Moreover, the "spies" affair had hopelessly shattered public respect for science. At the war's conclusion Boas gave up his evening custom of playing Beethoven sonatas on his piano, complaining that "he could not stand the emotional strain."[87] He did not want to be reminded of German culture which was destroyed by the war.

Although censured by several organizations and compelled to resign from the National Research Council, Boas remained the most influential member of America's anthropological community. He adopted a somewhat caustic attitude toward the entire incident, remarking that it was "salutory to be kicked out of an institution."[88] Despite the criticism and abuse directed toward him by fellow anthropologists, the events of the early 1920s well illustrated that his influence and status remained intact. They also served notice that he would continue to protest publicly when the occasion arose.

By the spring of 1920, Boas had grown increasingly concerned about the ability of German and Austrian libraries to purchase American books at the high rate of exchange. Accordingly, he worked through the rejuvenated Germanistic Society, attempting to solicit aid from wealthy patrons and men of science in the United States. He also became involved in attempts to provide food relief for Vienna. Eventually, he combined these charitable concerns by joining in the establishment of the Emergency Society in Aid of European Science and Art, dedicated to preventing the "intellectual starvation" of Europe.[89]

Unlike his silence during the war, Boas publicly attacked the punitive aspects of the Versailles settlement. He criticized the French treatment of German subjects in the occupied regions, and remained firmly convinced that the terrible conditions must be rectified if another outbreak of hostilities was to be avoided.[90]

Boas also witnessed how American wartime hysteria had increased xenophobia and racism. The repressive climate of opinion in the country that followed the fighting led to the passage of two immigration restriction acts. Furthermore, a renewed emphasis on "one hundred percent Americanism" and pseudoscientific race theory endangered the welfare of most non-Nordic peoples.

As early as 1916, with the publication of Madison Grant's *The Passing of the Great Race*, it became evident that the war had rekindled American anxiety about foreigners. Grant warned of the dangers that an influx of non-Nordic types would pose to American society. The great Aryan race was passing away, and the book mourned the loss. Grant, a eugenicist and Wasp, believed that controls were necessary lest America suffer a radical decline in stature. He cautioned against unrestricted immigration, and warned that "the maudlin sentimentalism that has made America 'an asylum for the oppressed'" was "sweeping the nation toward a racial abyss." Allowing immigration to continue unchecked would speed "the type of native American of Colonial descent" to an untimely demise.[91]

Recognizing the danger of such pseudoscientific beliefs and moved by his own loathing of anti-Semitism, Boas agreed to review Grant's volume. He did so in order to "expose the fallacies" on which it rested.[92] For Boas, the book was a "modern edition of Gobineau." It erred in discussing hereditary characteristics of the human race as a whole. It failed to illustrate environment's effect on the development of local types and badly misunderstood race mixture theory. Of course, Boas understood that the book had "not been written for the purpose of setting forth scientifically well founded data." Rather, Grant intended "to show that democratic institutions and the arrival of immigrants of non-northwest European types are a danger to the welfare of the American people."[93]

What made Grant's book so pernicious, in Boas's mind, was not simply its scientific errors but its eugenicist tone. Boas disagreed with eugenicists' fundamental assumptions. Although conceding that the dream of eliminating suffering through controlled breeding was attractive, Boas found major limitations to such a plan. From a biological perspective, only hereditary features could be "affected by eugenic selection."[94] Environmental factors could not be reshaped by selective breeding.

Moreover, there were ethical considerations that argued against deciding what characteristics were worthy of retention in breeding. Viewing the present as only "one phase in the development of mankind," Boas was wary of setting "standards for all time to come."[95] Eugenics could be useful in eliminating genetic defects that led to retardation, but should never attempt "to raise a race of supermen." For Boas eugenics did not represent "a panacea that will cure human ills," but was a "dangerous sword that may turn its edge against those who rely on its strength."[96]

However, the American public was enamored with scientific theories that proved the existence of a racial hierarchy. The failure of Wilson's Fourteen Points, combined with the Bolshevik revolution, convinced many Americans that their society was in grave danger. The Red Scare and Palmer raids, the execution of Sacco and Vanzetti, a wave of urban race riots, and the immigration restriction acts all testified to the insecurity of the times.

Writers in the popular tradition of Madison Grant mourned the passing of

Anglo-Saxon superiority. Lothrop Stoddard, in *The Rising Tide of Color*, warned that "swarthy races" were taking over the country. This national mania was nowhere more poignantly reflected than in F. Scott Fitzgerald's *The Great Gatsby*. During dinner conversation, Tom Buchanan's comments well illustrated the climate of opinion in the country: "Civilization's going to pieces. ... Have you read *The Rise of the Colored Empires* by this man Goddard? ... Well, it's a fine book, and everybody ought to read it. The idea is if we don't look out the white race will be—will be utterly submerged. It's all scientific stuff; it's been proved.... It's up to us, who are the dominant race, to watch out or these other races will have control of things."[97]

To Boas, Stoddard's arguments were worthless, since they emanated from an "abject fear of an equal development of all the members of mankind," and because they lacked any "convincing proof."[98] Throughout the 1920s, Boas continued a public assault on the race prejudice that had permeated the skin of America. Although not breaking any new ground, he kept alive the egalitarian impulse that became one of the crucial forces of the modern civil rights movement. He condemned the racism of writers such as Henry F. Osborn, who feared the passing of the Teutonic race and who were motivated more by their own status anxiety than by the acquisition of scientific knowledge.[99]

The 1924 Immigration Restriction Act increased Boas's anger. Based on a new, destructive type of nationalism, "nordic nonsense" to Boas, the new law discriminated against all individuals "not considered as representatives of the 'Nordic' type."[100] Writers such as Grant and Stoddard were "carried away by the ardent wish to establish the superiority" of their own ancestors, and thus proceeded without caution. They ignored evidence that all races contained "imbeciles, weaklings, emotionally unstable strains, as well as good sound stock of excellent nervous make-up and strong constitution."[101] Moreover, they viewed with too great an anxiety the crowded conditions of the urban ghetto, thus often painting a false portrait of immigrant abilities and the efficacy of the melting pot. On the contrary, in Boas's mind, "social resistance to Americanizing influences was weak among immigrants, leading to rapid assimilation."[102]

Prior to the bill's passage, New York congressman Emanuel Celler had contacted Boas regarding the congressional debate over restriction, informing him that Grant had "immeasurably influenced the members of the Immigration Committee."[103] Congress had been infected with "prejudice and biased knowledge"; the act was passed, despite Boas's personal appearance before the committee.[104]

Apart from the national context, Boas fought individual cases of discrimination. In 1924, United States authorities prohibited an Armenian family from gaining citizenship, contending that they were not members of a "white race."[105] Boas's involvement in the case of the *United States v. Cartosian* led the United States District Court of Oregon to uphold Armenians' rights to citizenship.[106] Although not a major victory, the trial's adjudication gave Boas hope that he could help defeat prejudice.

During the 1920s Boas remained in control of Columbia's anthropology department. Under his tutelage, Melville Herskovits began his investigations into Africa culture, which ultimately led to the publication of *The Myth of the Negro Past*.[107] Margaret Mead won a National Research Fellowship.[108] Boas assumed the role of father figure to his graduate students. Besides remaining in touch with his older pupils, such as Alfred Kroeber and Robert Lowie of the University of California, Edward Sapir of the Geological Survey of Canada and Leslie Spier at the University of Washington, Boas constantly looked after their interests. In 1924 he relinquished the editorship of the *Folk-Lore Journal*, passing the position on to Ruth Benedict.[109] He continued to advise Alexander Goldenweiser of the New School for Social Research, as well as Pliny Goddard of the American Museum of Natural History. Finally, he secured an instructorship for Gladys Reichard at Barnard. In communicating with Boas in 1922, Reichard vividly depicted the relationship he had with many of his students when she addressed him as "Dear Papa Franz."

During the decade, Boas's thought on cultural laws entered its third and final stage. Characterized by a realization that anthropologists could not discover evolutionary regularities, Boas's argument propounded that "the aims of anthropology should not include the discovery of laws," because historical laws did not exist. He lost interest in historical reconstruction and focused more on "psychological factors." Accordingly, his "most famous female students received their training and were sent out with his encouragement to probe the neglected relationship between the individual and culture."[110]

The wartime period challenged Boas's security. In lashing out at America's foreign policy both before and after the fact, he placed all that he had worked for in jeopardy. The *Nation* editorial, so characteristic of his inability to be silent, could have conceivably destroyed a less powerful figure. As it was, his influence over American anthropology seemed shaken in 1920. Yet Boas remained firmly in control. Through his postwar attacks on pseudoscience, he became an acknowledged leader in the battle against race prejudice. He fashioned the turning point in the debate over equality, which put "the racists . . . increasingly on the defensive."[111] Moreover, he still dominated the professionalization of anthropology by training a host of talented students at Columbia.

Boas's authority on scientific subjects was never disputed. He worked closely with Carter Woodson and the Center for the Study of Negro Life and Culture.[112] He also was appointed to a committee of the American Anthropological Association to investigate the issues raised by the Scopes trial.[113] Late in 1925, he was appointed chairman of the committee of the American Anthropological Association that submitted questions and advice to the National Research Council.[114] In an ironic twist, Michael Pupin, president of the American Association for the Advancement of Science, who had so vehemently denounced him as a "public nuisance,'" welcomed Boas as a member of the Association's Committee of One Hundred on Scientific Research.[115]

Boas did not lose power or influence as a result of the war. The reputation he had so carefully constructed since his arrival in America remained intact. At the same time, he had been loyal to his belief, "my country if right to keep right, if wrong to set right."[116] Boas looked forward to the second quarter of the twentieth century with a renewed sense of satisfaction. He had come a long way from the despair over his future that had plagued him in the early 1880s, and he optimistically welcomed new challenges. From the late 1920s up to his death, he would again have the opportunity to take a stand, motivated as always by his liberal heritage, his scientific integrity and his personal experience with prejudice.

# NOTES

1. Franz Boas, "The Race-War Myth," *Everybody's Magazine* 31 (December 1914): 672.

2. Ibid., p. 673.

3. Ibid.

4. Franz Boas to Ernst Boas, August 6, 1914, in Ronald Rohner, ed., *The Ethnography of Franz Boas: Letters and Diaries of Franz Boas Written on the Northwest Coast from 1886 to 1931*, ed. Ronald Rohner (Chicago: University of Chicago Press, 1969), p. 271. (Hereafter letters from this work will be cited as RR/FB.)

5. Boas to Marie Boas, August 7, 1914, RR/FB, p. 272.

6. Boas to Heini Boas, August 15, 1914, RR/FB, p. 275.

7. Boas to Berthold Laufer, March 18, 1915, American Philosophical Society, Boas Correspondence. (Hereafter cited as APS/BC.)

8. Boas to James E. Martine, August 7, 1915, APS/BC.

9. Ibid.

10. Ibid.

11. Franz Boas, "Warns of German Wrath," editorial, *New York Times*, December 11, 1915.

12. The Reverend William H. Morgan to Boas, December 11, 1915, APS/BC.

13. Franz Boas, "Why German-Americans Blame America," editorial, *New York Times*, January 8, 1916.

14. Arthur Walker to Boas, January 18, 1916, APS/BC.

15. E. W. Bulkley to Boas, January 19, 1916, APS/BC.

16. Franz Boas, "Our National Ideals," editorial, *Springfield Republican*, February 2, 1916.

17. Boas to Charles W. Eliot, March 15, 1916, APS/BC.

18. Boas to the *Evening Mail*, October 27, 1916, APS/BC.

19. Ibid.

20. Ibid.

21. Boas to Oskar Bolza, December 15, 1916, APS/BC.

22. Boas to Woodrow Wilson, February 5, 1917, APS/BC.

23. Franz Boas, "Professor Boas Dissents, Blames the President for the Break with Germany," editorial, *New York Times*, February 9, 1917.

24. Elsie Clews Parsons to the *New York Times*, March 9, 1917, APS/BC.

25. Boas to George McAneny, March 21, 1917, APS/BC.

26. Boas to the editor of the *Evening Mail*, March 30, 1917, APS/BC.

27. Boas to Allan Wiburg, April 11, 1917, APS/BC.

28. Boas to Abraham Jacobi, April 25, 1917, APS/BC.

29. Boas to Sylvester Viereck, June 19, 1917, APS/BC.

30. James McKean Cattell to Allyn A. Young, November 11, 1917, APS/BC.

31. Ibid.

32. Boas to Nicholas Murray Butler, September 29, 1917, APS/BC.

33. Boas to James McKean Cattell, October 2, 1917, APS/BC.

34. Boas to Henry H. Donaldson, October 12, 1917; Boas to William H. Welch, October 12, 1917; Boas to Edward Grant Conklin, October 12, 1917; Boas to Jacques Loeb, October 12, 1917; Boas to Robert A. Milliken, October 12, 1917, APS/BC.

35. William Welch to Boas, October 16, 1917, APS/BC.

36. Jacques Loeb to Boas, October 20, 1917, APS/BC.

37. James McKean Cattell to the trustees of Columbia University, September 2, 1921, APS/BC. For a detailed history of the complexities and charges of the Cattell case, see Carol S. Gruber, *Mars and Minerva: World War I and the Uses of Higher Learning in America* (Baton Rouge: Louisiana State University Press, 1975), pp. 187–206.

38. Charles D. Walcott to Leo J. Frachtenberg, October 30, 1917, APS/BC.

39. Frachtenberg to Walcott, October 31, 1917, APS/BC.

40. John R. Swanton to Boas, November 3, 1917, APS/BC.

41. Leo J. Frachtenberg to Boas, November 6, 1917, APS/BC.

42. Boas to Elsie Clews Parsons, November 26, 1917, APS/BC.

43. Boas to Robert H. Lowie, December 3, 1917, APS/BC.

44. Ibid.

45. Charles D. Walcott to the Civil Services Commission, February 4, 1918, APS/BC.

46. Ibid.

47. Alfred Kroeber, "Franz Boas: The Man," *American Anthropologist* 45 (1943): 18.

48. Boas to Alfred W. Tozzer, April 27, 1918, APS/BC.

49. J. A. Robinson to Boas, March 22, 1918, APS/BC.

50. Boas to Alfred W. Tozzer, April 27, 1918, APS/BC.

51. Ibid.

52. Franz Boas, "Scientific Progress and University Government," *The Nation* 106 (May 1918): 540.

53. Franz Boas, "Freedom for the School," *School and Society* 8 (1918): 740.

54. Franz Boas, "Freedom to Teach," *The Nation* 108 (January 1919): 88–89.

55. Ibid.

56. Franz Boas, "Freedom of Thought," lecture to anthropology class, November 1917, in Boas, ed., *Race and Democratic Society* (New York: J.J. Augustin, 1945), p. 184.

57. Franz Boas, "A Sturdy Protest," *The Nation* 107 (October 19, 1918): 487.

58. Honorary delegate certificate, December 24, 1918, APS/BC.

59. Franz Boas, "As an American of German Birth—I Protest," *Viereck's* 10 (1919): 185.

60. Ibid.

61. Franz Boas, "Colonies and the Peace Conference," *The Nation* 108 (February 15, 1919): 247–249.

62. Franz Boas, "Nationalism," *The Dial* 66 (March 1919): 237.

63. Ibid.

64. Letter to the *New York Evening Post*, November 6, 1919, in Boas, ed. *Race and Democratic Society*, p. 152.

65. Berthold Laufer to Boas, August 11, 1917, APS/BC.

66. Boas to Laufer, August 16, 1917, APS/BC.

67. Laufer to Boas, August 20, 1917, APS/BC.

68. Boas to James McKean Cattell, October 8, 1919; Cattell to Boas, October 11, 1919, APS/BC.

69. Franz Boas, "Scientists as Spies," *The Nation* 108 (December 1919): 797.

70. Ibid.

71. Charles D. Walcott to Boas, December 23, 1919, APS/BC.

72. Boas first learned of this in January 1918 during the Frachtenberg affair. Assistant Secretary of War Keppel to Boas, January 2, 1918, APS/BC.

73. Edward Grant Conklin to Charles D. Walcott, January 2, 1920, Franz Boas Folder, National Academy of Sciences. (Hereafter cited as BF/NAS.)

74. George Ellery Hale to Charles D. Walcott, January 3, 1920, BF/NAS.

75. Henry Fairfield Osborn to Charles D. Walcott, January 6, 1920, BF/NAS.

76. Ibid.

77. Michael Pupin to Charles D. Walcott, January 12, 1920, BF/NAS.

78. Resolution of the Anthropological Society of Washington, December 26, 1919, APS/BC.

79. Summary of the consideration given the Boas letter at the Cambridge meeting of the American Anthropological Association, December 31, 1919, BF/NAS. The vote on the resolution was by no means unanimous. Former Boas students Kroeber, Goddard, Lowie, Spier, Speck and Wissler dissented from the majority. Alfred Tozzer, Elsie Parsons, Charles Peabody and several others joined this group. Surprisingly, Roland Dixon voted against Boas. Predictably, most of the negative voting came from Washington-based scientists.

80. George Stocking, "Ideas and Institutions in American Anthropology: Thoughts Toward a History of the Interwar Years," in *Selected Papers from the American Anthropologist, 1921–1945*, ed. Stocking (Washington, D.C.: American Anthropological Association, 1976), p. 2.

81. Clark Wissler to Boas, September 27, 1919, APS/BC.

82. Boas to chairman of the committee on nominations, December 29, 1919, APS/BC.

83. Charles D. Walcott to Russell H. Chittenden, January 9, 1919, BF/NAS.

84. James Alden Mason to Boas, February 18, 1920, APS/BC.

85. Stocking, "Ideas and Institutions," pp. 1–2.

86. "The Reminiscences of Franziska Boas," Oral History Research Office, Columbia University, 1972, p. 22.

87. Ibid., p. 49.

88. Boas to Leo J. Frachtenberg, May 10, 1920, APS/BC.

89. Tract of the Emergency Society in Aid of European Science and Art, 1920, APS/BC.

90. Franz Boas, "In the Occupied Area," editorial, *New York Times*, October 20, 1923; Boas, "Rights of Invaded Regions," editorial, *New York Times*, November 4, 1923.

91. Madison Grant, *The Passing of the Great Race* (New York: Charles Scribner's Sons, 1916), p. 228.

92. Franz Boas, "Inventing a Great Race,'" *New Republic*, January 13, 1917, p. 305.

93. Ibid., p. 306.

94. Franz Boas, "Eugenics," *Scientific Monthly* 3 (1916): 471.

95. Ibid., p. 476.

96. Ibid., p. 478.

97. F. Scott Fitzgerald, *The Great Gatsby* (New York: Charles Scribner's Sons, 1925), p. 13.

98. Franz Boas, *The Rising Tide of Color*, by Lothrop Stoddard, *The Nation* 111 (1920): 656.

99. Franz Boas, " 'Lo, the Poor Nordic,' " editorial, *New York Times*, April 13, 1924, p. 19.

100. Franz Boas, "This Nordic Nonsense," *The Forum* 74 (October 1925): 502.

101. Ibid., p. 507.

102. Ibid., p. 511.

103. Emanuel Celler to Boas, February 11, 1924, APS/BC.

104. Celler to Boas, February 15, 1924, APS/BC.

105. Boas to Thomas L. Dabney, February 18, 1924; William Guthrie to Boas, February 26, 1924; Boas to Roland Dixon, March 1, 1924; William Guthrie to Dixon, March 21, 1924; Boas to Guthrie, March 21, 1924; Guthrie to Boas, March 24, 1924, APS/BC.

106. Attorney General J. G. Sargent to William Guthrie, December 30, 1925, APS/BC.

107. Boas to Columbia University's committee on fellowships, March 28, 1923, APS/BC.

108. Boas to E. L. Thorndike, April 23, 1925; Boas to Frank R. Lillie, May 12, 1925, APS/BC.

109. Boas to Paul Radin, November 12, 1924, APS/BC.

110. Marvin Harris, *The Rise of Anthropological Theory: A History of Theories of Culture* (New York: Thomas Y. Crowell, 1968), pp. 280–81.

111. Thomas F. Gossett, *Race: The History of an Idea in America* (New York: Schocken Books, 1965), p. 430.

112. Boas to Felix Warburg, December 19, 1924, APS/BC.

113. Boas to Thomas L. Dabney, June 25, 1925, APS/BC.

114. Boas to John C. Merriam, December 31, 1925, APS/BC.

115. Michael Pupin to Boas, October 6, 1925, APS/BC.

116. "The Reminiscences of Franziska Boas," p. 18.

# 8
# The End of an Era

For Boas a relative degree of tranquility characterized the second half of the 1920s, affording him the opportunity to concentrate on teaching and research. He continued his work on Indian languages, which he conducted with former students Edward Sapir and Paul Radin and with his longtime informant George Hunt.

More significantly, he expanded his investigations on racial issues in a number of ways. He played a major role on the National Research Council's Committee on the Anthropology and Psychology of the American Negro, and helped organize a Conference of Racial Differences, which was sponsored by both the NRC and the Social Science Research Council. Also, acting as an adviser to Melville Herskovits, who dealt with the physical anthropology of Afro-Americans; to Otto Klineberg and Zora Neale Hurston, who tackled differences in mental ability; and to Margaret Mead, who studied youth in Samoa, Boas was able to direct a wide-ranging assault on the notion that cultural differences were racially determined.

His increased conviction that race was irrelevant in determining mental ability also led him to step up his public condemnation of those scientists who advanced theories of racial supremacy, especially when they based their arguments on intelligence testing. Arguing that the tests did not provide "actual insight into the biologically determined functioning of the mind," Boas stressed that they usually demonstrated differences in environment. Criticizing the tests for failing to adjust for an individual's experience, he became an early critic of the cultural bias inherent in IQ testing, and renewed his emphasis on the importance of environment in determining mental ability.[1] The studies Boas directed supported his conclusions: the "cultural background of the individual" forcefully determined the "general approach to the test situation in such a manner as markedly to influence" test scores.[2]

Unlike his earlier efforts, which usually fell on deaf ears in the scientific community, by the mid–1930s his "viewpoint on issues of race and culture" were "on the verge of becoming social scientific orthodoxy."[3] By the end of the decade, "it had become axiomatic among many educated Americans that race did not determine intelligence or personality, and that environment, not genes, most influenced human behavior."[4] The nascent Afro-American civil rights movement quickly latched on to these opinions, welcoming the opportunity to use science to support the drive for equality.

The calm of the late 1920s, however, was not to endure. On the horizon loomed major disruptions in American life, which once again forced Boas into the public eye. As if an omen that the 1930s would be tumultuous for him, his wife Marie was killed in an automobile accident late in December 1929.

Another harbinger of change was the onset of the depression, which to Boas meant a shortage of funds needed to carry out further scientific research. He felt the impact of that economic crisis soon after the stock market crash, and began making plans to ensure that research would not suffer.[5] Initially, at least, his scientific endeavors proceeded smoothly. Moreover, in January 1931, at the age of 72, he was elected president of the American Association for the Advancement of Science, in recognition of his long and successful career.

Columbia University's Department of Anthropology also drew his attention and concern. He believed that the faculty of the department needed strengthening, and that the university had grown unsympathetic to the department's needs. Desiring to build "a center of anthropology" at Columbia, Boas tried to lure Alfred Kroeber and Edward Sapir back to their graduate school alma mater as professors. In neither case was he successful. Kroeber opted to remain at the University of California–Berkeley, while Sapir left the University of Chicago for a teaching post at Yale. Boas's disappointment signalled the beginning of his general dissatisfaction with his university's central administration, which would intensify during the years to come.

The 1930s also marked a change in Boas's health. A year to the day after Marie's death, he complained of "a sudden attack of weakness of the heart," which confined him "to the house for nearly three months."[6] After recovering, Boas declined the many dinner invitations he normally received, indicating that his health demanded rest and a restricted diet. Although cardiac problems remained with him, by no means did his health impede his activities during the decade. In fact, the growing problems in Germany, brought about by the rise of Adolf Hitler and the Third Reich, moved Boas to intense action on a wide variety of fronts, and forced him to grapple with anti-Semitism directly instead of behind the veil of other forms of prejudice.

Early in 1933, Boas first addressed himself to conditions in Germany; he believed that scientific activity there was being hampered by a lack of freedom of thought. To Boas, this subjugation was reflected in an increase of non-scientific opinions that were based solely on racial or political attitudes.[7] Accordingly, despite America's precarious financial situation, Boas sought funds to conduct and publicize research that would counter pseudoscientific misinformation. Thus, the environment versus heredity conflict was played out once again, with Boas arguing vehemently that the former, not the latter, determined mental behavior.

Unlike his earlier participation in this debate, Boas came armed with a wealth of information gleaned from his research over the decades. He had already demonstrated that no pure race existed, and that heredity had no place in defining racial makeup. Moreover, his head form studies and other growth investigations had proven that social strata and the subsequent environment in which an individual lived were the critical factors in determining a host of issues, ranging from psychological and social behavior to the "eruption of teeth among children" and criminality. Yet the difficulty, much as it had been earlier, was disseminating this information to the public as a way of offsetting the racial propaganda spread by Nazi scientists.[8]

Of course what most troubled Boas about the German situation was its virulent anti-Semitism. Unlike earlier efforts to mask his displeasure with such bigotry, he lashed out at Nazi prejudice in a number of overt ways. One of the most helpful was the aid he procured for German-Jewish scientists who had been expelled from their faculty positions due to their ancestry. Boas interrupted his scientific work to raise money to bring these scholars to America, and devoted a large amount of time to securing them teaching posts at American universities.[9] He attempted to do the same for German-Jewish graduate students, although in this effort he was much less successful.

German racial propaganda, and the danger of its spread to the United States, were the greatest irritants to Boas. He consequently devoted most of his energy to counteracting these threats. He enlisted the support of colleagues at Columbia to bar Nazi scientists from lecturing there and chaired the American Committee for Anti-Nazi Literature, which was dedicated "to wage a campaign of education and enlightenment against the Nazis."[10] Boas even accepted an invitation by Harvard University's Liberal Club to debate a pro-Nazi ideologue, but the confrontation was cancelled when his would-be opponent declined to match wits "against one of the greatest anthropologists in the world."[11]

Several major factors accounted for Boas's immediate, overt condemnation of Nazism. As usual, his liberalism and scientific integrity placed him diametrically at odds with German race theory and its correspondent suppression of freedom of thought. So too, his long-hidden battle against anti-Semitism forced him to act. Finally, the fact that all this hatred and propaganda was emanating from his homeland had a strong impact upon him. As a result, Boas launched his own private war on several fronts. On one level he carried out a strong, personal attack against Hitler, often colored by fond reminiscences of a vastly different Germany and what it could have become. On another plane, he presented a rational, detached scientific rebuttal to Nazi race theory. In both instances he strove to reach the widest possible audience, in order both to undermine Nazi propaganda by demonstrating its unscientific basis and to halt its spread to America.

Throughout the decade Boas unleashed his wrath against Hitler, characterizing him "a narrow minded fanatic" whose own writings underscored "his absolute lack of knowledge." For Boas, Hitler's "unpardonable sin" was the destruction of "freedom of thought and expression." Hitler single-handedly "degraded a free nation and transformed them into serfs without legal rights," thus undermining "the morale of the people" and turning them into "infamous informers."[12] The only logical place for Hitler and his "ruling clique," Boas felt, was an "insane asylum," where they would not be dangerous to the rest of the world.[13]

Not only did Germany stand as a menace to Jews because of its anti-Semitic actions, it endangered scientific progress as well, since its scientists were not free to think for themselves. While Boas privately goaded these scholars "to rise against the violence done to the human intellect," and castigated their sacrificing "the highest ideals for the sake of the itch for power," he publicly attempted to neutralize official Nazi scientific theory.[14]

This effort took several forms. Boas either joined or contributed to virtually every organization dedicated to anti-Nazi activity in the United States. His name appeared on letterheads of most of these groups, which would later have ramifications that he would have to address. Nevertheless, he forthrightly signed on as a member of the intellectual vanguard combating Nazism. Public lectures were another way of fighting this propaganda, and Boas frequently used the podium to attack anti-Semitism, pseudoscientific race theory and the suppression of free thought.

For Boas all these evils were interrelated. He argued repeatedly that the concept of a pure or master race was scientifically invalid. Bringing to the fore an overwhelming amount of evidence, he dispelled the concept of a chosen people. The "shallow twaddle about race" propounded by German scientists was an infamy to be eradicated, "since every *honest* scientist, whose view is not obscured by fanaticism," could "see through all the false premises and conclusions."[15] Yet, anti-Semitism could not be lightly dismissed simply because it rested on an unsound scientific foundation. Recognizing this, Boas attacked the underpinnings of Hitler's race theory, namely the division of people into "Aryans and Non-Aryans."

Boas contended that the term Aryan pertained solely to linguistic classifications, and that it was "a fiction to speak of a German race." Further, there was no "semitic" race either, since the migrations and intermixture of people over the centuries had made the concept of a pure race anachronistic from both a biological and ethnological viewpoint.[16] But Boas did not stop with his scientific denunciation of Nazism. In an obvious attempt to thwart the propaganda, he explained how Hitler used science to justify anti-Semitism, and derided the attempt as pseudoscientific. For Boas, a nation could not "be defined by its descent," but had to be classified by its language and customs.[17]

The substance of Boas's criticisms was contained in a small article appropriately titled "Aryans and Non-Aryans." According to Herskovits, "the German version, distributed by the anti-Nazi underground," received wide circulation and was "printed on tissue-thin paper, the better to be concealed as it was passed surreptitiously from hand to hand."[18]

Never forgetting that the hysteria of race hatred swelling in Germany could also spread to America if left unchecked, Boas diligently sought opportunities to counter its rise. To prevent such contamination, he tried to demonstrate the "hollowness of the arguments of those who claim the superiority of any one particular race." This led to his continued critique of Madison Grant's writings, which enjoyed immense popularity in the United States, despite their misinformation and pseudoscientific foundation. Grant's "careless handling of facts" to support "Nordic propaganda" infuriated Boas, not only because of the danger this racism posed to minorities in America but also because "serious scientific questions" never entered Grant's mind. Grant and supporters, such as Henry Fairfield Osborn, gave credence and respectability to Hitler's views, and thus to Boas's mind constituted a clear and present danger.[19]

Boas was also careful to treat anti-Semitism specifically, instead of directing his remarks to prejudice in general. He argued against the notion that Jews were uniform in descent, and thus weakened the attempts to classify them as one race. Moreover, he stressed the impact of environment in determining physical and mental capabilities, to point out the fallacy of notions of racial superiority or inferiority.[20] These arguments had long been attributed to Boas, since he had used them in defense of Afro-Americans and immigrant groups in the past. This time, however, he confronted anti-Semitism directly. No longer was he able to appear the detached, objective scientist, for he was no longer utilizing a surrogate cause to mask his true concern.

Given Boas's passionate denunciation of Hitler and Nazi Germany, it might seem inevitable for him to countenance American intervention in World War II. However, somewhat reminiscent of his stance in 1916, he argued against U.S. involvement. He supported neutrality partly because he remembered the repressive climate of opinion extant in America during the First World War, most notoriously characterized by the Red Scare and Palmer raids. Boas wrote: "The spying of Congressional Committees, of the Federal Bureau of Investigation, the numerous bills passed or proposed in Congress and legislatures, directed against the rights of minorities," were all "expressions of dangerous war hysteria."[21] Beyond the domestic ramifications of participation in war, Boas feared that if the conflict produced clear winners and losers, the same type of punitive, retaliatory peace treaty would result as at Versailles in 1919. Boas was certain that the onerous nature of that settlement had contributed mightily to Hitler's rise and the inexorable march to the Second World War.[22]

As the war intensified, however, Boas changed his mind somewhat. He began accepting America's involvement as inevitable, and urged that it be conditional upon an Allied promise not to exact "a vindictive peace if Germany should succumb."[23] Given Boas's pacifistic nature and his earlier defense of Germany in 1916, this shift demonstrated how profoundly he abhorred Hitler and all for which he stood.

By 1939, he had become so alarmed by the Nazi menace that he played a major role in founding the American Committee for Democracy and Intellectual Freedom. That organization was dedicated to "the protection and development of intellectual freedom in public life and particularly in education." It performed this function "not by investigating individual cases of suppression," which other agencies already did, "but by counteracting intolerant prejudice and systematic attempts to hamper free education and free discussion."[24] Boas's participation on the committee stemmed from a realization that "certain dangers in American life" were becoming more pronounced because of "growing tensions" in Europe. Accordingly, during the late 1930s he "intensified his support of academic freedom, of civil liberties, and other unpopular causes."[25]

His chief focus became intellectual freedom. Boas was convinced that American democracy, while not yet perfected to provide "the fullest measure" of freedom to all citizens, was still a treasure worth guarding. He believed this was especially relevant in the fight against prejudice, since "the results of honest research" had to be "accessible to all" as a means of combating bigotry.[26] Historically, American democracy had "developed as a natural and necessary action against outside interference with the freedom of the individual," and Boas hoped that the threat from Nazi Germany would not retard this progress. He had often warned that Americans should not yield to any attempts "to restrict freedom of thought and freedom of expression," because by so doing "scientific progress" would suffer. He challenged America to protect "freedom of thought by the most searching scrutiny of current opinion and of our minds." That process, he said, required "hard and courageous work to recognize where the irrational prejudices of the day" interfered with "rational thought."[27]

This general worry about intellectual liberty in American society was also reflected in Boas's concern about academic freedom. Nowhere was this more evident than at Columbia itself. Boas had become more and more displeased with the university's administration during the 1930s. Although he well understood the economic squeeze faced by most academic institutions during the depression, he blamed Columbia for not supporting faculty research and for continuing to ignore the staffing needs of the anthropology department. This hostility was exacerbated by Boas's forced retirement from teaching in 1936. At that time the board of trustees appointed him to the rank of Professor Emeritus in Residence, but he was angered by the reduced salary he would receive and felt slighted after his forty years of loyal service to the university.[28]

While these incidents still smoldered, and the war fever caused him to worry about a general curtailment of liberties, Boas vented his frustrations with the central administration of the university. He based his argument on a conviction that a faculty's intellectual and academic freedom was a paramount necessity and should not be hindered by a board of trustees, which played no significant role in teaching or research. Although freely admitting that he had never experienced any restriction on his own freedom while a member of the faculty, he believed that in general Columbia's trustees stripped professors of their freedom, relegating them to the classroom with no control over the institution itself. Further, in times of political crisis, such as during a war, Boas believed that a faculty "must be free, unhampered by political considerations, by whims of outsiders or fancies of members of the governing boards."[29]

Boas's anxiety over academic freedom soon extended beyond Columbia. He publicly stressed that America had to protect her children also, by guaranteeing their "right to be informed" so that they could "form an intelligent judgement" about their own "place in society." For Boas, primary education could do one of two things. It could foster "personal freedom"; or it could teach the young "to become subservient tools of the employer, be it the State, an individual, or a commercial, intellectual or spiritual organization." Abhorring the latter indoctrination, Boas wanted an atmosphere of freedom, where teachers and students could exchange views without fear of reprisal.[30] Only in that way could America continue its journey along the path of democracy.

Extending his critique of Columbia's board of trustees to education in general, Boas suggested that such a diffuse type of administration precluded "healthy development of intellectual and spiritual freedom" by removing educational responsibility from teachers. To prevent American democratic ideals from becoming bigoted, Boas urged that schools allow teachers the freedom to teach and students the freedom to learn, so that all Americans could come to their own opinions about issues affecting society.[31] Teachers had to "be the shock-troops of an intelligent understanding of democracy," the sine qua non of intellectual freedom.[32]

For this outcry against abridgements of academic freedom, and because of his conviction that American democracy was not yet ideal, as evidenced by the lack of equal opportunity for all, Boas paid a price. He was labelled a Communist in the popular press and found himself on the defensive simply because he spoke out against repression.[33] But he continued to be active. He even supported a general call for the release of Earl Browder, head of the Communist Party of the United States (CPUSA), who was serving a four-year sentence in Atlanta Penitentiary for violation of a passport statute.[34]

Privately Boas acknowledged that he had no use for the Communist Party's methods. He disagreed with "the demand for obedience of party members" and the corresponding limits placed on intellectual freedom that accompanied party membership. Nevertheless, he shared the CPUSA's "ideals of equality" and supported "united front" ventures, such as the defense of the Scottsboro Boys, in which the Communists were active. He justified his own activism on the grounds that political and religious differences should not interfere with "united work" in a field where individuals agreed on goals.[35] Moreover, he criticized the Dies Committee, established by Congress to investigate un-American propaganda, for being itself undemocratic and un-American.[36] Its creation was symptomatic, Boas felt, of the repression that accompanied wartime hysteria.

Significantly, Boas supported the American war effort in the wake of the attack on Pearl Harbor. He guarded against any suppression of civil liberties and accelerated his own private war against racism. He pressed on with his campaign for research funds to "undermine the pseudo-scientific basis of race prejudice," and highlighted its illogical, "emotional basis" by giving the usual lectures and publishing the usual essays. However, cognizant of popular culture's increasing influence in America, he added to his campaign a new weapon. He proposed the creation of a "popular film" that would propagandize "the absurdity of race prejudice" to the masses.[37] At a time when Hollywood itself was facing mounting pressure from the National Association for the Advancement of Colored People and others to reform its own racist practices, Boas's idea was visionary.

His critique of race prejudice in this period varied little from its earlier form. Fearing that America faced "a rising tide of . . . anti-semitism and anti-Catholicism," Boas sought to "drive home again the democratic principle that a citizen is to be judged solely by the readiness which which he fits himself into the social structure and by the value of his contributions to the country's development."[38] Education was the best means of counteracting "the race nonsense preached by Hitler," based as it was on fanatical ignorance. "The Negro problem," Boas instructed, "would disappear if we were willing to meet the Negro individually eye to eye." Personal contact would obviate the need to rely on racial stereotypes. In the same context, Boas spoke openly about anti-Semitism in America, which segregated Jews as a type, when in fact individuals in that group had little in common.[39]

Obsession with the race issue, depleted research funds and old age began to take their toll on much of Boas's other scientific activity. His investigations on race and development, much of his ongoing ethnological work on the Kwakiutls, and even some of the linguistic collections languished. Lamenting that he had little time to complete his many projects, he hoped to attract "some young people" who could become familiar with his work so that it would not be lost when he died.[40] Despite his pessimism over the future of his research, the period after his retirement from teaching was prolific in terms of output. His revised version of *The Mind of Primitive Man* appeared; in addition, he published a volume of collected scientific papers, *Race, Language and Culture*; a textbook entitled *General Anthropology*; the third volume of the *Handbook of American Indian Languages*; and a text of *Kwakiutl Tales*.[41]

However, Boas remained convinced that his research was hampered by his increased political activity. He saw the need for the scientist to play a dual role of researcher and educator. For him it was not sufficient to conduct investigations and report them to the scientific community. A scientist had an obligation to inform the public as well, and consequently he must stay "conscious of his duties." It was essential, Boas thought, to "extend the field of education so as to overcome bigotry."[42]

With this in mind, no doubt, Boas gave a luncheon at the Columbia Faculty Club in honor of Paul Rivet on December 21, 1942. Rivet, "an anthropological colleague," had left France after the Nazi take-over and had remained defiant in his opposition to Nazism and its racist practices. In many respects his career mirrored Boas's own social activism and proclivities. As the lunch progressed, Boas found himself in the usual position of discussing prejudice and the ways to combat it. As always, he concluded by instructing the gathering to be vigilant and to fight race prejudice wherever it existed. He then fell back into his chair and died, passing his still unfinished war on to a younger generation.[43]

## NOTES

1. Franz Boas, "Fallacies of Racial Inferiority," *Current History* 25 (February 1927): 681–82.

2. Otto Klineberg, "Race and Psychology," in *Race, Science, and Society*, ed. Leo Kuper (New York: Columbia University Press, 1975), p. 180.

3. George W. Stocking, Jr., "Anthropology as Kulturkampf: Science and Politics in the Career of Franz Boas," in *The Uses of Anthropology*, ed. Walter Goldschmidt (Washington, D.C., American Anthropological Association, 1979), p. 43.

4. Harvard Sitkoff, *A New Deal for Blacks: The Emergence of Civil Rights as a National Issue: The Depression Decade* (New York: Oxford University Press, 1978), pp. 190–91.

5. Boas to Herrn Staatsminister, December 23, 1929, American Philosophical Society, Boas Correspondence. (Hereafter cited as APS/BC.)

6. Boas to Howard Lee McBain, January 4, 1931; Boas to George Hunt, April 7, 1932, APS/BC.

7. Boas to Charles G. Abbott, April 17, 1933, APS/BC.

8. Boas to Sidney Wallach, April 24, 1937, APS/BC.

9. Boas to Alfred Tozzer, November 16, 1933, APS/BC.

10. Boas to John Dewey, May 31, 1934; Boas to Annie Nathan Meyer, July 28, 1936, APS/BC.

11. Bruce Bliven, Jr. to Boas, October 4, 1935, APS/BC.

12. Boas to (unnamed), October 8, 1935; Boas to Franz Termer, August 10, 1938, APS/BC.

13. Franz Boas, "Insane Asylum for Nazi Leaders," *PM* (January 4, 1943): 2.

14. Boas to Franz Termer, August 10, 1938, APS/BC.

15. Boas to (unnamed), October 8, 1935, APS/BC.

16. Franz Boas, "Aryans and Non-Aryans," *American Mercury* 32 (June 1934), 219 & 221.

17. Ibid., p. 223.

18. Melville Herskovits, *Franz Boas: The Science of Man in the Making* (New York: Charles Scribner's Sons, 1953), p. 117.

19. Franz Boas, "Nordic Propaganda," *New Republic* 78 (March 1934), 107.

20. "Remarks of Prof. Franz Boas at Meeting of Judaeans," March 4, 1934, APS/BC.

21. Statement to be read at Madison Square Garden at New York Peace Committee meeting on April 6, 1940, in Boas's absence, APS/BC.

22. Boas to Oswald Veblen, May 24, 1940, APS/BC.

23. Franz Boas, "Britain's War Aims?" *PM*, October 4, 1940, p. 2.

24. Franz Boas, letter to the editor, *Equality*, December 1, 1939, p. 40.

25. Herskovits, *Franz Boas*, p. 118.

26. Franz Boas, "Democracy and Intellectual Freedom," *American Teacher* 23 (March 1939): 9–10.

27. Franz Boas, "Freedom of Thought," in *Race and Democratic Society* (New York: J. J. Augustin, 1945), pp. 183–84.

28. Nicholas Murray Butler to Boas, November 7, 1935; Boas to Frederick Coykendall, March 10, 1936, APS/BC.

29. Boas to Butler, January 2, 1941, APS/BC.

30. Franz Boas, "Freedom Defined," *New York Teacher* 6 (June 1941): 25.

31. Franz Boas, "Freedom in Teaching," in *Race and Democratic Society*, pp. 201–2.

32. Franz Boas, "On Intellectual Freedom," *The New Masses* 30 (February 1939): 17.

33. "Walter Winchell on Broadway," *Daily Mirror* April 8, 1940; Boas to Walter Winchell, April 19, 1940, APS/BC.

34. Boas press release, December 21, 1941, APS/BC.

35. Boas to Earl Browder, May 17, 1941, APS/BC; Boas, "Freedom in Teaching," 202; Stocking, "Anthropology as Kulturkampf," 44–45.

36. Franz Boas, "Opinion Not Subject To Inquiry," *Forum* (March 1940): 157.

37. Boas to William Rosenwald, March 4, 1937, APS/BC.

38. Franz Boas, "Race Prejudice from the Scientist's Angle," *Forum* 98 (July 1937): 94.

39. Franz Boas, "Science in Nazi Germany," *Survey Graphic* 26 (August 1937): 416.

40. Boas to Edwin G. Conklin, October 23, 1941; Boas to Alfred Tozzer, May 9, 1939, APS/BC.

41. Herskovits, *Franz Boas*, p. 119.

42. Franz Boas, "The Role of the Scientist in Democratic Society," in *Race and Democratic Society*, p. 219.

43. Herskovits, *Franz Boas*, pp. 120–21.

# 9
# Conclusion

With Boas's death at age eighty-four, anthropology lost its most influential individual. His fundamental restructuring of the science professionalized the discipline and earned it increasing respect from both universities and the nation at large. His scientific acumen and refusal to speculate encouraged methodological rigor among his colleagues and students, which in turn expanded the areas in which ethnology could be applied. In a sense, Boas created order within his science. Much like other reformers of the Progressive period, he brought rationality and efficiency to a formerly chaotic endeavor, and by so doing transformed anthropology into a useful tool for analyzing the problems of society.

Of further significance in the building of a science of man in America was his role as a teacher. Boas trained many of the most prominent anthropologists of the twentieth century. Whether they remained loyal to him or not, all expressed their indebtedness to him. He was, for Margaret Mead, "a surprising and somewhat frightening teacher." He did not "discuss formal epistemology," but rather "presented material in such a way that his students simply absorbed the correct procedures."[1] Ruth Benedict was so heavily influenced by him that she hoped to emulate his style in her own career.[2]

Although some students, like Edward Sapir, sought to break away from his influence and referred to him critically as an "idealistic slave-driver," all were deeply affected by his teaching.[3] Upon learning of Boas's temporary illness, even Sapir illustrated the mythical dimensions of his mentor by lamenting: "it is with great regret that one is reminded that this beloved hero is subject to the frailties of the flesh."[4] In sum, Boas created a cadre of followers trained to respect scientific integrity. They did not all appreciate his paternalistic style, but all recognized how much they had benefited from his instruction.

Boas's influence extended beyond his students. He educated the public also, both by his discussions of prejudice and the need for tolerance and by his own social activism. His "quiet devotion to scholarship" and "refusal to bow the knee, when bowing was the way to popularity and power" profoundly affected colleagues and laymen alike. Many drew "inspiration and courage from the sturdy honesty" that characterized Boas's career and his life.[5]

Boas also left his mark as a thinker. He shaped anthropological theory in many respects. Perhaps his "greatest theoretical contribution" was "the concept of culture as a dynamic, changing force, to be understood only if it is recognized as a manifestation of the 'mental life' of man."[6] For Boas, not all cultures progressed to the same degree because they had not all experienced the same historical conditions. The fact of cultural relativity was critical to Boas's paradigm, since it permitted him to hypothesize that all cultures were of equal potential. They only needed to be influenced by similar historical events to exhibit similar levels of progress.

The logic of this argument led to Boas's critical reaction to both the comparative method of cultural analysis and evolutionary theory. If, in fact, cultures demonstrated equal potential, then the entire concept of ranking races according to mental ability based on their degree of civilization signified nothing. It demonstrated only that particular environmental conditions were dissimilar, and said little about intelligence or ability.

The constant tension between modern Western civilization and that of the "primitive man" permitted Boas to criticize his own society in "universalistic" terms, while in a "relativistic" sense "he defended the cultural alternative." Moreover, Boas implored his students to break the habit of evaluating other cultures by comparing them to their own. Non-Western cultures were essential, he believed, "for the achievement both of scientific knowledge in the social sphere and of the freedom of the individual in society." Without such "an external cultural reference point," no scientific progress could be made, and "true freedom" would never occur. In this sense, Boas's "lifelong fight for culture" was a crusade to build upon scientific knowledge and protect individual freedom.[7]

Boas also built a strong intellectual foundation for the development of physical anthropology. He added substantially to the study of man by proving the plasticity of the human physical form. His growth studies of children and his immigration report were major technical and theoretical contributions to physical anthropology. Moreover, "his observations on the retardation of children in orphanages were instrumental in altering child-care programs and in the adoption of the foster-home plan."[8] Unlike amateurs such as John W. Powell, Boas made physical anthropology "an integral part of his professional activity."[9] In fact, he was "the last man who can be said to have embraced the whole field of anthropology."[10] This was the case precisely because he had so greatly expanded the parameters of anthropological investigation that future ethnologists tended to focus on only one of the subspecialties within the discipline he had helped create.

In the area of linguistics, too, Boas framed the course of future research and laid the basis for much future progress. Not only did he gather masses of material in the form of texts and grammatical analyses, he also outlined the general methodological techniques and hypotheses for linguists of the next generation. He made it clear that language was "a cultural form, the components of which [were] to be investigated as [was] any other culture manifestation."[11] At times when foundations and philanthropists balked at his requests for funds to study the American race problem, Boas turned to his study of language as another way of attacking the problem of prejudice. His famous introduction to the *Handbook of Indian Languages* argued forcefully against any notion of racial rankings.

Despite his many and varied contributions to anthropological theory, Boas did not escape criticism. His hesitation to generalize led some skeptics to suggest that he retarded anthropological progress.[12] Boas did not develop a precise school of anthropological thought. Rather than build coherent theories that might not stand the test of future investigation, he was content to point out the shortcomings of existing hypotheses. In his role as a critic he promoted debate that ultimately led to progress along methodological and theoretical lines.

Other critics questioned Boas's belief in racial equality. Although his activism on behalf of Afro-Americans and his consistent opposition to immigration restriction painted him as a race champion, several detractors have viewed his dealings with the Indians of British Columbia as proof of his own prejudice. His grave-robbing activity in Canada has been brought forth as evidence of his lack of respect for Indian life. Boas, however, abhorred this aspect of his research. He recognized its implications, but felt the scientific importance outweighed all other considerations. As his relationship with George Hunt indicated, Boas had great respect for the Indians he studied. Although frequently criticizing Hunt for being lazy or wasting too much time, Boas had a deep affection for him. They developed a close personal friendship that transcended the scientific work in which they engaged.

It was in the area of race that Boas had his greatest impact on American society and on future intellectual thought. By emphasizing the importance of each culture's values and by promoting "an understanding of the human misery, degradation and demoralization that can result when one people imposes its way on another," Boas changed many minds both within academic circles and in the general community. His "tolerance for other ways of life than his own," and his willingness to proclaim this publicly and actively, significantly transformed American racial thought.[13] As a consequence, the emerging civil rights movement benefited, as did American democracy. Although it was not until World War II that many Americans saw the contradiction between fighting racism abroad while condoning it at home, it was Boas who planted the seed that prejudice was based on ignorance and fear.

Boas shifted science away from racist ideology to egalitarianism. Pseudo-scientists no longer monopolized the field. Although they continued their xenophobic campaigns against blacks and immigrants, Boas had dealt them a major setback. He initiated a chain of events that would place racists increasingly on the defensive and would ultimately smash the legal framework supporting discrimination.

The Boas legacy is complex and must be viewed quite broadly. In the strict scientific sense, much of his thought and practice became the foundation upon which other anthropologists would build. As the profession developed, the groundwork he laid tended to be less obvious; the theories he advanced became axiomatic, so much part of the discipline that their origins were forgotten. His contribution, however, remains monumental. Through his teaching, research and commitment to science, he transformed an amateur hobby into a professional discipline. For this reason alone Boas deserves to be called the father of American anthropology. His power and reputation became so formidable that even the upheaval surrounding two world wars and a major financial depression could not dislodge him.

More generally, Boas must be viewed as a symbol of his age. From his arrival in America in the 1880s to his death in 1942, he dealt with the profound changes in America that occurred as a response to modernization. As the nation's face became more urban, more industrial and more ethnically diverse, significant upheavals took place that required immediate solutions. Since Boas himself fell victim to these changes, he had strong reason to become involved. Although his liberalism and commitment to professional science can never be overlooked in assessing his intellectual contributions and social activism, it was his own experience with anti-Semitism that usually pushed him to act. This factor led him to attack evolutionary theory, to challenge the structure of white, Anglo-Saxon Protestant science, and to defend American minority and immigrant groups. He had varying degrees of success in these battles, but he always managed to keep his own revulsion against anti-Semitism in the background. With the rise of Nazism, however, it came to the fore, and he intensified his lifelong fight against prejudice with a passion that consumed him during his final years.

That Boas could only begin to show America the way to solve its social problems stands testimony to the complexity of such a national transformation. He recognized on the eve of his death that prejudice and racism still existed. That is why his final words pertained to their eradication. Yet he refused to be pessimistic. He saw in America the possibility of a true democracy, which while not yet ideal, could become so. Boas adhered to a Hegelian notion of progress, believing that each advance in knowledge moved human beings closer to true freedom and made them more civilized. With this in mind, Boas dedicated his life to the education of his country and the world.

In the final analysis, he was concerned with the human condition. He championed the causes of individuals in trouble, often placing his own reputation in jeopardy. "In all his work, whatever its approach, he continuously stressed the innate worth of the human being, the dignity of all human culture."[14] Above all else, Boas was a humane man who was tormented by humankind's imperfections, and who desired nothing more than to help overcome them. This quest for human progress on all fronts remains Franz Boas's most enduring legacy.

## NOTES

1. Margaret Mead, *Blackberry Winter: My Earlier Years* (New York: William Morrow, 1972), pp. 122, 228.

2. Margaret Mead, *An Anthropologist at Work: Writings of Ruth Benedict* (Boston: Houghton Mifflin, 1959), p. 65.

3. Edward Sapir to Ruth Benedict, June 14, 1925, in Mead, *An Anthropologist at Work*, p. 180.

4. Ibid., p. 228.

5. H. R. Mussey to Franz Boas, January 16, 1929, American Philosophical Society, Boas Correspondence.

6. Melville Herskovits, *Franz Boas: The Science of Man in the Making* (New York: Charles Scribner's Sons, 1953), p. 72.

7. George W. Stocking, Jr. "Anthropology as Kulturkampf: Science and Politics in the Career of Franz Boas," in *The Uses of Anthropology*, ed. Walter Goldschmidt (Washington, D.C.: American Anthropological Association, 1979), p. 47.

8. Ruth Bunzel, introduction to Franz Boas, *Anthropology and Modern Life* (New York: W. W. Norton, 1962), p. 8.

9. George W. Stocking, Jr., ed. *The Shaping of American Anthropology, 1883–1911: A Franz Boas Reader* (New York: Basic Books, 1974), p. 14.

10. Leslie Spier, "Some Central Elements in the Legacy," *American Anthropologist* 61 (October 1959): 146.

11. Ibid., p. 152.

12. See chapter 3 for more detail of these criticisms.

13. Herskovits, *Franz Boas*, p. 100.

14. Ibid., p. 7.

# Selected Bibliography

## MANUSCRIPTS

The Franz Boas Folder, The National Academy of Sciences.
The Franz Boas Papers, 1858–1942, American Philosophical Society (APS/BC).
The W J McGee Papers, Manuscript Division, Library of Congress.

## WORKS BY BOAS

### Articles

"The Anthropological Position of the Negro." *Van Norden's Magazine* (April 1907):
40–47.
"Anthropological Research, Petition." *Science* 25 (May 1907): 756–57.
"An Anthropologist's Credo." *The Nation* 147 (August 1938): 201–4.
"Anthropology." *Science* 9 (January 1899): 93–96.
"Are the Jews a Race?" *The World Tomorrow* 6 (January 1923): 5–6.
"Aryans and Non-Aryans." *American Mercury* 32 (June 1934): 219, 221.
"As an American of German Birth—I Protest." *Viereck's* 10 (1919): 185.
"Britain's War Aims?" *PM*, October 4, 1940, p. 2.
"The Bureau of American Ethnology." *Science* 16 (November 1902): 828–31.
"The Cephalic Index." *American Anthropologist*, n.s. 1 (1899): 448–61.
"Colonies and the Peace Conference." *The Nation* 108 (February 1919): 247–49.
"Commencement Address at Atlanta University." *Atlanta University Leaflet*, no. 19,
May 31, 1906.
"Democracy and Intellectual Freedom." *American Teacher* 23 (March 1939): 9–10.
"The Department of Anthropology." *Columbia University Quarterly* 10 (1908): 303–
7.
"The Development of The American Museum of Natural History: Department of An-
thropology." *American Museum Journal* 2 (June 1902): 47–53.

"The Ethnological Significance of Esoteric Doctrines." *Science* 16 (November 1902): 872–74.

"Eugenics." *Scientific Monthly* 3 (1916): 471–78.

"Evolution of Diffusion." *American Anthropologist* 26 (1924): 340–44.

"Fallacies of Racial Inferiority," *Current History* 25, (February 1927): 681–82.

Foreword to Mary White Ovington, *Half a Man, the Status of the Negro in New York* pp. vii–ix. New York: Longmans, Green, 1911.

"Form of the Head as Influenced by Growth." *Science*, n.s. 4 (January 1896): 50–51.

"The Foundation of a National Anthropological Society." *Science*, n.s. 15 (May 1902): 804–9.

"Frederick Ward Putnam." *Science* 42 (September 1915): 330–32.

"Freedom Defined," *New York Teacher* 6 (June 1941): 25.

"Freedom for the School." *School and Society* 8 (December 1918): 739–40.

"Freedom to Teach." *The Nation* 108 (January 1919): 88–89.

"The Growth of Children." *Science*, n.s. 5 (April 1897): 570–73.

"The Growth of the First-Born Children." *Science*, n.s. 1 (April 1895): 402–4.

"The Head-Forms of the Italians as Influenced by Heredity and Environment." *American Anthropologist* 15 (1915): 163–88.

"Heredity in Anthropometric Traits." *American Anthropologist* 9 (1907): 453–69.

"Heredity in Head Form." *American Anthropologist* 5 (1903): 530–38.

"The History of the American Race." *Annals of the New York Academy of Sciences* 21 (January 1912): 177–83.

"The History of Anthropology." *Science* 20 (October 1904): 513–24.

"How Can Endowments Be Used Most Effectively for Scientific Research." *Science* 17 (April 1903): 574–77.

"Human Faculty as Determined by Race." *Proceedings of the American Association for the Advancement of Science* 43 (September 1894): 301–27.

"The Industries of African Negroes." *Southern Workman* 38 (1909): 217–29.

"The Influence of Environment upon Development." *Proceedings of the National Academy of Sciences* 6 (1920): 489–93.

"Influence of Heredity and Environment upon Growth." In *Race, Language and Culture*, ed. Franz Boas, pp. 82–85. New York: Macmillan, 1940.

"Insane Asylum for Nazi Leaders," *PM*, January 4, 1943, p. 2.

"International School of American Archeology and Ethnology in Mexico." *American Anthropologist* 14 (1912): 192–94.

"In the Occupied Area." Editorial, *New York Times*, October 20, 1923.

"Inventing a Great Race." *New Republic* 13 (January 1917): 305–7.

Lecture before Barnard College class in anthropology, November 1717. In *Race and Democratic Society*, ed. Boas, pp. 178–84.

"The Limitations of the Comparative Method of Anthropology." *Science*, n.s. 4 (December 1896): 901–8.

" 'Lo, The Poor Nordic.' " Editorial, *New York Times*, April 13, 1924.

"The Mental Attitude of the Educated Classes." *The Dial* 65 (September 1918): 145–48.

"The Mind of Primitive Man." *Journal of American Folk-Lore* 14 (1901): 1–11.

"Mixed Races." *Science*, o.s. 17 (March 1891): 179.

"Modern Populations of America." *Proceedings of the Nineteenth International Congress of Americanists*, December 15, 1915, pp. 569–75.

"Museums of Ethnology and Their Classification." *Science*, o.s. 9 (1887): 587–89, 614.

"Nationalism." *The Dial* 66 (March 1919): 232–37.

"The Negro and the Demands of Modern Life." *Charities* 15 (1905): 85–88.

"New Evidence in Regard to the Instability of Human Types." *Proceedings of the National Academy of Sciences* 2 (1916): 713–18.

"Nordic Propaganda," *New Republic* 78 (March 1934), 107.

"The Occurrence of Similar Inventions in Areas Widely Apart." *Science*, o.s. 9 (1887): 485–86.

"Our National Ideals." Editorial, *Springfield Republican*, February 2, 1916.

"Physical Characteristics of the Tribes of British Columbia." *Report of the British Association for the Advancement of Science*, 1898, with Livingston Farrand.

"The Problem of the American Negro." *Yale Review* 10 (1921): 384–95.

"Professor Boas Dissents, Blames the President for the Break with Germany." Editorial, *New York Times*, February 9, 1917.

"Program for Equal Educational Opportunity." *New York Call*, December 7, 1919.

"Psychological Problems in Anthropology." *American Journal of Psychology* 21 (1910): 371–84.

"The Question of Racial Purity." *The American Mercury* 3 (1924): 163–69.

"Race Prejudice from the Scientist's Angle," *Forum* 98 (July 1937): 94.

"Race Problems in America." *Science* 29 (May 1909): 839–49.

"The Race-War Myth." *Everybody's Magazine* (December 31, 1914): 671–74.

"The Real Race Problem." *The Crisis* 1 (1910): 22–25.

"The Relations between the Variability of Organisms and That of Their Constituent Elements." *Science* 15 (January 1902): 1–5.

"Remarks on the Theory of Anthropometry." *Quarterly Publications of the American Statistical Association* 3 (1893): 569–75.

Response to Address by the President of Columbia University on the Occasion of the Formal Presentation of the Boas Anniversary Volume, at a Meeting of the University Council." *American Anthropologist* 9 (April 1907): 646–49.

Review of *The Negro Races*, by Thomas Dowd. *Political Science Quarterly* 23 (1908): 727–31.

Review of *The Races of Europe*, by William Ripley. *Science* 10 (September 1899): 292–96.

Review of *The Rising Tide of Color*, by Lothrop Stoddard. *The Nation* 111 (December 8, 1920): 656.

"Rights of Invaded Regions." Editorial, *New York Times*, November 4, 1923.

"Rudolf Virchow's Anthropological Work." *Science*, n.s. 16 (September 1902): 441–45.

"Science in Nazi Germany," *Survey Graphic* 26 (August 1937): 416.

"Scientific Progress and University Government." *The Nation* 106 (May 1918): 539–40.

"Scientists as Spies." *The Nation* 108 (December 1919): 797.

"Some Philological Aspects of Anthropological Research." *Science* 23 (April 1906): 641–45.

"Some Principles of Museum Administration." *Science*, n.s. 25 (June 1907): 921–33.

"Some Problems in North American Archaeology." *American Journal of Archaeology* 6 (1902): 1–6.

"Some Recent Criticisms of Physical Anthropology." *American Anthropologist*, n.s. 1 (1899): 98–106.

"Some Traits of Primitive Culture." *Journal of American Folk-Lore* 17 (1904): 243–54.

"Statistical Study of Anthropometry." In *Race, Language and Culture*, ed. Franz Boas, pp. 131–37.

"A Sturdy Protest." Editorial, *The Nation* 107 (October 19, 1918): 487.

"This Nordic Nonsense." *The Forum* 74 (October 1925): 502–11.

"Warns of German Wrath." Editorial, *New York Times*, December 11, 1915.

"What is a Race?" *The Nation* 120 (January 1925): 89–91.

"What the Negro Has Done in Africa." *The Ethical Record* 5 (1904): 106–9.

"Why German-Americans Blame America." Editorial, *New York Times*, January 8, 1916.

## Books

*Anthropology and Modern Life*. New York: W. W. Norton, 1928.

*Changes in Bodily Form of Descendants of Immigrants*. Reports of the Immigration Commission, Senate Documents, 61st Congress, 2nd Session, 1909–1910. Vol. 64. Washington, D.C.: Government Printing Office, 1911.

*Introduction to Handbook of American Indian Languages*. Bulletin 40, part 1, Smithsonian Institution Bureau of Ethnology (Washington, D.C.: Government Printing Office, 1911). Repr. Lincoln: University of Nebraska Press, 1966.

*The Mind of Primitive Man*. New York: Macmillan, 1913. Rev. ed., 1938.

*The Publications of the Jesup North Pacific Expedition*. Vol. 1, 1898.

(Ed.) *Race and Democratic Society*. New York: J. J. Augustin, 1945.

(Ed.) *Race, Language and Culture*. London: Collier-Macmillan, 1940.

## WORKS ON BOAS

Beardsley, Edward H. "The American Scientist as Social Activist: Franz Boas, Burt G. Wilder and the Fight for Racial Justice, 1900–1915." *Isis* (March 1973): 50–66.

Benedict, Ruth. "Franz Boas." *Science* 97 (1943): 60–62.

———. "Franz Boas as an Ethnologist." *American Anthropologist* 45 (September 1943): 27–34.

Benison, Saul. "Geography and the Early Career of Franz Boas." *American Anthropologist* 51 (1949): 523–26.

Boas, Franziska. "The Reminiscences of Franziska Boas." Oral History Research Office, Columbia University, 1972.

Buettner-Janusch, John. "Boas and Mason: Particularism versus Generalization." *American Anthropologist* 59 (1957): 318–24.

Cartwright, Walter J., and Thomas R. Burtis. "Race and Intelligence: Changing Opinions in Social Science." In *Blacks in the United States*, ed. Norval D. Glenn and Charles W. Bonjean, pp. 168–84. San Francisco: Chandler Publishing, 1969.

Cole, Fay-Cooper. "The Concept of Race in Light of Franz Boas' Studies of Head-Forms among Immigrants." In *Methods in Social Science*, ed. S. A. Rice, pp. 582–85. Chicago: University of Chicago Press, 1931.

Emeneau, Murray B. "Franz Boas as a Linguist." *American Anthropologist* 45 (September 1943): 35–38.

Goddard, Pliny E. "American Anthropology and Franz Boas." *The American Mercury* 7 (1926): 314–16.

Goldschmidt, Walter, ed. "The Anthropology of Franz Boas: Essays on the Centennial of His Birth." *American Anthropologist* 61 (October 1959), Memoir no. 89.

Goldstein, Marcus S. "Franz Boas' Contributions to Physical Anthropology." *American Journal of Physical Anthropology* 4 (1948): 144–61.

Gruber, Jacob. "Horatio Hale and the Development of American Anthropology." *Proceedings of the American Philosophical Society* 111 (1967): 1–37.

Herskovits, Melville J. "Franz Boas as Physical Anthropologist." *American Anthropologist* 45 (September 1943): 39–51.

———. *Franz Boas: The Science of Man in the Making.* New York: Charles Scribner's Sons, 1953.

Hinsley, Curtis M. and Bill Holm. "A Cannibal in the National Museum: The Early Career of Franz Boas in America." *American Anthropologist* 78 (1976): 306–16.

Hrdlicka, Ales. "Franz Boas." *American Philosophical Society Yearbook* (1942): 333–36.

Hyman, Stanley Edgar. "Freud and Boas: Secular Rabbis?" *Commentary* (March 1954): 264–67.

Hymes, Dell. "The Use of Anthropology: Critical, Political, Personal." In *Reinventing Anthropology*, ed. Dell Hymes, pp. 3–82. New York: Random House, 1969.

Klineberg, Otto. "Race and Psychology," in *Race, Science, and Society*, ed. Leo Kuper. N.Y.: Columbia University Press, 1975.

Kluckhohn, Clyde and Olaf Prufer. "Influences during the Formative Years." *American Anthropologist* 61 (October 1959): 4–28.

Kroeber, Alfred. "Franz Boas: The Man." *American Anthropologist* 45 (September 1943): 5–26.

———. "The Place of Boas in Anthropology." *American Anthropologist* 58 (1956): 151–59.

Kunkel, Peter. "Boas, Space and Time." *American Anthropologist* 56 (1954): 115.

Lesser, Alexander. "Franz Boas." *International Encyclopedia of the Social Sciences*. New York: Macmillan, 1968.

Levenstein, H. A., "Franz Boas as Political Activist." *Papers of the Kroeber Anthropological Society* 29 (1963): 15–24.

Lewis, David Levering, "Parallels and Divergences: Assimilationist Strategies of Afro-American and Jewish Elites from 1910 to the Early 1930s," *Journal of American History* 71 (December 1984).

Lowie, Robert H. "Biographical Memoir of Franz Boas, 1858–1942." *National Academy of Sciences Biographical Memoirs* 24 (1947): 303–22.

———. "Boas Once More." *American Anthropologist* 58 (1956): 159–63.

———. "Franz Boas, His Predecessors and His Contemporaries." *Science* 97 (February 1943): 202–3.

———. "The Progress of Science." *Scientific Monthly* 56 (1943): 182–84.

Mason, James Alden. "Franz Boas as an Archaeologist." *American Anthropologist* 45 (September 1943): 58–66.

Mead, Margaret. "Apprenticeship under Boas." *American Anthropologist* 61 (October 1959): 29–45.

Parmenter, Ross. "Glimpses of a Friendship: Zelia Nuttall and Franz Boas." In *Pioneers of American Anthropology*, ed. June Helm, pp. 83–147. Seattle: University of Washington Press, 1966.

Ray, Verne F. "Rejoinder." *American Anthropologist* 58 (1956): 164–69.

Reichard, Gladys. "Franz Boas and Folklore." *American Anthropologist* 45 (September 1943): 52–57.

Rohner, Ronald. "Franz Boas: Ethnographer on the Northwest Coast." In *Pioneers of American Anthropology*, ed. June Helm, pp. 149–212. Seattle: University of Washington Press, 1966.

———. ed., *The Ethnography of Franz Boas: Letters and Diaries of Franz Boas Written on the Northwest Coast from 1886 to 1931*. Chicago: University of Chicago Press, 1969.

Shipton, C. K. "Franz Boas." *Proceedings of the American Antiquarian Society*, 53 (1943): 15–16.

Smith, Marian. "Boas' 'Natural History' Approach to Field Method." *American Anthropologist* 61 (October 1959): 46–60.

Spier, Leslie. "Franz Boas and Some of His Views." *Acta Americana* 1 (1943): 108–27.

———. "Some Central Elements in the Legacy." *American Anthropologist* 61 (October 1959): 146–55.

Stocking, George W., Jr. "Anthropology as Kulturkampf: Science and Politics in the Career of Franz Boas." In *The Uses of Anthropology*, ed. Walter Goldschmidt. (Washington, D.C.: American Anthropological Association, 1979).

———. "Franz Boas and the Founding of the American Anthropological Association." *American Anthropologist* 62 (1960): 1–17.

———, ed. *The Shaping of American Anthropology, 1883–1911: A Franz Boas Reader*. New York: Basic Books, 1974.

Tanner, J. M. "Boas' Contributions to Knowledge of Human Growth and Form." *American Anthropologist* 61 (October 1959): 76–111.

Voget, F. W. "Franz Boas." *Dictionary of Scientific Biography*. New York: Charles Scribner's Sons, 1970.

Wax, Murray. "The Limitations of Boas' Anthropology." *American Anthropologist* 58 (1956): 63–74.

White, Leslie, *The Ethnology and Ethnography of Franz Boas*. Austin: Texas Memorial Museum, 1963.

Williams, J. L. "Boas and American Ethnologists." *Thought* 11 (1936): 194–209.

Willis, William S. "Skeletons in the Anthropological Closet." In *Reinventing Anthropology*, ed. Dell Hymes, pp. 121–52. New York: Random House, 1969.

## OTHER RELATED WORKS

Ackerknecht, Erwin H. *Rudolf Virchow, Doctor, Statesman, Anthropologist*. Madison: Wisconsin University Press, 1953.

Allen, Robert L. *Reluctant Reformers: The Impact of Racism on American Social Reform Movements*. Washington, D.C.: Howard University Press, 1974.

Bean, Robert Bennett. "The Negro Brain." *Century Magazine* 72 (1906): 778–90.

Benedict, Ruth. *Race: Science and Politics.* New York: Macmillan Co., 1940.

Bledstein, Burton J. *The Culture of Professionalism.* New York: W. W. Norton, 1976.

Brew, J. O., ed. *One Hundred Years of Anthropology.* Cambridge: Harvard University Press, 1968.

Brooks, Van Wyck. *The Confident Years, 1885–1915.* New York: E. P. Dutton, 1952.

Caulfield, Mina Davis. "Culture and Imperialism: Proposing a New Dialectic." In *Reinventing Anthropology,* ed. Dell Hymes, pp. 182–212. New York: Random House, 1969.

Darnell, Regna. "American Anthropology and the Development of Folklore Scholarship, 1890–1920." *Journal of the Folklore Institute* 10 (1973): 23–39.

————. *The Development of American Anthropology 1879–1920: From the Bureau of American Ethnology to Franz Boas.* Unpublished Ph.D. diss., University of Pennsylvania, 1969.

————, ed. *Readings in the History of Anthropology.* New York: Harper and Row, 1974.

Darrah, W. C. *Powell of the Colorado.* Princeton: Princeton University Press, 1951.

Delaguna, Frederica, ed. *Selected Papers from the American Anthropologist, 1888–1920.* Evanston, Ill.: Row, Peterson, 1960.

Filler, Louis, *randolph bourne.* New York: Citadel Press, 1943.

Fitzgerald, F. Scott. *The Great Gatsby.* New York: Charles Scribner's Sons, 1925.

Flack, J. Kirkpatrick. *Desideratum in Washington: The Intellecutal Community in the Capital City, 1870–1900.* Cambridge: Schenkman Publishing, 1975.

Freeman, John F. "University Anthropology: Early Departments in the United States." Paper read before the Kroeber Anthropological Society, April 25, 1964, Berkeley, California.

Fredrickson, George M. *The Black Image in the White Mind: The Debate on Afro-American Character and Destiny, 1817–1914.* New York: Harper and Row, 1971.

Furner, Mary O. *Advocacy and Objectivity: A Crisis in the Professionalization of American Social Science, 1865–1905.* Lexington: University Press of Kentucky, 1975.

Goldschmidt, Walter, ed. *The Uses of Anthropology.* Washington, D.C.: American Anthropological Association, 1979.

Gossett, Thomas F. *Race: The History of an Idea in America.* New York: Schocken Books, 1965.

Grant, Madison. *The Passing of the Great Race.* New York: Charles Scribner's Sons, 1916.

Gruber, Carol S. *Mars and Minerva: World War I and the Uses of Higher Learning in America.* Baton Rouge: Louisiana State University Press, 1975.

Haller, John S. *Outcasts from Evolution: Scientific Attitudes of Racial Inferiority, 1859–1900.* New York: McGraw-Hill, 1975.

Handlin, Oscar. *The Uprooted.* Boston: Little, Brown, 1951.

Harris, Marvin. *The Rise of Anthropological Theory: A History of Theories of Culture.* New York: Thomas Y. Crowell, 1968.

Hays, Samuel. *The Response to Industrialism, 1885–1914.* Chicago: University of Chicago Press, 1957.

Helm, June, ed. *Pioneers of American Anthropology.* Seattle: University of Washington Press, 1966.

Hemenway, Robert E. *Zora Neale Hurston: A Literary Biography*. Urbana: University of Illinois Press, 1977.

Herskovits, Melville J. *Franz Boas: The Science of Man in the Making*. New York: Charles Scribner's Sons, 1953.

————. *The Myth of the Negro Past*. Boston: Beacon Press, 1958.

Higham, John. *Strangers in the Land: Patterns of American Nativism, 1860–1925*. New York: Atheneum, 1963.

Hofstadter, Richard. *Social Darwinism in American Thought*. Philadelphia: University of Pennsylvania Press, 1944.

Hurston, Zora N. *Mules and Men*. Philadelphia: J. B. Lippincott, 1935.

Judd, Neil M. *The Bureau of American Ethnology: A Partial History*. Norman: University of Oklahoma Press, 1967.

Kardiner, Abram and Edward Preble. *They Studied Man*. New York: World Publishing, 1961.

Keesing, Roger M. and Felix M. Keesing. *New Perspectives in Cultural Anthropology*. New York: Holt, Rinehart and Winston, 1971.

Keller, Morton. *Affairs of State: Public Life in Late Nineteenth-Century America*. Cambridge, Mass.: Belknap Press, 1977.

Kennedy, John Michael. "Philanthropy and Science in New York City: The American Museum of Natural History, 1868–1968." Ph.D. diss., Yale University, 1968.

Kessner, Thomas. *The Golden Door: Italian and Jewish Immigrant Mobility in New York City, 1880–1915*. New York: Oxford University Press, 1977.

Kroeber, Alfred. "A Half-Century of Anthropology." In *The Nature of Culture*, ed. Alfred Kroeber, pp. 139–43. Chicago: University of Chicago Press, 1952.

Laufer, Berthold, ed. *Boas Anniversary Volume: Anthropological Papers Written in Honor of Franz Boas*. New York: Stechert, 1906.

Mason, Otis T. "The Occurrence of Similar Inventions in Areas Widely Apart." *Science*, o.s. 9 (1887): 534–35.

————. "Resemblances in Arts Widely Separated." *American Naturalist* 20 (1887): 246–51.

Mead, Margaret. *An Anthropologist at Work: Writings of Ruth Benedict*. Boston: Houghton Mifflin, 1959.

————. *Blackberry Winter: My Earlier Years*. New York: William Morrow, Inc. 1972.

————, and Ruth L. Bunzel, eds. *The Golden Age of American Anthropology*. New York: George Braziller, 1960.

Mitra, Panchanan. *A History of American Anthropology*. Calcutta: University of Calcutta Press, 1933.

Nash, Roderick. *The Nervous Generation: American Thought, 1917–1930*. Chicago: Rand McNally and Co., 1970.

Newby, I. A. *Jim Crow's Defense: Anti-Negro Thought in America, 1900–1930*. Baton Rouge: Louisiana State University Press, 1965.

Nye, Russel B. *This Almost Chosen People: Essays in the History of American Ideas*. East Lansing: Michigan State University Press, 1966.

Powell, John W. "Museums of Ethnology and Their Classification." *Science*, o.s. 9 (1887): 612–14.

Ross, Dorothy. *G. Stanley Hall: The Psychologist as Prophet*. Chicago: University of Chicago Press, 1972.

Stanton, William. *The Leopard's Spots: Scientific Attitudes Toward Race in America, 1815–1859*. Chicago: University of Chicago Press, 1960.

Stegner, Wallace. *Beyond the Hundredth Meridian: John Wesley Powell and the Second Opening of the West*. Boston: Houghton Mifflin, 1953.

Stocking, George W., Jr. "American Social Scientists and Race Theory: 1890–1915." Ph.D. diss., University of Pennsylvania, 1960.

———. *Race, Culture, and Evolution: Essays in the History of Anthropology*. New York: Free Press, 1968.

———. *Selected Papers from the American Anthropologist 1921–1945*. Washington, D.C.: American Anthropological Association, 1976.

Stoddard, Lothrop. *The Rising Tide of Color against White World Supremacy*. New York: Charles Scribner's Sons, 1920.

Szwed, John F. "An American Anthropological Dilemma: The Politics of Afro-American Culture." In *Reinventing Anthropology*, ed. Dell Hymes, pp. 153–81. New York: Random House, 1969.

Wiebe, Robert. *The Search For Order, 1877–1920*. New York: Hill and Wang, 1967.

Wolf, Eric R. "American Anthropologists and American Society." In *Reinventing Anthropology*, ed. Dell Hymes, pp. 251–63. New York: Random House, 1969.

# Index

## About the Author

MARSHALL HYATT is the director of the Center for Afro-American Studies at Wesleyan University. He received his Ph.D. in American History from the University of Delaware and has taught at Delaware and at Harvard University. His areas of special interest include civil rights history, cultural and intellectual thought, race theory, and the semiotics of film. His writings have appeared in *The Journal of Negro Education*, *The Western Journal of Black Studies*, *The Negro History Bulletin*, and *Perspectives in American History*. He is the author of *The Afro-American Cinematic Experience* (1983).